BLACK WOMEN IN
UNITED STATES HISTORY

Editor

DARLENE CLARK HINE

Associate Editors

ELSA BARKLEY BROWN
TIFFANY R.L. PATTERSON
LILLIAN S. WILLIAMS

Research Assistant

EARNESTINE JENKINS

A CARLSON PUBLISHING SERIES

See the end of the fourth volume of this title for a comprehensive guide to this sixteen-volume series.

Black Women in American History

THE TWENTIETH CENTURY

Edited with a Preface by Darlene Clark Hine

IN FOUR VOLUMES

Volume Four

CARLSON
Publishing Inc

BROOKLYN, NEW YORK 1990

See the end of the fourth volume of this title for a comprehensive guide to the sixteen-volume series of which this title is Volumes Five through Eight.

Library of Congress Cataloging-in-Publication Data

Black women in American history : the twentieth century / edited with
  a preface by Darlene Clark Hine.
        p.   cm. — (Black women in United States history ; v. 5-8)
     Includes bibliographical references.
     ISBN 0-926019-15-5 (set)
     1. Afro-American women—History—20th century. 2. Afro-
Americans—1877-1964. I. Hine, Darlene Clark. II. Series: Black
women in United States history ; v. 5, etc.
E185.86.B543   vol. 5-8
973'.0496073 s—dc20
[973'.0496073022]
[B]   90-1392

Case design: Allison Lew

The index to this book was created using NL Cindex, a scholarly indexing program from the Newberry Library.

Printed on acid-free, 250-year-life paper.

Manufactured in the United States of America.

Contents of the Set

Volume One

Volume Two

Volume Three

Volume Four

(continued)

Black Women
in American History

Black Women and American Social Welfare: The Life of Fredericka Douglass Sprague Perry

Wilma Peebles-Wilkins

Biographical research and the study of mutual-aid networks provide invaluable data to document the historical contributions of black women to American social welfare. The achievements of these black women role models can be an inspiration to contemporary social workers. The caregiving and community social welfare activities of one such woman, Fredericka Douglass Sprague Perry, are discussed in this article.

The contributions of black women to American social welfare have largely been ignored in mainstream social work journals and social welfare history. Data from primary and secondary sources, retrieved from the late nineteenth and early twentieth centuries, demonstrate some of the community social welfare activities that were initiated by black women. Janie Porter Barrett of Virginia, founder of the Locust Street Settlement in 1902, and Eartha M. White of Florida, who coordinated war-camp services during World War I and founded the Clara White Mission for the homeless in 1928, are just two examples of such women (see Gary, 1986; Peebles-Wilkins, 1987a, 1987b). Autobiographies and biographical accounts provide excellent source material for documenting the historical development of contributions by black women to American social welfare. This article focuses on

AFFILIA, Vol. 4 No. 1, Spring 1989 33-44
● 1989 Women and Social Work, Inc.

the life of one black woman, Fredericka Douglass Sprague Perry, the granddaughter of antislavery leader and suffrage advocate Frederick Douglass, and a pioneer in the reform of child welfare for black adolescents.

This account was developed from data collected in relation to a broader funded study on the mutual-aid activities of black women during the period, 1895-1930. Data from primary sources were obtained from the Frederick Douglass Papers (cited in the text with box and folder numbers) and the Mary Church Terrell Papers, both at the Moorland-Spingarn Research Center, Howard University, Washington, DC. Other resources include data from news accounts obtained from the Missouri Valley Room of the Kansas City Public Library; resources obtained from Lincoln University, Jefferson City, Missouri; the autobiography of John Edward Perry (1947), husband of Fredericka Perry; related autobiographical and biographical publications; a publication of the original records of the activities of the National Association of Colored Women (NACW, 1933) and periodicals published by the black press.

THEORETICAL BACKGROUND

The recent literature on social history reveals that in the late nineteenth and early twentieth centuries the activities of the colored women's movement paralleled those of its white counterparts. In addition to being involved in activities to promote suffrage, to abolish lynching, and to advance the political power of black people, black women were involved in benevolent activities that contributed to the development of social welfare services in the black community between 1895 and 1930. This period encompassed several landmark events in American history: the Progressive movement, World War I, and the Great Depression. Some black scholars hold that residual social welfare activities provided by local communities for both blacks and whites declined after the Great Depression when legislation shifted the responsibility for caregiving to governmental agencies. Before the Great Depression, however, the three major sources of caregiving among blacks were the extended family, the church, and women's clubs (Martin & Martin, 1985). Hine (1986) indicated the need for the continued study of the role of black club women in social reform and self-help activities prior to the emergence of institutionalized social welfare. She stated (pp. 237-238):

980

Although considerable attention has been devoted to the club women's movement, there still remains a great deal to be done in the area of black women's involvement in voluntary and self-help associations. In virtually every city and rural community in twentieth century America there existed an organized grouping of black women, often led by a cadre of elite educated black middle-class matrons. These clubs and organizations gradually added to their primary concern of upgrading sexual images a concern for women's suffrage and progressive social reform.

Such efforts by black women have been noted by other scholars as well. For example, over 65 years ago, McDougald (1925), a black social worker, teacher, and journalist, called attention to black women's efforts to combat double discrimination through group activism in New York. Such community organization activities resulted in services for delinquents and the elderly and a range of other recreational and educational programs for black children and youths. Women's clubs in New York and other parts of the country were formed, in part, because of the "exclusion of Black women from white clubs" (Terborg-Penn, 1978, p. 21), out of black women's "efforts to elevate the race" (Terrell, 1901, p. 437), and from attempts to "band together to do good" (Terrell, 1899, p. 345). In existence as early as the 1830s in both northern and southern communities and using the motto "Lifting As We Climb," these local clubs were unified in 1896 with the formation of the NACW (Lerner, 1973, pp. 435-437). By 1916, the NACW had a membership of some 50,000 women from 28 federations and over 1,000 clubs. Members of this organization were educated, middle-class women who were strong believers in the Protestant Ethic (Giddings, 1984, p. 95).

981

Typically, black women like Janie Porter Barrett and Eartha White were part of mutual-aid networks composed of other black women and were affiliated with or were leaders of the NACW. Voluntary associations including the black women's clubs, performed caregiving, organizing, and reform activities. Such patterns of activities in the black community are forms of mutual aid that exemplify the black helping tradition.

Martin and Martin (1985) suggested that West African kinship practices and the philosophical and cultural traditions based on group interest and cooperation, rather than individualism and competition, are the antecedents of mutual aid in the black community. The benevolence in traditional African society, documented in anthropological writings, is also noted in Martin and Martin's theoretical framework. Gutman (1977) discussed the transformation of black family obligations to non-kinship-network obligations. His final stage of this transformation is "the development of inter- and intra-generational linkages between slave families accompanied by the transformation of conceptions of family and kin obligation rooted in blood and marriage into conceptions of quasi-kin and non-kin social obligations" (p. 223). The naming practices of slaves; the postslavery care of orphaned children and the provision of schooling; and communal practices, such as "each putting in according to his means" (Gutman, p. 229), are manifestations of this transformation.

982

When communities throughout the United States were segregated, collective efforts or mutual-aid networks were essential. The leadership activities of individual black women were helpful in providing needed services to families and children in local communities.

On the basis of the early writings in black publications and of historical documentation in secondary sources, four propositions may be stated about the organized caregiving activities of black women: (1) They were manifestations of the black helping tradition, (2) they were combined with leadership or active roles in the NACW or its organizational affiliates, (3) they represented an interplay of race, class, and gender in this society, and (4) they declined after the Great Depression and were replaced by governmental support in the new social welfare structure. In this article, these propositions are illustrated by the life of one black woman. It is hoped that this article will encourage other social work researchers to investigate these propositions using biographical as well as quantitative information to study the historical development of contributions by black women to social welfare.

FREDERICKA PERRY

Fredericka Douglass Sprague Perry, born about 1872, was the fifth oldest child of the seven children of Rosetta Douglass Sprague and Nathan Sprague. Rosetta Douglass Sprague was the oldest daughter of Frederick Douglass. Her husband, Nathan Sprague, was a poorly educated ex-slave who was often unemployed and was eventually imprisoned for a year for removing the contents of letters while working in a post office in Rochester, New York, where Frederick Douglass helped him obtain employment. After his release from prison, he joined Rosetta, who had moved to Washington, DC, and was working as a government clerk in the office where her father was the recorder of deeds. Although Rosetta provided the primary support for the couple's six children, she and her husband were able to rely on the resources of Frederick Douglass and were not living in poverty, as a description such as this might suggest. After Douglass's death, Rosetta kept her father's memory alive through speaking engagements. She was a speaker at the founding meeting of the NACW (Sterling, 1984, p. 422). Her article "Anna Murray Douglass—My Mother As I Recall Her" (Sprague, 1923) indicated the support that her mother provided to her father, Frederick Douglass. Rosetta Douglass Sprague has been called an "exponent for equal rights and a restless agitator for the cause of humanity" (Majors, 1893, pp. 194-195).

983

Rosetta's daughters, Fredericka Perry and Rosabelle Sprague Jones, were active members of the NACW and were leaders of the Kansas City Federation of Colored Women's Clubs, as well as literary and other clubs for black women in Kansas City, Missouri. Like her sister, Rosabelle was deeply involved in voluntary associations. She was married to physician Thomas A. Jones and was the mother of Thomas Perry Jones, the youngest black licensed aviator at the time of his death in a plane crash in 1931 (NACW, 1933, p. 278). Rosabelle was the treasurer of the Book Lover's Club (founded in 1903) from 1934 to 1935 and Fredericka was listed as a member in 1930 (Frederick Douglass Papers, Box 28, Folder 98). Rosabelle was president of the Kansas City (Missouri) Federation of Colored Women's Clubs, an organization composed of 25 clubs in the city. Her presidential address revealed that a group of "race women" were actively involved in legislative and political activities with the NAACP as well as in community social welfare activities. At this time, the major social welfare activities of this federation included two annual visits and a program for the Old Folks Home and the Boy's Industrial Home, distribution of clothing to needy children and toys to hospitalized children, and fund-raising activities coordinated with the Community Charities Chest Committee (Frederick Douglass Papers, Box 28, Folders 93-96).

A "History of the Woman's League of Kansas City, Missouri" (NACW, 1933, pp. 412-413) reveals that from its founding in 1893, a strong emphasis was placed on helping youths, particularly young women. The Home for Working Girls was established, and a six-room house was eventually purchased and used for both "employed and unemployed girls and strangers." This home was eventually deeded to the Kansas (City) Black Young Woman's Christian Association, whose establishment was inspired by the (Colored) Women's League of Kansas City, Missouri in 1913. Juvenile delinquency was another concern of the league from its inception. Through interracial cooperation, Kansas club women were instrumental in founding a county institution, the Children's Improvement Association, modeled on a farm for "neglected, orphaned, and homeless boys." Both granddaughters of Frederick Douglass were involved in the membership and activities of this organization, which "called forth and developed the finest abilities of women" (NACW, 1933, p. 413).

In some instances, the identities of the two sisters, Rosabelle and Fredericka were fused in accounts of club activities. For example, in the 1933 organizational history of the NACW, the nine-paragraph section entitled "Biography of Mrs. Rosabelle Douglass Sprague Jones" has only one paragraph about Rosabelle; the rest of the section contains biographical material on her sister, Fredericka.

Fredericka Douglass Sprague was educated in the public schools of the District of Columbia and at the Mechanics Institute in Rochester, New York. She moved to Missouri where, in 1906, she was an instructor in cooking and developed the home economics curriculum at Lincoln Institute (Lincoln University) in Jefferson City (Lincoln Institute, 1906-07). Later, she organized the home economics program for black girls at Lincoln High School in Kansas City (Frederick Douglass Papers, Box 28, Folder 83). In 1912, she married a physician, John E. Perry. They had one son, Eugene Boone Perry, who was also a physician ("Mrs. John E. Perry," 1943).

In 1910, Dr. Perry founded the Wheatley Provident Hospital (previously called the Perry Sanitarium), the first private hospital for blacks in Kansas City. Many of Fredericka's community activities were associated with her husband's career, and she served as his "faithful co-partner" in his efforts to improve health care in the black community (Perry, 1947, p. 318). Fredericka organized many fundraising activities to support the hospital and the hospital's nursing program. The Wheatley Provident Hospital Auxiliary No. 1 and the Wheatley Hospital Beacon Club are examples of these activities (Frederick Douglass Papers, Box 28, Folder 83). Although her activities at the Perry Sanitarium are not directly discussed in Perry's

984

(1947) autobiography, Fredericka is pictured among the early lecturers at the hospital. Although this article is concerned with her community efforts on behalf of delinquents and her programs for young black girls, Fredericka's interests were obviously varied. In addition to fund-raising, she was involved in cultural and historic preservation and the legal defense of blacks. She helped found the Civic Protective Association to help "persecuted and friendless" blacks in Kansas City. The activities of this organization were later subsumed by the Legal Defense Fund of the NAACP (Frederick Douglass Papers, Box 28, Folder 83). Along with other members of the NACW, Fredericka was a trustee of the Frederick Douglass Memorial and Historical Association; she was also active in the John Brown Memorial Association (Coles, 1943).

985

In 1923, she initiated the formation of the Missouri State Association of Colored Girls, sponsored by the senior women's association; Kansas City was one of the first cities to have such a group ("Mrs. Perry Resigns," 1940). A "girls' department" was a typical part of the organizational structure of the senior association of colored women's clubs in each state. At one time, Fredericka also served as the chairperson of the National Association of Colored Girls. She composed the words of the state song "Show Me" and the motto "Learning As We Climb" for the Missouri State Association of Colored Girls (NACW, 1933, p. 279). Before her death in 1943, she was quoted as saying that the Missouri Girls' Association provided "an opportunity for young girls to become useful women." She "strongly advocated membership [in the NACW] of all young girls and women, believing that a race can rise no higher than its women" (Coles, 1943). At the time of her resignation in 1940, there were about 19 such clubs in Missouri.

Fredericka's concern about delinquency among black girls developed during her employment with the Kansas City Juvenile Court system and led to the organization of the Missouri Girls' Association. Her husband had this to say about her interest in this area:

> Her vision was very acute and accurate. At least a quarter of a century ago, she predicted the problem of juvenile delinquency that is such a disturbing factor in the minds of the American people. Her contention was that home life was weakening in its potency as a guiding influence in the lives of youths. She predicted the crime wave that is currently sweeping the country. (Perry, 1947, p. 320)

In 1934, Fredericka Perry, along with a small group of other black women, developed a program to curtail delinquency among neglected black teenage girls. Using the name, the Colored Big Sister Association of Kansas City, these women participated in home-finding activities for 12-year-old girls who were released from the Frank C. Niles Orphan Home. When no homes were available, the court system sent these girls to a state institution for juvenile delinquents until they were aged 17. Many of these girls were not youthful offenders, and this placement interrupted their education. Although home placement was a standard social service of the local Community Charities Chest Committee, at that time, it was not part of the services provided to black adolescents.

When the association's home-finding efforts failed, the Colored Big Sister Association involved other members of the black community and persuaded a juvenile court judge, Ray G. Cowan, to rent a residence for such girls on an experimental basis. Fredericka Perry served as superintendent of the residence, which was called the Colored Big Sister Home for Girls. Home furnishings and financial aid were provided by "sympathetic colored men and women" and later, ice was provided by the Salvation Army. Food and other donations were given by local bakeries and cookie and potato chip companies. During the first year, "fifteen girls were successfully clothed, fed and schooled." A well-to-do black woman, Rosetta W. Gibson, gave up a comfortable home to volunteer for 2 years as housemother. The girls were taught homemaking skills; when they were not in school, they worked as helpers in private homes. After over a year of success, the women appealed to the local Community Charities Chest Committee for help. With the intent of eventually closing the home, the committee offered $50 a month for four months to operate the home and to hire a black caseworker to find homes for the girls; it assumed that the girls would be placed in white homes as domestic workers. In 1936, in the belief that girls who left the orphan home did not need to be placed in correctional facilities but still needed help with their transition to other environments, Fredericka Perry made a public appeal to the citizens of Kansas to help maintain the home through "assured assistance": "We refrained from asking white friends for help until we had demonstrated our real ambition to carry forward this necessary program" ("Negro Home for Girls," 1936).

Although data on the final outcome of the home has not yet been located, it has been documented that the home was still in existence in

July 1943—seven years after Fredericka's public appeal for support and three months before her death ("First Ladies," 1943).

CONCLUSIONS

The life of Fredericka Douglass Sprague Perry is a case study of caregiving in the black community. Her biography illustrates several features of the theory of the black helping tradition and Gutman's (1977) fourth stage of transformation of kin obligations to social obligations. Her name is the feminine form of Frederick, her grandfather's name. Not only are naming practices symbolic of affectional ties, they "epitomize personal experiences, historical happenings, attitudes to life, and cultural ideas and values" (Gutman, p. 185). Fredericka Perry's leadership in caregiving activities illustrates the support networks in the black community that were developed by black women during the early decades of the twentieth century. The efforts of such women represented strong cultural commitments to the uplift of their race and to community problem solving.

987

As an organization, the NACW mirrored the race, class, and gender issues of the early twentieth century. The black women activists who belonged to this group were "race women," committed to improving the quality of life of the black masses. They were strong supporters of black men and committed to home life. Terrell (1899, pp. 352-353) described this commitment as follows:

> If I were called upon to state in a word where I thought the Association should do its most effective work, I should say unhesitantly, "in the home." The purification of the home must be our first consideration and care. It is in the home where woman is really queen, that she wields her influence with the most telling effect. It is through the home, therefore, that the principles which we wish to promulgate can be most widely circulated and most deeply impressed. In the mind and heart of every good and conscientious woman, the first place is occupied by home.

Terrell's words are emulated in the life of Fredericka Perry, who operated within the gender conventions of her time. In addition to being a strong source of support and encouragement to her husband, she also took several children of relatives into their home, cared for them, and helped them aspire to be good citizens. Her husband put it this way:

Love and loyalty were among her principal assets. Love for home and those who dwelled therein was everpresent in her mind. No sacrifice was too great for her in making contributions for the comfort and care of the household. Tenderly, she devoted her life to husband and children who came under her supervision. With kind words and noble deeds, she so indelibly stamped her personality upon the minds of those with whom she was most closely associated that she will always be affectionately remembered. Her love for humanity carried her activities beyond the home, far out among the unfortunate and less privileged. (Perry, 1947, p. 320)

988

Like other early members of the NACW, Fredericka was of a high socioeconomic status in the black community. She was a teacher, was married to a prominent physician, and was committed to supporting his career. She received limited recognition as the granddaughter of Frederick Douglass and for her own work with young black girls. However, it is not unlikely that, like her grandmother, Anna Murray Douglass,

her identity became so merged with that of her husband, that few . . . knew and appreciated the full value of the woman . . . in adversity or prosperity, she was the same faithful ally, guarding as best she could every interest connected with [him], his lifework and the home. (Sprague, 1923, pp. 94, 100)

The study of the lives of such women as Fredericka Douglass Sprague Perry provides invaluable insight into the role played by black women activists in organizing and caregiving efforts in the black community through voluntary associations. At least in this instance, caregiving persisted after the Great Depression and culminated in Fredericka Perry's attempts to sustain the Colored Home for Girls as a private form of charity. The operation of this home was a significant contribution to improved child welfare practices for black adolescents in Kansas City. Such efforts may be considered extensions of the helping tradition within the black community and should be publicized and reclaimed as significant for inclusion in the study of American social welfare. Community-action activities, such as those described, contributed to the betterment of social conditions for black Americans and created cooperative efforts that stimulated other social welfare services. Yet, these efforts have been lost to history and as guides to contemporary services in the black community.

Today, social work students learn a great deal about black women recipients of social welfare services but little about the role of black women as developers and providers of services. The study of the pioneering efforts of black women has significant implications for future social work leadership. Germain and Hartman (1980) noted the role that historical content plays in the formation of a professional identity and the understanding of ideological tensions. Prospective and current practitioners, both black and white, can benefit from and be inspired by the historical achievements of black women role models. In addition, the lives of such women as Fredericka Douglass Sprague Perry illuminate for social workers the historical context of contemporary gender issues and gender behavior in the black community.

989

REFERENCES

Coles, A. (1943, October 29). Relative of great abolitionist passes. *Rochester Voice*. In Frederick Douglass Papers. Washington, DC: Moorland-Spingarn Research Center, Howard University.

First ladies of colored America—No. 11 (1943, July). *Crisis Magazine*, p. 209.

Gary, L. (1986). Eartha M. White. In W. I. Trattner (Ed.), *Biographical dictionary of social welfare in America* (pp. 753-756). New York: Greenwood Press.

Germain, C., & Hartman, A. (1980). People and ideas in the history of social work practice. *Social Casework, 61*(6), 323-331.

Giddings, P. (1984). *When and where I enter*. New York: William Morrow.

Gutman, H. G. (1977). *The black family in slavery and freedom, 1750-1925*. New York: Random House.

Hine, D. C. (1986). Lifting the veil, shattering the silence. In D. C. Hine (Ed.), *The state of Afro-American history: Past, present, and future*. Baton Rouge: Louisiana State University Press.

Lerner, G. (Ed.). (1973). *Black women in white America: A documentary history*. New York: Random House.

Lincoln Institute. (1906-07). *35th annual catalogue*. Jefferson City, MO: Inman E. Page Library, Lincoln University.

Majors, M. A. (1893). Mrs. Nathaniel Sprague. In M. A. Majors (Ed.), *Noted Negro women* (pp. 194-195). Atlanta, GA: Atlanta Public Library Special Collection.

Martin, J. E., & Martin, E. P. (1985). *The helping tradition in the black family and community*. Silver Spring, MD: National Association of Social Workers.

McDougald, E. J. (1925, March). The double task: The struggle of Negro women for sex and race emancipation. *Survey Graphics*, pp. 689-691.

Mrs. J. E. Perry resigns as girls club supervisor. (1940, July 5). *The Call*. In Frederick Douglass Papers. Washington, DC: Moorland-Spingarn Research Center, Howard University.

Mrs. John E. Perry (death). (1943, October 25). *Kansas City Times.* In
    Clipping Files, Missouri Valley Room, Kansas City Public Library.
National Association of Colored Women. (1933). *Lifting as they climb.*
    Jefferson City, MO: Inman E. Page Library, Lincoln University.
Negro home for girls. (1936, September 20). *Kansas City Journal Post.* In
    Clipping Files, Missouri Valley Room, Kansas City Public Library.
Peebles-Wilkins, W. (1987a). Eartha M. White. In *Encyclopedia of social
    work* (18th ed., Vol. 2, pp. 945-946). Silver Spring, MD: National
    Association of Social Workers.
Peebles-Wilkins, W. (1987b). Janie Porter Barrett. In *Encyclopedia of social
    work* (18th ed., Vol. 2, pp. 914-915). Silver Spring, MD: National
    Association of Social Workers.
Perry, J. E. (1947). *Forty cords of wood: Memoirs of a medical doctor.*
    Jefferson City, MO: Lincoln University Press.
Sprague, R. D. (1923). Anna Murray Douglass—My mother as I recall her.
    Journal of Negro History, 8, 93-101.
Sterling, D. (Ed.). (1984). *We are your sisters: Black women in the nineteenth
    century* (pp. 418-423). New York: W. W. Norton.
Terborg-Penn, R. (1978). Discrimination against Afro-American women in
    the women's movement, 1830-1920. In S. Harley & R. Terborg-Penn
    (Eds.), *The Afro-American woman: Struggles and images* (pp. 17-27). Port
    Washington, NY: National University Publications.
Terrell, M. C. (ca. 1899). The duty of the National Association of Colored
    Women to the race. *Church Review,* pp. 340-354. In Mary Church Terrell
    Papers. Washington, DC: Moorland-Spingarn Research Center, Howard
    University.
Terrell, M. C. (1901). Club work of colored women. *Southern Workman,*
    30(8), 435-438. In Mary Church Terrell Papers. Washington, DC: Moorland-
    Spingarn Research Center, Howard University.

990

*Wilma Peebles-Wilkins is Associate Head and Director, Social Work
Program, Department of Sociology, Anthropology, and Social Work,
North Carolina State University, Raleigh. Initial funding for the
research reported in this article was provided by the College of
Humanities and Social Sciences Research Fund, North Carolina
State University. This article is a revised version of a paper presented
at the Social Welfare History Symposium, Annual Program Meeting,
Council on Social Work Education, Atlanta, Georgia, March 7, 1988.*

A Mother's Wages

Income Earning Among Married Italian and
Black Women, 1896–1911

■

ELIZABETH H. PLECK

IN RURAL AREAS black as well as white wives were productive laborers, often working in the fields alongside their husbands. In urban areas white wives labored in their homes but did not earn wages; black wives did both. A far higher proportion of black wives were earning wages than any other group of married women: even with her husband at work, a black wife often continued to earn a living. In 1900 the rate of wage earning was 26 percent for married black women and 3.2 percent for married white women.[1] Nor does

Originally published in *A Heritage of Her Own: Toward a New Social History of American Women*, Nancy F. Cott and Elizabeth H. Pleck, eds. (New York: Simon and Schuster, 1979).

the contrast of black and immigrant wives narrow this difference. In nearly all American cities in 1900, the rate of employment for black married women was anywhere from four to fifteen times higher than for immigrant wives.[2]

A host of diverse economic, cultural, and demographic grounds have been given in accounting for the high rate of labor-force participation among black married women.[3] Many argue that slavery destroyed any vestige of domesticity and left in its place a black wife and mother hardened to back-breaking drudgery. Others refer to the menial jobs and frequent unemployment of black husbands. Because these men could not find work, it has been said, black wives had to secure jobs as domestics, laundresses, or cooks. As a result of this imbalance, many marriages broke up: husbands separated or deserted and wives were forced to support the family. Then, too, it is claimed that black mothers could easily accept paid jobs because of the availability of grandmothers or other elderly relatives as child caretakers.

Another set of explanations has been given for the absence of immigrant wives from the urban labor market. Among the immigrants Italian women have received particular attention. Italian wives rarely earned wages, despite low incomes and severe unemployment among their husbands. In her study of Italian families in early twentieth-century Buffalo, Virginia Yans-McLaughlin found very few single or married Italian women took jobs. She argued that Italian culture prohibited these women from working, even at the price of family economic well-being.[4] On the other hand, Louise Tilly suggested alternative economic and demographic explanations, such as the large number of mothers with young children or the absence of demand for women workers in Buffalo.[5]

On this subject opinions are strongly held; alas, with little empirical investigation. Survivals of peasant customs can encourage, limit or prohibit specific behavior; old cultural patterns can be enlivened by new economic circumstances or destroyed in the process.[6] Two cultures may respond in a different manner to similar economic circumstances, and a particular culture may also vary its response as economic circumstances change. Too often in recent historical writing family norms have been pitted against economic imperatives without appreciating the context of family needs and economic choices.[7] It is not a question of choosing between economic, demographic and cultural factors but of showing the interaction between these factors. A systematic comparison of groups roughly similar in economic condition is required. Because of the large body of available information and the extent of historical writing, Italians have

992

A Mother's Wages

been compared with blacks, although another European immigrant group could have been selected. Before making the comparison, some background is provided. First, special surveys of Italian and black families around the turn of the century form the basis of the comparison. A portrait of the general economic condition among blacks and Italians demonstrates that both groups lived in desperate poverty. Differences in the higher rate of wage earning for black than for Italian wives are examined in the context of similar as well as changing family conditions and economic opportunities. Finally, some of the reasons for this difference are suggested. Taken together, a black wife faced economic need and found cultural support for working; an Italian wife, often at the edge of poverty, encountered cultural barriers toward her employment which could only be offset by the offer of higher wages.

993

I

Several government documents permit a direct contrast of urban black and Italian wives. The U.S. Bureau of Labor in 1896 surveyed 6,773 Chicago Italians near Hull House. The same year the Bureau assigned black investigators to study living conditions among 2,748 blacks in Atlanta, Cambridge, Massachusetts, and Nashville. Fifteen years later Senate investigators conducted another survey asking similar questions. The subsequent report, issued by the Senate Committee on the Investigation of the Condition of the Immigrants, known as the Dillingham Commission, ran into forty-six volumes. Two volumes concerned black and immigrant families in seven cities: these seven differed in size, ethnic composition, and most importantly, economic opportunities for working women. Whether it was Cleveland, Boston, or any of the large cities, there was always some demand for women workers as servants. But, in addition, in four of these cities—Philadelphia, Chicago, Boston, and New York —garment industries employed many women workers. The other three—Milwaukee, Cleveland and Buffalo—dominated by aluminum and steel industries, breweries or oil refineries, offered few jobs other than service for women workers.

A comprehensive profile of women's work can be drawn from these documents. Compared with the federal census for the same period, these surveys were far more complete in delineating women's work. The federal census inquired about boarders in the household and women's paid employment but failed to inquire about wages (for women or men) and piece work performed at home.

These surveys in 1896 and 1911 included these questions and much more: data concerning hours of work, weeks of unemployment, and family income. By combining three separate pieces of information from the surveys—paid employment, taking boarders, and piece work—we are able to more accurately contrast wage earning among black and Italian wives.

One can always doubt the accuracy of this information. Surveys have rarely recorded the full range of women's work, but there is little reason to conclude that the wage earning of Italian wives was more carefully noted than for blacks. In 1896 the Bureau of Labor employed black men and women, at least one a lawyer, another a college professor, as surveyors. They asked questions similar to those in the Bureau of Labor report on Chicago's Italians the same year. Blacks have often been underenumerated in surveys, but the absent group generally consists of young black men, not married women. If, for any reason, these surveys failed to count many impoverished black wives, the percentages reported here represent conservative estimates of black women's rate of working: missing women were just as likely, if not more likely to work, as other black women.

Seen from a distance, one might have suspected that Italian wives were more tradition bound and less likely to earn a living than other immigrant women. They were raised in a Catholic, Mediterranean culture which circumscribed a woman's dress and demeanor.[8] A man's honor was a precious but fragile commodity: in her daily actions a wife had to avoid bringing shame on her husband.[9] As recent arrivals in American cities, such wives spoke no English and knew very little about finding employment. Then, too, Italian migration consisted mostly of men. Because this was so, Italian women were likely to marry, often at a young age, and if their husbands found work, it was less necessary for them to do so.

Closer scrutiny of documents for 1896 and 1911 shows that Italian wives were no more confined to the home than other immigrant wives. Peasant wives in Italy were expected to contribute to the family by field work as well as their performance of traditional female tasks. In the blistering Mediterranean sun, Italian wives picked grapes at harvest time and mowed, winnowed, bundled, and hauled sheaves of grain. In a contemporary account about women in Sicily, only the poorest wives worked alongside their husbands in the fields, yet most of the women carried heavy bags of water to the men.[10] Even in Sicily, the wives planted vegetable gardens and sold the surplus, slaughtered pigs, cut wood, dug and weeded mattock.

In American cities few married women from any immigrant

994

background were employed, according to the survey in 1911. Italian wives were as likely to work as German or Irish wives and more often employed than Polish or Russian Jewish married women (Table 1). Nor did Italian traditionalism prevent daughters from working in American sweatshops and factories, generally with parental approval. In depression-ridden Chicago in 1896, the one city for which information is available, about half of unmarried Italian girls between the ages of fifteen and nineteen were employed.[11] Ruth True, a New York City social reformer, recognized that Italian values, the importance of the family above individual preference, actually encouraged the employment of teenage daughters. She noted: "The girl herself is as eager to go to work as her parents are to have her. She takes it for granted that she should help in the family income. Carlotta gets a job not because she feels the need of self-support as an expression of individuality, or self-dependence, but because she feels so strongly the sense of family obligation."[12] A New York Italian daughter who quit parochial school at age twelve echoed these conclusions: "My father was a stone mason, you know how it is. He didn't have steady work and my mother used to talk all the time about how poor we were. So I had my mind on work all the time. I was thinking how I could go to work and bring money home to my mother."[13]

995

There are additional reasons for doubting the uniqueness of the Italian situation. Unfamiliarity with a city or with American life was never an effective barrier to employment; the level of employment rose only slightly as Italian wives became accustomed to America. For those Chicago Italian wives in 1896 residing in the city more than ten years, 16 percent were employed, only 3 percentage points higher than for wives resident in Chicago six to ten years, or 6 points higher than for wives in America less than six years.[14] Knowledge of spoken English was never a prerequisite for paid employment, at least in the kind of jobs immigrant wives were forced to accept. The typical Italian wife from any one of seven American cities in 1911 was far less likely to speak English than the Jewish, Polish, or German wife, but she was just as likely and sometimes even more likely to be employed than these women.[15] Even within the Italian community, the ability to speak English was not a necessary job qualification. Among Chicago Italian wives in 1896 the rate of labor-force participation was only 2 percentage points higher for wives speaking English compared with non-English-speaking wives (10 percent vs. 8 percent).[16] Finally, the excess of men failed to alter the rate of working women among Italians. For instance, there were 132 Italian men for every 100 New York City Italian women in 1905.[17] Nonetheless,

TABLE 1

Proportion of Black and Italian Families with Income Contributed by Wives, Children, and Lodgers[a]

Group, City and Date	% with Wives Working	% with Children Working	% with Lodgers	N
Blacks, Atlanta, 1896	65	10	8	240
Blacks, Nashville, 1896	55	12	6	199
Blacks, Cambridge, 1896	44	8	8	88
Blacks, New York, 1905	na	na	42	3014
Blacks, New York, 1911	51	10	27	145
Blacks, Philadelphia, 1911	54	13	41	71
Italians, Chicago, 1896[b]	15	36	16	1227
Italians, Chicago, 1911	19	25	17	219
Italians, Buffalo, 1905	14	19	na	na
Italians, Buffalo, 1911	0	9	37	115
Italians, New York, 1905	na	na	21	2945
Italians, New York, 1911	36	19	20	333
Italians, Philadelphia, 1911	8	23	16	195
Italians, Boston, 1911	16	25	39	210
Italians, Cleveland, 1911	10	22	41	111
Germans, New York, 1911	30	35	0	308
Germans, Chicago, 1911	8	44	11	208
Germans, Milwaukee, 1911	5	28	14	163
Poles, Chicago, 1911	7	21	43	410
Poles, Philadelphia, 1911	7	10	60	159
Poles, Boston, 1911	11	4	61	95
Poles, Cleveland, 1911	4	4	43	131
Poles, Buffalo, 1911	2	28	9	178
Poles, Milwaukee, 1911	5	24	17	150
Russian Jews, New York, 1911	1	31	56	452
Russian Jews, Chicago, 1911	8	30	38	187
Russian Jews, Boston, 1911	15	41	40	226
Irish, New York, 1911	5	18	20	272
Irish, Philadelphia, 1911	28	50	19	98
Irish, Boston, 1911	27	49	18	197
Irish, Cleveland, 1911	5	36	10	122

Sources: Computed from data in "Condition of the Negro in Various Cities," *Bulletin of the Department of Labor*, Vol. II, No. 10 (May 1897), pp. 257–360; Carroll D. Wright, *The Italians in Chicago: A Social and Economic Study* (Washington, D.C., 1897), Table 1, pp. 52–273; Virginia Yans-McLaughlin, "Patterns of Work and Family Organization: Buffalo's Italians," *Journal of Interdisciplinary History*, Vol. II, No. 2 (Autumn, 1971), pp. 111–126; U.S. Senate Reports, 62nd Cong. 1st sess., *Immigrants in Cities*, Vol. 2 (Washington, D.C., 1911), Table 401, pp. 546–548; Herbert G. Gutman, *The Black Family in Slavery and Freedom, 1750–1925* (New York, 1976), Table B-4, p. 530.

[a] Data pertains to families with both husჟand and wife present.
[b] All evidence for Italians is for South Italians only.

the rate of labor-force participation among Italian wives was higher there than in any other American city in 1911—almost a third of Italian wives were employed.[18] Since single women were removed as competitors for New York City jobs, it may have been slightly easier for Italian wives to find work. Or, more likely, the balance of the sexes may have had less bearing on the employment of wives than the economic demand for women in New York's garment industry.

II

Three dimensions of poverty—low family income, chronic male unemployment, and unskilled labor for men—plagued Italian as well as black families. In these conditions, Italians suffered as much as blacks from low incomes and more from severe unemployment, but they were less concentrated in dead-end and demeaning jobs. Working women from both groups were employed in low wage, low skill jobs, but black women were largely excluded from factory employment. In terms of family income, Italian poverty matched that of blacks. For Chicago Italians in 1896 the median income for a male-present family was $235 compared with black family incomes that year of $393.50 in Nashville, $374 in Atlanta, and $584 in Cambridge.[19] Fifteen years later, despite an increase in real wages, both groups continued near subsistence. Philadelphia's Italians in 1911 earned ten or twenty dollars less than blacks, and New York City's Italians earned virtually the same as blacks.[20]

Severe male unemployment was even more pronounced among Italians than blacks. During a national depression in 1896, a black father in any of eighteen northern or southern cities was out of work an average of 11.7 weeks.[21] Chicago Italian fathers, unemployed on the average thirty-six weeks during the year in 1896,[22] spent the rest of the time in "idleness and almost absolute inactivity in poorly ventilated rooms."[23] Pursuing the question of how families subsisted during hard times, the Bureau of Labor found no unemployed Italian fathers who depended on their wives' wages and only a few who relied on their children. Instead, most Italian families were living on savings or a combination of savings and credit.[24] "When no more money," one Italian father in New York City made plain, "me take out trust at grocery man."[25] An Italian daughter in New York City stated simply: "If there is no money, we eat less."[26] Asked about their means of subsistence, black families also listed savings or credit, but in addition, eleven families in Atlanta, ten in Cambridge, and seventeen in Nashville mentioned the wife's earnings.[27]

Italian as well as black husbands were heavily concentrated in unskilled labor. About one quarter of Italian husbands in Chicago or black men in Atlanta, Nashville, or Cambridge were common laborers.[28] In the other jobs available, Italians differed from blacks: they had access to jobs which in the present offered low wages and high unemployment but which held some promise for the future. Aside from unskilled labor, Italian men earned their livings as tailors, carpenters, barbers, and fruit peddlers. Among New York City Italian male workers in 1905, the racial gap is clear: almost two out of ten Italians were employed in the garment industry and another three out of ten in skilled trades; in contrast, only one out of ten employed black men was in one of these two types of work.[29] Most black husbands not employed as unskilled laborers were servants and waiters and elevator operators: in sum, low-wage jobs, paying almost half what one made in unskilled labor.

An unskilled but racially segregated labor market was even more apparent among the women. Italian daughters, not their fathers, entered factories, mostly sewing pants, shirts, dresses, and gloves, and making boxes, candy, and artificial flowers.[30] More Italian than black women found work in Philadelphia clothing factories; the few black women in this industry were confined to low-paying jobs as pressers, or they sewed the cheaper garments like middy blouses, overalls, and housedresses.[31] Most black women were excluded from factories in the North except as strike breakers or as extra laborers during wartime. Social worker Mary White Ovington summarized the difference between white and black women's work in New York City around the turn of the century:

> She [the black woman] gets the job that the white girl does not want. It may be that the white girl wants the wrong thing, and that the jute mill and tobacco shop and flower factory are more dangerous to health and right living than the mistress' kitchen, but she knows her mind and follows the business that brings her liberty of action when the six o'clock whistle blows.[32]

Two jobs were the mainstay of black women workers: laundry work and domestic service. At these two occupations eight out of ten black wives were employed in 1900. Laundry work was largely the preserve of black mothers. These women, who wanted to remain at home, worked "at their tubs or ironing boards from Monday morning until Saturday night,"[33] often at wages lower than in service. This condition, Mary White Ovington noted, "makes the tenement rooms, tiny enough at best, sadly cluttered, but it does not deprive the children of the presence of their mother, who accepts a smaller

998

income to remain at home with them."[34] Single as well as married black women disliked service. Philadelphia black working women, interviewed in 1919, preferred their work in a rag factory to domestic service because they could enjoy free evenings, holidays, and Sundays.[35] If all else failed, a black mother entered service: five times as many black as foreign-born domestics in 1900 were married.[36] When mothers were compelled to become maids, they often left their children with "babytenders." Although some of these caretakers must have had years of experience, others were unable to properly supervise children and incapable of giving sufficient milk to infants.[37]

Despite the many similarities in economic need for both Italian and black families, there was one defining difference: black wives were far more often breadwinners than Italian wives. There is no mistaking the extent of this racial difference. First of all, the rate of black wives at work was 44 percent in Cambridge, 55 percent in Nashville, and 65 percent in Atlanta in 1896; the rate of Chicago Italian wives at work that year was 15 percent. Fifteen years later, it appears from Table 1, over half of Philadelphia and New York City black wives were employed, but just one out of six Italian wives in these cities were working.

Black mothers were also more likely to supplement the family budget by doing paid work at home.[38] The Dillingham Commission of 1911, which inquired about the number of wives working in the family's quarters, found about one in five black wives in New York City and Philadelphia working at home, usually as laundresses. The photographic record of New York City Italian mothers making artificial flowers or sewing shirts around the kitchen table harmonizes with the statistical reality. In 1911 one-third of Italian wives in New York City were earning wages at home, mostly as tailoresses. But these women were the exception for Italian immigrants: few Italian wives elsewhere were doing piece work, whether in Buffalo or Boston, Chicago or Milwaukee (Table 2).

Black and Italian wives were probably equally as likely to earn money by a third method, taking lodgers. From the percentages in Table 1, it is impossible to give the edge to blacks or Italians in this regard. The number of lodgers varied between years and between cities, perhaps coinciding with the waves of migrants reaching each locale. It is also puzzling to explain the relative absence of lodgers from black homes in Atlanta, Nashville, or Cambridge for 1896. Nevertheless, among black and Italian families in the same city, there was a tendency for blacks to house lodgers more often than Italians. Lodgers were twice as common among black than Italian New York City households in 1905,[39] although six years later the gap

999

TABLE 2
Percentage of All Italian and Black Wives Employed at Home, 1911

	%	N
Blacks, New York City	23	273
Blacks, Philadelphia	17	139
South Italians, New York City	22	402
South Italians, Philadelphia	3	349
South Italians, Boston	5	309
South Italians, Buffalo	1	205
South Italians, Chicago	3	349
South Italians, Milwaukee	1	145

Source: U.S. Immigration Commission, *Immigrants in Cities*, Vol. II, Tables 24, 78, 126, 290, 340, pp. 39, 83, 127–129, 239, 293–298, 350–352.

1000

between the groups was erased. For Philadelphia in 1911, lodgers were almost three times as common in black as Italian households.

By any measure of income earning, black wives were more often breadwinners than Italian wives. They often took lodgers, earned money doing laundry in their homes, and worked as domestics or cooks. Italian wives frequently housed lodgers, avoided piece work (except in New York City), and very rarely held paid employment.

III

Common sense explanations for why black wives were so often breadwinners have rarely been subjected to systematic comparison. The idea is that some hidden difference in group composition between Italians and blacks accounted for the difference in the rate of wage earning. One by one, seven possible reasons are evaluated: that Italians differed from blacks in terms of income, male unemployment, the presence of young children at home, attitudes toward children's schooling, reliance on child labor, availability of childcare, or marital stability. Any of these seven differences may have produced the lower rate of wage earning among Italian than black wives. The research method examines differences in wage earning, holding each of these factors constant.

First of all, even with husbands earning identical incomes, a black wife was more likely to work than an Italian wife. Among the poorest families in 1896, those with husbands earning less than $200 a year, almost all black wives in Atlanta, Nashville, or Cambridge

TABLE 3

*Percentage of Wives in Paid Employment According to
Husband's Income, Among Chicago's Italians and Blacks in
Atlanta, Nashville, and Cambridge, 1896*

| | $0–100 | | $101–200 | | $201–300 | | $301–400 | | $401–500 | | $501+ | |
	(%)	N	(%)	N	(%)	N	(%)	N	(%)	N	(%)	N
Italians, Chicago	20	334	12	379	12	178	9	89	5	55	7	43
Blacks, Cambridge	100	2	100	3	25	8	64	11	41	17	29	38
Blacks, Atlanta	80	10	77	39	66	62	40	42	36	14	28	32
Blacks, Nashville	60	15	68	19	56	43	48	48	11	19	41	27

Sources: Carroll D. Wright, *The Italians in Chicago: A Social and Economic Study* (Washington, D.C., 1897), Table 1, pp. 52–273; "Condition of the Negro in Various Cities," *Bulletin of the Department of Labor*, Vol. II, No. 10 (May 1897), pp. 257–360.

were working, whereas the same desperation sent only a fifth of Italian wives in Chicago to work. At all income levels, Table 3 demonstrates that black wives were far more likely to work than Italian wives. One also needs to include taking boarders as women's income, information which is only available for 1911 (Table 4). The inclusion of this additional income does not alter the basic difference. For every income category, black wives were still more likely to earn wages *and* admit boarders.

When her husband became unemployed, a black wife was more likely to work than an Italian wife.[40] Since the 1911 study by the Dillingham Commission did not include information on unemployment, this comparison depends on computations for 1896. Among Italian wives whose husbands were unemployed at least twenty-one weeks a year, only one in six wives earned wages. For Nashville, Cambridge, and Atlanta black wives in this predicament, the percentage of working wives was at least three times greater. The racial gap appeared whether a husband was unemployed a few weeks or most of the year; in either of these circumstances, a black wife was more likely to work than an Italian wife.

Even with young children at home, black mothers more often took paid jobs than Italian mothers.[41] It is almost a universal condition that mothers of young children find it too difficult to accept paid work; yet the presence of young children was less of a barrier to the employment of black than Italian mothers. For mothers with pre-

TABLE 4
*Percentage of Wives Earning Wages or Taking in Boarders by
Husband's Income for Black and Italian Families, 1911*

	Husband's Income					
	0–$399	N	$400–$599	N	$600+	N
Blacks, New York City	90%	42	71%	38	61%	28
Blacks, Philadelphia	72	29	60	20	83	6
Italians, New York City	47	71	53	170	29	72
Italians, Philadelphia	25	130	16	43	8	13

Source: U.S. Senate Reports, 62nd Cong., 1st sess., *Immigrants in Cities*, Vol. 1, Table 69, p. 230, 410.

school children, probably youngsters under age six in 1896, the data in Table 5 indicates that black mothers in Atlanta, Nashville, and Cambridge were almost four times as likely to earn wages as Italian mothers of young children.

It might be thought that black mothers accepted jobs because they could depend on their kin for childcare. In *The Black Family in Slavery and Freedom*, Herbert Gutman demonstrated the importance of kin networks among slave and emancipated black families. In cities kin were not always available; the evidence suggests female kin were far more frequent in Italian than black urban households. One approximate measure of the availability of female caretakers was the residence of adult women relatives in the household. Yet the odds were one and a half times greater that an Italian household in Chicago included a female relative compared with a black household in Cambridge, Atlanta, or Nashville for 1896.[42] In 1905 the likelihood was that a New York City Italian rather than black household included relatives (23 percent for Italians, 16 percent for blacks).[43] Even when Italian kin did not occupy the same living quarters, they often lived nearby. In studying Italian families of Providence, Rhode Island, in 1915, Judith Smith found that three out of five Italian families were related to at least one other household in the city, and almost all of these kin lived less than eight blocks from their families.[44]

Another possible source of the difference might lie in parental attitudes toward schooling. There is at least substantial reason to think that black parents held more favorable attitudes toward children's education than Italians. If a black mother chose to keep her older children in school rather than sending them to work, she may have been compelled to earn the extra income for her family. To be sure, black children were more likely to attend school than Italian

TABLE 5

Relationship of Mother's Wage Earning to the Presence of Children Among Italians in Chicago, and Blacks in Atlanta, Nashville, and Cambridge, 1896

	Percentage of Mothers at Work						
	No Children at Home	N	Children at Home	N	Children at School	N	Children at Work	N
Italians, Chicago	15%	180	12%	848	18%	124	23%	75
Blacks, Cambridge	48	25	41	32	43	14	67	3
Blacks, Atlanta	49	65	60	108	61	31	50	8
Blacks, Nashville	51	51	44	89	57	37	65	17

Sources: Carroll D. Wright, *The Italians in Chicago: A Social and Economic Study* (Washington, D.C., 1897). Table I, pp. 52–273; "Conditions of the Negro in Various Cities," *Bulletin of the Department of Labor*, Vol. II, No. 10 (May 1897), pp. 257–360.

youngsters. The rate of school attendance was almost twice as great for black sons in Atlanta, Cambridge, or Nashville compared with Chicago Italian sons (aged ten to fourteen) in 1900. Similar disparities appeared in the rate of school attendance among schoolage Italian and black daughters in those cities.[45] Beyond the legal age requirements for school attendance, the pattern of difference held true. Black teenagers of both sexes in Atlanta, Cambridge, and Nashville in 1900 were more likely to attend high school than Italian adolescents. Nonetheless, there is reason to doubt that keeping children in school was the motive behind more black than Italian mothers working. If this had been the case, then one might expect such mothers to quit their jobs when their children finished school. The exact opposite situation occurred for both black and Italian mothers. Both groups of women (with the exception of black wives in Atlanta) were more inclined to work than mothers with school children.

Italian youngsters, who often dropped out of school at an early age, were contributing their wages to the family. In city after city, child labor was more common among Italians than blacks. Can we then conclude that black wives worked because the family could not rely on child labor? To test this suggestion, we can compare Italian and black mothers of child laborers. Even black mothers who could send their children to work still earned wages. Only a quarter of Chicago Italian mothers in 1896 with working children were employed, whereas between one-half and two-thirds of the black mothers of employed children in Cambridge, Atlanta, or Nashville in 1896 still earned a living.

A final explanation for black women's greater participation in the work force is rooted in the short-lived duration of many black marriages. Households with a missing (dead, deserted, or separated) husband were far more common among blacks than Italians, according to a New York City sample from the state census in 1905. In studying two Italian and black neighborhoods in New York City, one in Greenwich Village and the other in San Juan Hill, Herbert Gutman found such female-headed households were almost four times as common among blacks as Italians.[46] Given these differences, it might be argued that black wives anticipated an end to their marriages, and therefore held jobs as a form of economic insurance for the future. Evidence from my research on blacks in late-nineteenth-century Boston is relevant to this argument. The rate of marital dissolution was determined for black couples listed in the manuscript census schedules of the federal census for 1880 who were traced to the same records for Boston twenty years later. (If one or both spouses had died in the intervening period, as certified by Boston death records, they were eliminated from the trace.) Boston black wives whose husbands had left them by 1900 were no more likely to have been employed in 1880 than black wives in stable marriages lasting the two decades, but the 7 percent difference was not statistically significant. In sum, a wife's wage earning bore little connection to her husband's subsequent absence. It is still possible that taking paid employment expressed a wife's doubt about the future of her marriage, but if that was the case, her calculations were inaccurate.

To summarize these comparisons, we have seen that no single economic or demographic condition accounts for the higher rate of wage earning among black than Italian wives. Even if her husband was unemployed or earning very low wages, an Italian wife generally decided against employment, whereas her black counterpart generally took a job. More black than Italian mothers of young children went to work, despite the fact that the supply of female relatives as caretakers was greater in Italian than black households. As Italian children entered the labor force, a mother became the manager of the family finances; even after her working children contributed to the household, a black mother continued to earn an income as well as oversee family affairs. When an Italian mother could rely on the wages of her working children, she did not enter the labor market, while black mothers of working children remained in the labor force. It is true that black wives, who were more often living without husbands than Italian wives, needed to work. But there is no reason to conclude that uncertainty about the future of a marriage was the impetus behind a black wife working.

IV

Faced with similar conditions, blacks and Italian wives acted differently. Confronted with changing conditions, how did they respond? Evidence from Tables 1 through 6 illustrate the effect of changes in the economics of the family environment on the labor-force participation of Italian and black wives. Three factors—family economic need, the composition of the household, and the wage rate for women workers—led to higher rates of working among black as well as Italian wives.

1005

As a first principle, growing immiserization was an inducement to work. The poorer her husband, the more likely that a black wife sought employment in Cambridge, Atlanta, or Nashville in 1896 or in New York City in 1911. Perhaps due to the small number of families studied, this was not true for Philadelphia black wives in 1911: there the wives of wealthier husbands were even more likely to work than more impoverished married women. The same economic squeeze compelled Italian wives to work, whether in Chicago in 1896 or New York and Philadelphia in 1911. A glance at Tables 3 and 4 demonstrates that wage earning for the Italian wife increased as her husband's wage decreased.

The evidence from Table 6 suggests a second conclusion: that chronic unemployment for either the Italian or black husband sent his wife to work. As the number of weeks a husband was unemployed mounted, the wife's rate of employment climbed. Cambridge black wives in 1896, whose incomes were higher, rarely sought work until a husband lost his job. Once that happened, they, like black wives elsewhere, entered the labor force in large numbers. Sustained unemployment for an Italian husband also increased the likelihood of a wife working. For Chicago in 1896, Italian wives with husbands unemployed at least twenty-one weeks a year were twice as likely to work as wives with fully employed husbands.

The age of her children also influenced a mother's willingness to work. All mothers of young children were more likely to remain at home before reentering the work force when their children were grown. Black mothers from Cambridge or Nashville in 1896 slightly decreased their participation in the labor market during the childbearing years but later reentered the work force in large numbers. Atlanta black mothers never dropped out of the labor force even as young matrons. Freedom from childcare responsibilities also made it easier for Italian mothers to take paid jobs. The tendency to work

1006

TABLE 6
Percentage of Wives Working Due to Husband's Unemployment, Among
Chicago's Italians and Blacks in Atlanta, Nashville, and Cambridge, 1896

	Fully Employed	N	Unemployed for Some Time During the Year	N	Number of Weeks Husband Unemployed					
					1–10	N	11–20	N	21–52	N
Italians, Chicago	10%	370	17%	767	15%	66	9%	68	18%	633
Blacks, Cambridge	16	30	53	49	42	26	53	13	80	10
Blacks, Atlanta	50	134	64	66	58	38	63	16	83	12
Blacks, Nashville	48	127	47	53	43	21	38	16	63	16

Sources: Carroll D. Wright, *The Italians in Chicago: A Social and Economic Study* (Washington, D.C., 1897), Table 1, pp. 52–273; "Condition of the Negro in Various Cities," *Bulletin of the Department of Labor*, Vol. II, No. 10 (May 1897), pp. 257–360.

among Chicago Italian mothers was twice as strong for mothers of adult children compared with mothers of preschoolers.[47]

Outside of the family's circumstances, the offer of "higher wages" persuaded more Italian as well as black wives to work.[48] A fair comparison must exclude the black women in southern cities, working at disastrously low wages. In northern cities the offer of higher wages led to expanded levels of paid employment for both sets of wives. For instance, in Philadelphia where black women in 1911 made an average of $170 a year, about half of black wives were earning wages; in New York City that year, where the median wage was $215 a year, seven out of ten black wives worked. When offered slightly higher wages, Italian wives in 1911 were also more willing to work. At a wage of $100 a year, the average for Italian working women in Cleveland and Philadelphia, one out of ten wives worked. With a twenty-dollar increase in pay, the rate in Chicago, two out of ten wives worked. An additional sixty dollars in pay persuaded one-third of New York City Italian wives to work. Just taking the two cities where comparable information was available, Philadelphia and New York, shows that both black and Italian wives responded to economic incentives. An additional sixty-five dollars in wages increased the Italian woman's rate of working by 14 points; a slightly smaller wage increase raised the black woman's rate of working about the same level.[49]

V

A number of possible reasons often advanced to explain the higher rate of employment among black than Italian married women have been eliminated. However, no clear alternative has emerged. There remains one suggestive economic difference: that black women's wage earning was a means of coping with long-term income inadequacy. Like black husbands, Italian men suffered from low wages and chronic unemployment, but their jobs in skilled crafts, the expanding garment industry, or in retail trade offered more future promise: better pay, on-the-job training, and promotions. The jobs of black men as waiters, cooks, and elevator operators were more often dead ends. From the available evidence one can neither confirm nor deny the possibility of this kind of economic difference. However, short of this kind of proof, and having eliminated a large number of economic and demographic explanations, we are forced to consider a residual factor: cultural differences between Italians and blacks.

For Italians cultural attitudes acted as a barrier to the employment of married women. This barrer was less a high stone wall than a low chain fence. Prohibitions applied to married women, especially mothers, but did not extend to daughters. Prior to marriage, Italian daughters often earned wages: after marriage, Italian wives managed finances, cared for the home, gave birth to children, and looked after youngsters. Yet even Italian cultural prohibitions could be overcome with the offer of higher wages, especially for wives doing piece work at home or employed along with other women in neighborhood factories.

For black women the natural tendency is to trace their pattern of wage earning to the legacy of slavery. If bondage fundamentally reshaped the role of slave women, then we would expect to find nearly all of them in the labor force a generation or two after emancipation. This was clearly not the case. Nor was it true that black married women behaved in a manner similar to poverty-stricken white married women. There was a fundamental cultural difference. We need to identify the connection between the slave experience and black attitudes about the involvement of wives in productive labor and in the family. Despite the magnificent new research on slave culture, consciousness, and family life, we are still far from answering this question. What follows are suggestions about how slave culture (defined here as ways of living) related to the wage

1007

earning of black married women. It is beyond the scope of this paper to analyze the *origins* of this slave culture (in West African tradition, learning from whites, or the blending of the two experiences amidst generations of life as slaves); rather what concerns us here is to pinpoint the slave ways of life which support black women's wage earning after emancipation. More specifically, we can suggest that black women's wage earning was influenced by three patterns, husband-wife relations, child-rearing, and the emphasis on children's schooling. However, for all the cultural support favoring women's employment, black husbands and wives approached this subject with considerable ambiguity. In fact, these three cultural elements were necessary to offset strong objections to paid employment.

Among black husbands slavery left as its first legacy negative attitudes toward the employment of wives. It is true that contemporary studies, such as a 1970 survey, indicate more favorable opinions toward working wives among black than white men.[50] Another survey in 1966 also found that black husbands, even those born prior to 1911, were less opposed to the employment of mothers with school-age children than white husbands.[51] Nonetheless, contemporary surveys cannot be grafted onto the past. During Reconstruction black husbands vehemently prevented their wives from working in the fields.[52] All over the South freedmen, who demanded a man's wage to support their families, believed their wives should remain at home with the children. One Louisiana plantation mistress noted in 1865 that "Pete is still in the notion of remaining but chooses to feed his wife out of his wages rather than to get her fed for her services."[53] A cotton planter lost money because he had to support "on an average twenty-five to thirty negro (*sic*) women and children in idleness, as the freedmen will not permit their wives and children to work in the fields."[54] This idleness would continue, according to an Alabama cotton grower, because "it is a matter of pride with the men to allow exemption from labor to their wives. . . ."[55] Long after Reconstruction black husbands refused to allow their wives to work for white families. One ex-slave father in the South confessed his ambition "to support his family by his own efforts; never to allow his wife and daughters to be thrown in contact with Southern white men in their homes."[56] In the early twentieth century, an Alabama sharecropper kept his wife from doing laundry for whites. He said, "I didn't want any money comin into my house from that. My wife didn't wait on white folks for their dirty laundry. There was plenty of em would ask her and there'd be an answer ready for em."[57]

Three countervailing cultural tendencies were necessary to set aside these attitudes. The first of these was the pattern of relations between husbands and wives which arose out of slavery. These patterns of interaction were not simple character traits but rather a bundle of contradictions: belief in the husband's responsibility to support his family but doubts about his ability to do so, forthright self-assertion as well as subtle influence and crafty manipulation. The small body of evidence available indicates ex-slave wives also believed in the husband's role as family breadwinner. In the early years of emancipation, freed wives on Henry Watson's Alabama plantation refused to work. They told him "they never mean to do any more outdoor work, that white men support their wives, and they mean that their husband shall support them."[58] Throughout the South the Freedman's Bureau received complaints about black wives who "would not work at all" or others, like the freedwomen in Wharton, Texas, who "left their cabins late and quit the field early."[59] At the same time slavery also taught black women that a husband could not always provide for his family. Many slave fathers died or were sold: perhaps as many as one out of every four husbands or wives were separated by sale.[60] Even when separation did not occur, the slave family did not by itself provide for its needs. Slaves realized that the work of fathers, mothers and children contributed to food and clothing, but the master was the middleman: he not only distributed food and clothing, but also made crucial decisions about the family's future. At the same time the slave wife, who labored in the fields and often cared for her family in her husband's absence, developed more respect for her own ability to assist the family.

1009

Given that freed women did not want to work outside their homes during Reconstruction, how do we explain their unusually high rate of wage earning by 1900? One can only speculate about how this reconciliation occurred. It appears that a black wife recognized the need for more income for the family (which probably was used to purchase food) and then identified her own responsibility for providing some of the cash for the family's needs. Even if a wife decided to seek employment, she often encountered objections from her husband. Most black wives, it appears, successfully overcame their husband's doubts. One cannot uncover this entire process of decision making in black families, except at the final stage: when a wife tried to overcome her husband's objections to her employment. Wives often defined their role in terms of "helping out." As a young girl, Hannah Shaw chopped and picked cotton and milked cows. When she married, her husband insisted she quit working in the field. But she persisted, as he recalled.

"I'd be in the field at work and my wife—I'd look around, see her comin out there with a hoe. I'd say, "what you comin out here for."

"I thought I'd come out here and help you."[61]

Years later the testimony of Hannah Shaw's husband demonstrates the success of her strategy: "Every step she took, to my knowledge, was in my favor."[62] Martha Harrison, an ex-slave mother, was equally successful in overcoming her husband's objections to her employment. She confessed her tactics:

1010

> My husband never did like for me to work: he used to ask me how come I work; he was doing all he could to give me what I wanted. "Looks like you don't appreciate what I'm trying to do for you." But I'd say, "Yes, I do honey I just help you cause I don't want you to break down. If you put a load on a horse it will pull him down but two horses can pull it jest as easy."[63]

Since there are no parallel examples of black husbands persuading their wives to work, we can assume that black women changed their own minds about employment and then persuaded their husbands. Identifying this process may also reveal what kept Italian wives outside the labor force. To begin with, it might have been the case that they did not define a higher standard of living as a family goal or that they did so, but saw wage earning as the responsibility of the husband and children. Or they may have defined their economic responsibilities in a manner similar to black wives, but simply have been unable to overcome a husband's objection to their employment. The research task is to identify where in this process Italian wives differed from blacks, but so far no documentary material has been uncovered which makes this clear.

The pattern of child rearing in black families was a second reason black mothers found it easier to work than Italian mothers. Italians believed in close supervision of children, blacks in training for independence. Properly raised Italian children (*ben educati*) were never left alone. Mothers told their children to play with siblings and other relatives rather than with neighbors. The extent of supervision probably increased in the New World not only because of dangerous living conditions but also for fear "America . . . will take our children."[64] Far different patterns of child rearing for blacks were the result of slavery. Because mothers as well as fathers worked in the fields, elderly black nurses sometimes cared for children, but more often older siblings supervised the young. It seems plausible to suggest that slave parents rarely connected their physical presence with good parenting; an obedient youngster remained out of trouble when left alone. However, the withdrawal of women from field labor in Reconstruction again suggests that ex-slave mothers wanted to invest more time in child rearing. It seems it was with some reluctance that black families devised patterns of child rearing which taught self reliance at an early age. A working mother was forced to train her children to care for themselves and for each other. One home economist, studying the budgets of Philadelphia blacks between 1916 and 1918, observed that black children often prepared the meals and purchased food for the family at the corner store.[65] In *The Philadelphia Negro* DuBois noted that the chief employment of black children was in "helping about the house while the mother was at work."[66]

1011

A third cultural underpinning for black women's work consisted of parental attitudes towards children's education. Even as slaves blacks desperately sought to read and write. They connected literacy with being able to read the Bible; they gave their greatest respect to fellow slaves who could read aloud passages from Scripture. Ex-slave parents reacted to their deprivations on the plantation: they wanted to read the Bible, write their names, correspond with relatives, keep accounts and much more. In the first years after emancipation, children of the slaves flocked to the newly opened missionary schools and sometimes their parents accompanied them. The belief in education persisted among black parents. We have already seen that even in 1900 the rate of school attendance was far higher among blacks than Italians. But the value of education for children operated within an economic context: because of racial discrimination in hiring, black children found it difficult to secure employment. Moreover, it is too simple to conclude that keeping children in school was the major reason a mother worked. As we have observed, mothers continued to earn wages, even when their children were grown. Instead, the importance of education for children helped a mother overcome doubts about women's wage earning.

This emphasis on children's education was imbedded within a family's plans for its survival. Both groups may have shared the same parental concern for provision in old age, but expressed the concern through different strategies: for Italians, through the continued presence of at least one adult child as a wage earner in the household; for blacks, through the education and social mobility for the children. Both groups tried to plan for the future, but a black family may have placed greater emphasis on a child's schooling as the means of meeting long-term family needs. Thus, both Italians and blacks believed in self-sacrifice, but with a difference. Whereas Italian children often submerged their needs to those of their parents, especially their mothers, black mothers deprived themselves of necessities for the sake of their children. According to a New York City social investigator, the Italian daughter was taught to "subordinate her individual desire" to family needs.[67] Such children, when they went out to work, knew their wages belonged to the family. In contrast, black mothers worked extra hours to help educate their children. Ex-slave mothers in the South "make great sacrifices to spare their own children during school-hours."[68] Mothers in demeaning jobs justified their work in terms of the dignity conferred by educating one's children. One Raleigh, North Carolina, black mother in 1869 stated proudly, "I don't care how hard I has to work if I can only send Sallie and the boys to school looking respectable."[69] We can suggest that in their relations with their husbands, their training of independent children, and their self-sacrifice for children's education, black wives and mothers found strength and support for their wage earning, but at this stage of research, these remain tentative ideas which can only be demonstrated by reexamining how black families in slavery and in the early years of emancipation made choices about women's involvement in work and in the family.

1012

NOTES

A previous version of this paper was presented at the Newberry Library Colloquium on Family and Community History, November, 1975. The author wishes to acknowledge the helpful criticisms of this paper from Miriam Cohen, Leonore Davidoff, Douglas L. Jones, Claudia Goldin, Maurine Greenwald, Nancy Hafkin, Karen Mason, Leslie Page Moch, John Modell, Joseph Pleck, Sheila Rowbotham, and Louise Tilly.

1. U.S. Bureau of the Census, *Twelfth Census of the United States: 1900, Supplementary Analysis and Derivational Tables* (Washington, D.C., 1906).

2. U.S. Bureau of the Census, *Statistics of Women at Work* (Washington, D.C., 1900), Table 29, pp. 311, 315, 323, 325, 353–354, 359, 363–364, 373–374, 387; U.S. Bureau of the Census, *Population*, II (Washington, D.C., 1902), Table 32, pp. 311–314, 325, 337, 342.

3. Studies concerned with the higher rate of wage earning among black women include Glen C. Cain, *Married Women in the Labor Force: An Economic Analysis* (Chicago, 1966); William G. Bowen and T. Aldrich Finegan, *The Economics of Labor Force Participation* (Princeton, 1969); Duran Bell, "Why Participation Rates of Black and White Wives Differ," *Journal of Human Resources*, Vol. 9, No. 4 (Fall, 1974), pp. 465–479; Claudia Dale Goldin, "Female Labor Force Participation: The Origin of Black and White Differences, 1870 and 1880," *Journal of Economic History*, v. xxxvii, No. 1 (March, 1977), pp. 87–112; Edwin Harwood and Claire C. Hodge, "Jobs and the Negro Family: A Reappraisal, *The Public Interest*, No. 23 (Spring, 1971), pp. 125–131.

4. Virginia Yans-McLaughlin, "A Flexible Tradition: South Italian Immigrants Confront a New Work Experience," *Journal of Social History*, Vol.

7, No. 4 (Summer, 1974), pp. 442–445. See also Virginia Yans-McLaughlin, "Italian Women and Work: Experience and Perception," in *Class, Sex, and the Woman Worker*, ed. Milton Cantor and Bruce Laurie (Westport, Connecticut, 1977), pp. 101–119.

5. Louise A. Tilly, "Comments on the Yans-McLaughlin and Davidoff Papers," *Journal of Social History*, Vol. 7, No. 4 (Summer, 1974), pp. 452–459. An excellent analysis of Italian women's work that emphasizes changes in the economy is Miriam Cohen, "Italian-American Women in New York City, 1900–1950: Work and School," in *Class, Sex and the Woman Worker*, pp. 120–143.

6. John Bodnar, "Immigration and Modernization: The Case of Slavic Peasants in Industrial America," *Journal of Social History*, Vol. 10, No. 1 (Fall, 1976), pp. 44–71.

7. A more balanced approach, emphasizing family needs as well as the demands of the industrial environment, is presented in Tamara K. Hareven's "Family Time and Industrial Time: Family and Work in a Planned Corporation Town, 1900–1924," *Journal of Urban History*, Vol. 1, No. 3 (May, 1975), pp. 365–389.

8. Since Sicilian wives were more home bound than other Italian immigrants, their presence in certain cities may have accounted for the absence of Italian married women from the labor market. In point of fact, low rates of wage earning characterized Chicago and Philadelphia Italian women, despite the fact that 8 percent of Chicago's Italians and 12 percent of Philadelphia's Italians were born in Sicily, and high rates of wage earning prevailed among New York City's Italians, about half of whom were Sicilian. Carroll D. Wright, *The Italians in Chicago: A Social and Economic Study* (Washington, D.C., 1897), Table V, p. 372; U.S. Senate Reports, 62nd Cong., 1st sess., *Immigrants in Cities*, Vol. 1 (Washington, D.C., 1911), Table 13, p. 358 and Table 17, p. 175.

9. Jane Schneider, "Of Vigilance and Virgins: Honor, Shame and Access to Resources in Mediterranean Society," *Ethnology*, Vol. 10 (January, 1971), pp. 1–24. This tradition applied especially to Italian women from the South.

10. Leonard Covello, *The Social Background of the Italo-American School Child* (Totawo, New Jersey, 1972), p. 296.

11. Computed from data in Ninth Special Report of the Commissioner of Labor, *The Italians in Chicago: A Social and Economic Study* (Washington, D.C., 1897), Table I, pp. 52–273.

12. Ruth S. True, *The Neglected Girl* (New York, 1914), p. 109.

13. Louise C. Odencrantz, *Italian Women in Industry* (New York, 1919), pp. 175–176.

14. Computed from data in Commission of Labor, *Italians in Chicago*, Tables I and II, pp. 52–351.

15. U.S. Senate, *Immigrants in Cities*, Vol. 2, Table 401, pp. 546–548.

16. Computed from data in Commission of Labor, *Italians in Chicago*, Tables I and II, pp. 52–351.

17. Herbert G. Gutman, *The Black Family in Slavery and Freedom, 1750–1925* (New York, 1976), Table B-1, p. 527.

18. U.S. Senate, *Immigrants in Cities*, Vol. 2, Table 401, pp. 546–548.

19. Computed from data in Commissioner of Labor, *The Italians in Chicago*, Table I, pp. 52–273 and "Condition of the Negro in Various Cities," *Bulletin of the Department of Labor*, Vol. II, No. 10 (May, 1897), pp. 257–360.

1013

In weekly wages Italian male laborers earned less than blacks in Cambridge, Nashville, or Atlanta. Italian wives heading households were also poorer than similar black wives.

20. U.S. Senate, *Immigrants in Cities*, Vol. I, Table 64, p. 226.

21. Computed from data in Department of Labor, "Condition of the Negro in Various Cities," pp. 257–360.

22. Computed from data in Commissioner of Labor, *Italians in Chicago*, Table I, pp. 52–273.

23. Ibid., p. 722.

24. Ibid., pp. 52–273.

25. Odencrantz, *Italian Women in Industry*, p. 163.

26. Ibid.

27. Computed from data in Department of Labor, "Condition of the Negro in Various Cities," pp. 257–360.

28. U.S. Senate, *Immigrants in Cities*, Vol. 1, Table 55, p. 216 and Table 52, p. 396; U.S. Bureau of the Census, *Occupations*, Table 43, pp. 486–489, 506–509, 618–621.

29. Gutman, *Black Family*, Table B-2, p. 527.

30. Commissioner of Labor, *Italians in Chicago*, pp. 379–380.

31. Barbara Klaczynska, "Why Women Work: A Comparison of Various Groups—Philadelphia, 1910–1930," *Labor History*, Vol. 17, No. 1 (Winter, 1976), pp. 73–87.

32. Mary White Ovington, *Half A Man: The Status of the Negro in New York* (New York, 1911; New York 1969), p. 162.

33. Ibid., p. 62.

34. Ibid.

35. Ibid.

36. U.S. Bureau of the Census, *Statistics of Women at Work*, Table 27, pp. 215–217.

37. Ovington, *Half A Man*, p. 58.

38. In New York City large numbers of Italian women were occupied earning wages, generally sewing in their apartments, and fewer wives took in lodgers. This substitution of a mother's wages for a lodger's income was true only in New York City. In other cities wives earned wages as well as taking in lodgers, and elsewhere wives did not work and did not accept lodgers.

39. Gutman, *Black Family*, Table B-4, p. 530.

40. In modern American cities male unemployment depresses the rate of female participation in the labor market, but around the turn of the century, male unemployment led to increases in the number of women working. The contemporary evidence is summarized in James Sweet, *Women in the Labor Force* (New York, 1973), p. 23.

41. Was the absence of other wage earners the reason a black wife had to work? Taking into account the number of wage earners in the family, black wives were still more likely to work than Italian wives. When an Italian family relied on one other income source, generally the husband's wage, one out of ten Chicago Italian wives worked in 1896, compared with one-third to one-half of black wives in Atlanta, Cambridge, and Nashville. With three additional incomes, about seven in ten black wives in Cambridge, Atlanta, and Nashville worked, compared with two out of ten of Chicago's Italian wives in 1896.

42. Wright, *Italians in Chicago*, Table VII, p. 374; Department of Labor, "Condition of the Negro in Various Cities," Table I, pp. 287–288.

1014

43. Gutman, *Black Family*, Table B-4, p. 530.

44. Judith Smith, "Work and Family Patterns of Southern Italian Immigrant Women in Providence, Rhode Island, 1915," unpublished paper delivered at the Berkshire Conference on Women's History, June, 1976.

45. For school attendance figures among black children, I substituted data from the 1900 federal census, which employed a division by age unavailable in the Bureau of Labor survey. Wright, *Italians in Chicago*, Table XVI, p. 385; U.S. Bureau of the Census, *Population*, Part II, Table 54, pp. 396–397, Table 9, pp. 122–136.

46. Gutman, *Black Family*, Table B-4, p. 530.

47. The greater the number of contributors to the family's economy, the higher the rate of wives at work. If just one additional member of an Italian family was employed, then only 10 percent of the wives worked. If at least three other members of the family worked, 17 percent of Italian wives did so. Black wives also increased their rate of working as more family members entered the labor force. For Cambridge black wives, the rate of labor-force participation rose from 36 percent with one additional income earner to 60 percent in families with at least three extra incomes. The rate of working increased from 43 percent to 63 percent for Atlanta wives, and from 53 percent to 67 percent for Nashville wives.

48. A working wife could never expect to match her husband's income; hence, the availability of work for women never adequately replaced a man's wages. Nevertheless, the ratio of male to female wages was higher for blacks than Italians. In Philadelphia the wages of a black wife in 1911 were 42 percent of those of her husband, and 71 percent in New York City. By contrast, among New York and Philadelphia Italians, a wife earned one-third what her husband made. U.S. Senate, *Immigrants in Cities*, Vol. 1, Tables 66–67, pp. 228–229, 408–409.

49. U.S. Senate, *Immigrants in Cities*, Vol. 1, Table 57, p. 64; Table 65, p. 448; Table 67, p. 229; p. 409; Table 70, p. 583; Table 72, p. 746; Table 76, p. 324.

50. Karen Oppenheim Mason and Larry L. Bumpass, "U.S. Women's Sex Role Ideology, 1970," *American Journal of Sociology*, Vol. 80, No. 5, (March, 1975), pp. 1212–1219.

51. James Morgan, I. Sirageldin, and Nancy Baerwaldt, *Productive Americans: A Study of How Individuals Contribute to Economic Progress* (Ann Arbor, 1966), Figure 19-4 p. 330. Consult also John Scanzoni, "Sex Roles, Economic Factors and Marital Solidarity in Black and White Marriages," *Journal of Marriage and the Family*, Vol. 37, No. 1 (February, 1975), pp. 130–144; Leland J. Axelson, "The Working Wife: Differences in Perception Among Negro and White Males," *Journal of Marriage and the Family*, Vol. 32, No. 3 (August, 1970), pp. 457–464; D. D. Lewis, "The Black Family: Socialization and Sex Role," *Phylon*, Vol. 36, No. 3 (1975), pp. 221–237.

52. Eugene D. Genovese, *Roll, Jordan, Roll*, p. 490; Vernon Burton, "Black Household Structure in Edgefield County, South Carolina," unpublished paper, 1976; Robert Abzug, "The Black Family during Reconstruction," in *Key Issues in the Afro-American Experience*, ed. Nathan I. Huggins, Martin Kilson, and Daniel M. Fox, Vol. 2 (New York, 1971), pp. 26–41.

53. Gutman, *Black Family*, p. 168.

54. Ibid.

55. Ibid.

56. Gerda Lerner, *Black Women in White America: A Documentary History* (New York, 1973), p. 292.

A Heritage of Her Own

57. Theodore Rosengarten, *All God's Dangers: The Life of Nate Shaw* (New York, 1974), p. 128.

58. Gutman, *Black Family*, p. 168.

59. Ibid.

60. Ibid, pp. 146–155; John Blassingame, *The Slave Community: Plantation Life in the Ante-Bellum South* (New York, 1972), p. 90; Herbert Gutman and Richard Sutch, "The Slave Family: Protected Agent of Capitalist Masters or Victim of the Slave Trade?" in Paul A. David, Herbert G. Gutman, Richard Sutch, Peter Temin, and Gavin Wright, *Reckoning with Slavery: A Critical Study in the Quantitative History of American Negro Slavery* (New York, 1976), Table 3, p. 129.

61. Rosengarten, *All God's Dangers*, p. 127.

62. Ibid., p. 475.

63. Lerner, *Black Women*, p. 15.

64. Covello, *The Social Background of the Italo American School Child*, p. 296.

65. Sadie Tanner Mossell, "The Standard of Living Among One Hundred Negro Migrant Families in Philadelphia," *Annals of the American Academy of Political and Social Science*, v. XCVIII, No. 187 (November, 1921), p. 186.

66. W. E. B. DuBois, *The Philadelphia Negro: A Social Study* (Philadelphia, 1899, New York, 1967), p. 111.

67. Mary Van Kleeck, *Artificial Flower Makers* (New York, 1913), p. 86, as quoted in Miriam J. Cohen, "The World of Work and the Family: New York City Italians, 1900–1950," unpublished paper, 1977.

68. Lerner, *Black Women*, p. 246.

69. Ibid., p. 102.

Section B: Maria Louise Baldwin, 1856-1922

DOROTHY B. PORTER

Curator, Moorland Collection, Howard University Library

MARIA LOUISE BALDWIN, ONE OF THE BEST SCHOOL TEACHERS, regardless of color, developed in the United States, was born in Cambridge, Massachusetts, September 13, 1856, the oldest daughter of Peter L. and Mary E. Baldwin. All her education was obtained in the schools of Cambridge. At the age of five years, she entered the Sargent Primary School. Later, she attended the Allston Grammar School. In June 1874, she graduated from the Cambridge High School. One year later, Maria Baldwin was graduated from the Cambridge training school for teachers.

For two years, Maria Baldwin, taught in Chestertown, Maryland. In 1881, she received an appointment as a primary grade teacher in the Agassiz Grammar School in Cambridge, Massachusetts, where she taught all grades from the first to the seventh. A member of the School Board in Cambridge said of her elementary school career: "From the first day I saw her I realized she was a rare character. . . . Her poise and dignity, her calmness and beautiful voice struck me at once, and I felt that her mere presence must be a valuable lesson to all children. Several parents told me their children realized this and always spoke of her in admiration and affection. . . . When the principal of the school was to be changed the superintendent told me it would be my duty to appoint a new principal. 'Why' I said, 'you know as well as I do there is only one suitable person, Miss Baldwin.' 'I think so too,' he said, 'but I was not sure about color.' 'It is not a question of color,'

I said, 'it is a question of the best.' " Miss Baldwin was thus made principal of the Agassiz School in 1889 and for forty-one years served with gentleness and capacity, as its director.

In 1915, the old school building was torn down and a new one erected at a cost of $60,000. The position of principal was raised to that of "Master" in the autumn of 1916.

As "Master" of the Agassiz School, Maria Baldwin supervised the teaching of twelve teachers, all white, who had in their charge more than five hundred children, many of whom were from old Cambridge families and children of Harvard professors. An admirer of Miss Baldwin stated that the understanding features of her character were "her strict adherence to duty and her loyalty to teachers and pupils." She was never known to say an unkind word to any boy or girl. Serious differences between teachers and pupils were unknown in her school. Her lovable and amiable qualities commanded only respect from students, teachers and parents.

Maria Baldwin was civic minded and alert to all community problems. She was a member of the Twentieth Century Club of Boston, the Boston Ethical Society, of which she served as president for one term and the League of Women for Community Service, of which she was president for many years. In addition, she belonged to the Cantabriga Club, Teacher's Associations and other organizations.

An excellent lecturer, Maria Baldwin was the first woman of any race to give the annual Wash-

1017

Originally published in *Journal of Negro Education*, 21 (Winter 1952).

ington's Birthday Memorial Address before the Brooklyn, New York Institute. On this occasion she selected for her subject—"The life and Services of the Late Harriet Beecher Stowe." *The Brooklyn Eagle* commented on this lecture in these words: "She is a type quite as extraordinary in one way as Booker T. Washington is in another. Her English is pure and felicitious, her manner reposeful and her thoughts and sympathies strong and deep." Several schools required her services as a teacher in their summer schools.

Maria Baldwin possessed a deep concern for her people. A strong advocate for equal justice to all men, she was a fervent opponent of American class segregation and prejudice. She earnestly believed that the idea of "fencing off is equally harmful to all concerned. In affairs of her country, she believed there should be one common standard by which all should be judged.

Throughout the years Maria Baldwin continued to study at Harvard University and other colleges. Her fine personal library was evidence of intensive and extensive reading. Her Prospect Street home was the headquarters for various literary club activities. Among her friends, who were of the highest culture, were many noted persons—Alice M. Longfellow, Edward Everett Hale, Thomas Wentworth Higginson, Alice Freeman Palmer, Edward D. Chaney and Elizabeth C. Agassiz.

On the night of January 9, 1922, while she was addressing the Council of the Robert Gould Shaw House Association, at the Copley-Plaza in Boston, Maria Baldwin collapsed and within a few minutes died. The shocked audience was dismissed by the Reverend Dr. Alexander Mann, Rector of Trinity Church.

Funeral services were held on January 12th at the Arlington Street Church, which will be remembered as the church of William E. Channing, one of the early abolitionists. White pall-bearers, some of them descendants of great revolutionary sires bore her body into the church. Her death was not only a shock to the people of Cambridge but also to the people of the United States, for she had become well-known as a result of her teaching activities.

A memorial number of *The Agassiz*, the school paper, contains many tributes from her associates and pupils who welcome the opportunity to acknowledge her worth and work and to indicate the high regard in which she was held by the community where she had so many years rendered unselfish service.

About one year after her death the Agassiz School unveiled a tablet to her memory, the gift of the class of 1922, the last she taught. The ceremony was held under the auspices of the Agassiz Parent-Teachers Association of Cambridge. The inscription on the tablet reads: "In grateful memory of Maria L. Baldwin, 1856 - 1922. Forty-one years inspiring teacher, wise and beloved Master of this school. A Scholarship has been founded and this room has been named Baldwin Hall."

In her day, Maria Baldwin, without a doubt held one of the most distinguished positions in the teaching field in this country. It is very fitting that one of the new girls' dormitories at Howard University has just been named in her honor. May her name serve as an inspiration to the many young women who will pass through the portals of Maria Baldwin Hall.

1018

REFERENCES USED

Brawley, Benjamin G. *Negro Builders and Heroes.* Chapel Hill, The University of North Carolina Press, 1937.

Brown, Hallie Q. *Homespun Heroines and Other Women of Distinction.* Xenia, O., The Aldine Publishing Co., 1926.

Ferris, William H. *The African Abroad.* . . . New Haven, Conn., The Tuttle, Morehouse & Taylor Press, 1913. v.2

Gibson, John W. Progress of a Race. . . Naperville, Ill., J. L. Nichols and Co., 1920.

1020

B. Joyce Ross

Mary McLeod Bethune and the National Youth Administration: A Case Study of Power Relationships in the Black Cabinet of Franklin D. Roosevelt

Mary McLeod Bethune, who rose from poverty to become one of the nation's most distinguished Afro-American leaders, had three different careers: as an educator, she was the architect of Florida's Bethune-Cookman College; as founder and president of the National Council of Negro Women, she was a central figure in the development of the black women's club movement; and, as a worker in politics, she was one of the few blacks who held influential posts in the federal bureaucracy during the administration of Franklin D. Roosevelt.

B. Joyce Ross's essay, reprinted from the Journal of Negro History, *deals with Bethune's career in a New Deal agency, the National Youth Administration, and is a case study in how the members of what was popularly dubbed the "black cabinet" functioned. While occupying the highest posts in the federal service that blacks had had since the early part of the century, these officeholders all served as special advisors on Negro affairs. Among the most important of them, in addition to Bethune, were Frank Horne, a specialist in housing; William H. Hastie, who served in various capacities, including civilian aide to the secretary of war during the first part of World War II; and Robert C. Weaver, who advised on housing and labor policies, and who would subsequently be the first Negro elevated to a cabinet post when Lyndon B. Johnson made him secretary of the Department of Housing and Urban Development.*

While supposedly representing black interests, the members of the "black cabinet" all found themselves working under serious constraints imposed by membership in the federal bureaucracy. Each individual handled this problem in his own way. Weaver, operating with great care, proved to be the most durable of this group of officeholders; Hastie, on the other hand, militantly resigned his post in the War Department because of the intransigent policy of discrimination and segregation that pervaded the Army's operations. In dealing with the only woman member of this "black cabinet," Ross illuminates the problems faced by these officials, and the limited progress they had to settle for, as they worked to advance Negro interests in the New Deal agencies.

1021

191

Originally published in the *Journal of Negro History*, 60 (Jan. 1975), pp. 1-28. Reprinted here from *Black Leaders of the Twentieth Century*, John Hope Franklin and August Meier, eds. (Urbana: University of Illinois Press, 1982).

1022

IN TERMS of black people's history, the New Deal primarily is important because it marked for the first time since the Reconstruction era the revival of the principle of federal auspices of racial equality. Second, it is important because not since the Reconstruction era did Negroes enjoy such a large number of significant governmental posts on the national, state, and local levels. Such New Deal provisions as the Fair Employment Practices Act, ostensibly equitable consideration of blacks under the federal housing program, and the authority and the avowed policy of federal agencies such as the National Youth Administration to force equitable representation and participation of blacks in even deep southern states marked the first occasion since the passage of the Thirteenth, Fourteenth, and Fifteenth amendments and the Civil Rights Acts of the 1860s and 1870s that the federal government assumed a major portion of the responsibility for insuring the equality of Negroes within the larger society. Indeed, the passage of the Voting Rights Act and other federally sponsored legislation during the 1960s has led some historians to describe the administration of Lyndon Johnson as the "Second Reconstruction." Yet, because it was the principle of federal auspices of racial equality which constituted the most important facet of the civil rights movement of the Reconstruction era, the initial revival of this principle during the 1930s rather than in the 1960s suggests that it was the New Deal which technically deserves the sobriquet "Second Reconstruction."

Nevertheless, the New Deal's application of the principle of federal auspices of racial equality was unique among the three eras, for unlike the Reconstruction era and the 1960s, federal auspices of racial equality during the Roosevelt administrations often enhanced the trend toward separate but equal accommodations for Negroes. On the other hand, the bulk of the federal civil rights legislation of the 1860s and 1960s decidedly favored an integrated society; Negroes were federally supported in their right to sit where they chose on interstate public carriers and to be served and seated without racial considerations in restaurants, theaters, and other public establishments. President Roosevelt often needed the support of the powerful southern bloc in Congress; therefore, he did not lend the full weight of his office to overturning southern laws and customs which had long governed the region's race relations. Despite the lobbying of the National Association for the Advancement of Colored People and other groups, he would not lend his personal support to anti-lynching legislation. Historians such as Charles Abrams convincingly have argued that, in the final analysis, New Deal housing legislation actually enhanced residential segregation.[1] In the case of agencies like the National Youth Administration (NYA), the administration's policy was tacit acceptance of separate, albeit ostensibly equal, consideration of blacks in the programs of the southern and border states. Thus, the greatest shortcoming of the New Deal was its failure to link inextricably the principle of federal auspices of racial equality with the concept of a desegregated society.

Though New Deal racial stances are vital to this study, its concerns are the power and interpersonal relationships surrounding Mary McLeod Bethune,[2] one of the members of the so-called black cabinet of Franklin D. Roosevelt—that coterie of blacks including Bethune, Robert Weaver, H. A. Hunt, William Hastie, Lawrence Oxley, Frank Horne, and others who served as "advisors," "assistants," and "directors" of Negro affairs in both the myriad of New Deal relief and recovery agencies, as well as in the majority of cabinet divisions of government. Though a projected full-length study of the black cabinet is not yet completed, the basic methodological questions that will be asked of the study are instructive of the role of Bethune and other appointees of the group.

1023

More than a dozen black New Deal appointees are loosely classified as members of the black cabinet; an in-depth study of each is neither entirely feasible nor necessary. The study will seek to focus upon eight to ten carefully selected appointees whose tenure, when viewed collectively, will reflect a wide spectrum of variables. Not all of the cabinet members served contemporaneously; indeed, it might well be argued that there were several black cabinets during Roosevelt's extensive tenure. Hence, while Bethune is an excellent representative of those individuals whose service primarily spanned the depths of the Depression and the pre–World War II period, it is also imperative to select an appointee such as Hastie, the assistant to the secretary of war for Negro Affairs, who attained prominence near the end of the Roosevelt administration and after the outbreak of hostilities. Such a comparison in time aids in determining how cabinet members' influence was affected. Such factors as the importance of Negroes to the war effort as a determinant in the comparative authority accorded black advisors in peace and war time, their relative strength during the two time periods of the major civil rights organizations, their role, if any, in enhancing the cabinet members' authority, and nuances of change over time in the social and political thought of the larger black community are significant. Meanwhile, the extent to which the respective cabinet members' personal and public philosophies reflected currents of black thought is also important.

Needless to say, it is even more important to focus upon Bethune and Weaver who did serve contemporaneously. Since all of the black cabinet members occupied top-level administrative posts, the primary perspective from which they must be studied is that of power relationships—the degree to which the individual cabinet member was able to influence the policies of his respective agency toward Negroes. It is not premature to project the conclusion that in addition to the pressure which black community groups were able to exert upon the administration, there were other major determinants. Two of these determinants were the influence that any given cabinet member could exercise over the relative authority officially and technically accorded his office within the total administrative structure of the agency, and the extra-official means available to white superiors and subordinates for circumventing or enhancing the cabinet member's official authority. A study of the latter two variables in regard to several cabinet members who served simultaneously illuminates such factors as the varying policies of the several agencies toward black affairs and the public and personal attitudes of white superiors and subordinates within each agency. Taken as a whole, such comparisons should do much toward explaining the fundamental question of why some of the black cabinet members apparently were more influential than others.

These cabinet members were appointed by federal officials rather than selected by the black community per se; the study does not accept as a foregone conclusion that they necessarily were spokesmen of the mainstream of contemporary black thought. Indeed, the forthcoming full-length study of the black cabinet will reveal that there were instances in which highly placed blacks in agencies other than the NYA were virtually publicly taken to task by the NAACP for pronouncements which the organization deemed racially conservative. Thus, a study of the interpersonal relationships among black cabinet members and their black subordinates within the respective agencies is imperative. It provides one of the most important yardsticks for measuring the extent to which the respective cabinet members were entitled to be designated as spokesmen of the mainstream of black thought during the 1930s and early 1940s. In other words, a comparison of Bethune's racial philosophy with that of black contemporaries who served as her assistants and subordinates within the NYA provides a major approach to determining whether her racial philosophy can be termed conservative, moderate, or radical.

1024

194

However, this study assumes that an even more valid means of placing personal racial philosophies within a broad spectrum is the use of
the official public racial stances during the period under consideration
of two of the nation's black advancement organizations—the NAACP
and the National Urban League. These organizations were chosen because they claimed the largest contingents of black followers during
the period under consideration. Hence, to utilize a hypothetical case,
if at a given time the NAACP held a position on segregation that differed significantly from the public position on this issue taken by Bethune, then this study assumes that there are reasonable grounds for
suspecting that her approach to that particular issue was not representative of an appreciable, and perhaps not the major, segment of the
contemporary black community.

1025

Some of these fundamental questions are applied to Bethune's tenure as director of the NYA's Division of Negro Affairs from the
division's inception in 1935 until its termination in 1943. The most important result was the failure of Bethune's division in many instances
to challenge the Roosevelt administration's reluctance to demand a
desegregated society.

The pertinent files show Bethune to have been a Janus-faced figure
who presented a public position to biracial and white groups that often
differed appreciably from her privately expressed attitudes. When addressing biracial groups, her appeals for racial equality often were
couched in terms which could only be flattering to white people, while
her demeanor was usually that of a supplicant whose primary approach
lay in appeals to white people's consciences and sense of fair play. Her
remarks in 1939, to the predominantly white NYA National Advisory
Committee, a group of thirty-five civic and professional leaders appointed by President Roosevelt to formulate NYA policy, typify her
public approach to biracial groups. In appealing for more blacks to be
appointed to NYA state and local posts, she was quoted by the stenog-
rapher as stating that she would "like to see more of those darkies dot-
ting around here."[3] When asked to make a few remarks at the close of
the same meeting, Bethune noted: "After being down in Harlem, I'm
glad to have the opportunity of being up here in the Waldorf-Astoria
with you white folks. I wish more of my people could share this opportunity."[4] Extemporaneous remarks and speeches were usually pro-
fusely laced with religious homilies and southern-style analogies, of
which one of her best was that of the chicken: "You white folks have
long been eating the white meat of the chicken. We Negroes are now
ready for some of the white meat instead of the dark meat."[5]

195

Nor can the general tenor of these remarks be dismissed as growing out of any initial timorousness which Bethune may have experienced as a result of occupying an important national office, for her pronouncements before the National Advisory Committee were made as late as 1939, more than four years after she had assumed office. Moreover, in light of the fact that the late 1920s and early 1930s had witnessed a protracted struggle by the NAACP, the Association for the Study of Negro Life and History,[6] and other groups to have the term Negro recognized as a proper noun, it seems fair to view Bethune's public reference to darkies as being decidedly passé in 1939.

However, the demeanor within which Bethune's public remarks were couched should not be confused with the content of her pronouncements. When her statements to the National Advisory Committee and her other public pronouncements are viewed collectively, it is apparent that despite her homespun homilies and subdued approach, she explicitly advocated a program centered in equitable representation of blacks in every level of the NYA's administration. Black youth were included in activities that prepared them for skilled, high-salaried positions in the labor market and for total equality for Negroes in every facet of the American society. Thus, the same NYA National Advisory Committee members who heard Bethune unabashedly utilize the term darkies also listened to the following mettlesome comments: "May I advise the committee that it does not matter how equipped your white supervision might be, or your white leadership, it is impossible for you to enter as sympathetically and understandingly, into the program of the Negro, as the Negro can do."[7] In the final analysis Bethune presented the public image of a woman who was so affable that even southern whites could hardly be offended by her approach, but who, at the same time, clearly expressed a vision of racial equality.

More important, the forcefulness of Bethune in her private behind-the-scenes official and interpersonal relationships with white and black administrators more than atones for her public shortcomings. As will be discussed shortly, she pragmatically accepted segregated consideration of Negroes under the NYA program and, therefore, only rarely utilized her personal and official power in demanding desegregation. The value of her tenure as NYA director of Negro Affairs was her unyielding demand, especially in her private contacts with colleagues, upon absolutely co-equal, albeit often separate, consideration of blacks.[8] A discussion of Bethune's officially designated power relationship within the NYA administrative hierarchy more appropriately

1026

belongs to a later section of this study. Suffice it to say at this point that in the wake of southern white state NYA officials' attempts to circumscribe the number of black state appointees, she stood firm, with the backing of black leaders, in demanding that white NYA national officials overrule southern administrators.[9] Indeed, it is not an exaggeration to state that her constant pressure in regard to the appointment of increasing numbers of black NYA officials on the state and local levels was perhaps her most outstanding administrative accomplishment and, in itself, justified the existence of her office and the Division of Negro Affairs. Similarly, for example, her behind-the-scenes correspondence with NYA white administrators regarding the inclusion of black youth in NYA work projects that afforded training aimed at the skilled and semiskilled positions in the job market yields the portrait of an aggressive and often outspoken woman. "It is about time," she told the NYA national director in 1937, "that white folks recognize that Negroes are human too, and will not much longer stand to be the dregs of the work force."[10] In the final analysis it would, therefore, appear that Bethune's subdued public approach probably was not an engrained part of her personality, but, rather, was a deliberate act, consciously and adeptly performed.

1027

Perhaps historians will be left to speculate as to whether Bethune's public approach was the most advantageous for her race at that particular point in history. It is instructive that the demeanor and approach of the only other black member of the National Advisory Committee, Dr. Mordecai Johnson, the president of Howard University, was antithetical to hers. Described by one contemporary as being "extremely fair complexioned but in reality very black," Johnson presented to the advisory committee the image of an articulate, candid black representative who spoke in terms of the "right" of Negroes to equality, the "consequences" to the nation of segregating itself into two distinct races, and the validity of the "demands" which blacks advanced. Indeed, one can only imagine what thoughts must have gone through his mind when his colleague spoke at the 1939 meeting and employed the term darkies. Nevertheless, though Johnson presented a forceful public image, unlike Bethune, he was rarely obliged to test his pronouncements within the context of official or semi-official NYA power relationships. During virtually the entire existence of the NYA, one of the shortcomings of the National Advisory Committee was rooted in the fact that the preoccupation of its highly prestigious members with personal professional concerns precluded the service which they were able to render as NYA advisors. Within a year after being appointed to the committee, Johnson admitted that his duties as a university president severely circumscribed his attendance at meetings and greatly diminished even his awareness of the committee's policies and activities. In fact, it was not uncommon for him to call upon Bethune during meetings to apprise him of developments in NYA Negro activities.[11] Thus, in comparison to the director of the Division of Negro Affairs, the more publicly forceful Johnson was not a major figure within the power relationships surrounding Negro activities of the NYA. It was largely the Janus-faced Bethune who stood in the midst of the proverbial lion's den.

1028

Bethune's racial philosophy can be closely defined through a comparison of her philosophy with that of her black subordinates within the NYA. The official administrative structure of the national NYA Division of Negro Affairs designated the major officers as Bethune in the top ranking position of director, followed by an "administrative assistant" to the director, then several stenographers and clerks. In 1937 T. Arnold Hill, an executive of the National Urban League, became an advisor to Bethune on industrial relations. This post was necessitated by the division's desire, in the wake of the resolutions of an NYA conference on the problems of the Negro, to incorporate more black youth into skilled manpower training programs and private industrial employment. Though Bethune served as the division's director during its existence, the turnover rate of her administrative assistants was high, which Bethune basically and correctly attributed to better job and salary opportunities elsewhere. The more well-known assistants included Juanita J. Saddler, a young national executive of the student division, YWCA; Horne, assistant superintendent of education in Fort Valley, Georgia; and Charles P. Browning, who was elevated to the post following his service as state director of Negro NYA affairs in Illinois (the counterpart of Bethune's position on the state level). The administrative assistants were charged with the responsibility of devising techniques for implementing the director's program, serving as liaisons between the national Division of Negro Affairs and the NYA Negro agencies on the state and local levels, and providing firsthand information to the director regarding state and local Negro activities through field trips to black projects in the several states. Thus, in terms of sheer numbers, Bethune commanded a relatively modest work force.[12]

A discussion of the philosophies of all of Bethune's assistants is not practical in a study of this length. However, Saddler[13] deserves special mention, although she served for less than two years. Saddler, aside from Bethune, probably was the most impressive administrator in the national Division of Negro Affairs during the organization's formative period. There is a possibility that she might have been a better choice than Bethune for the position of director. Bethune's official reports and her correspondence with white and black co-workers lacked depth of analysis on the programmatical problems that confronted the Division of Negro Affairs. She visited black NYA programs in every state of the union as director; her written reports were largely detailed. These reports were analytically superficial accounts of what she had seen, together with her speaking itinerary and notations regarding the group that had been her host. Her annual reports and official reports to such groups as the National Advisory Committee largely consisted of statistical and factual data, which were more descriptive than analytical. Furthermore, some of these reports, and especially those prepared during the formative period of the division, obviously were presented verbatim by Bethune from original drafts bearing Saddler's signature. Similarly, the content of her official and personal correspondence to co-workers suggests that while she clearly possessed a vision of equal participation of blacks in the NYA program, she rarely advanced commentaries on the underlying racial, economic, and social problems that governed the attainment of her goal. Nor does this preclude recognition of the fact that much of Bethune's correspondence was deliberately guarded—especially that which pertained to delicate racial matters. For example, when Ralph W. Bullock, a black southern NYA official, complained to her regarding southern white people's inequitable treatment of Negroes, she indicated that she would rather discuss the matter privately during her next visit to the South. There were also other memorable occasions on which Bethune, in the avowed interest of privacy, invited black state or local officials to visit her in Washington rather than convey her opinions in written communications.[14] In the final analysis, the files simply do not yield a clear conception of her intellectual prowess.

1029

Among national NYA black administrators, one who wishes an astute, in-depth analysis of the formative phase of the program of Negro activities should turn to Saddler's field reports and correspondence rather than to the files of Bethune. After visiting a given area, Saddler usually proved adept at concisely and candidly analyzing the total economic, social, and political milieus of the community. Her observations regarding the impact of intergroup relations among blacks upon NYA Negro activities are perhaps the most illuminating in the NYA files. For example, she pointed out to one NYA state director that friction had developed in the conduct of Negro activities because he had afforded representation to one black religious domination on the local advisory committee but had omitted its major rival. In the case of another state she warned that the Urban League official who had been appointed to the local advisory committee was not the best representative of blacks in that area. In reports which were designed for white NYA administrators as well as for Bethune, she did not hesitate in denouncing ostensibly liberal whites in agencies such as the YWCA for deliberately seeking to control local NYA Negro activities. In a number of instances she made field trips to southern states that were openly hostile to black participation in the NYA program, and, for example, in Texas she was largely responsible for inducing the then racially conservative state director, Lyndon B. Johnson, to afford blacks representation in the administration of the program in the form of a segregated all-black Texas state advisory committee. Moreover, Saddler often advanced her ideas and conclusions directly to white national officials over her own signature.[15]

1030

More important, Saddler questioned more candidly than any other national black NYA administrator the propriety of both the NYA's and the Roosevelt administration's position on desegregation. She expressed her ideal of integration openly and forcefully, though she often was obliged to accept much less in reality. Not only was she opposed to enforced segregation of blacks by the larger society, but she also maintained that the only grounds (particularly in reference to the NYA program) which justified Negroes voluntarily segregating themselves was when they might "have a chance for initiative and self-expression and the development of latent abilities within the group itself." Even when she discovered that whites in parts of upstate New York were attempting to control local NYA Negro activities, she agreed only reluctantly to the establishment of all-black local policy-making bodies, maintaining that "I, myself, question whether [segregation] is ever a wise step to take." Saddler perceived that federal funding of programs like NYA afforded an opening wedge for altering the South's historic racial attitudes. For example, when Johnson proved reluctant to place blacks in policy-making and supervisory positions, she suggested to him that "the fact that the Government is aiding and supporting various projects in the State [of Texas], seems to me to allow leeway for liberal and tolerant groups and individuals in the community to try to make the social patterns more just and equitable for all the people in the community." Though Saddler candidly spoke her ideal, the refusal of white

200

national NYA administrators to "press" Johnson led her to accept the "half-loaf" of a segregated Texas committee.[16]

In contrast, Bethune adopted the pragmatic position that segregation was an unfortunate reality and that while it remained a reality, Negroes must seek to insure equal, though separate, consideration. She told the National Advisory Committee in 1936: "In places where there is no need for a separate program, for Negro and white groups, we most heartily recommend the one program. And in fields where it is necessary for us to have a separate program, we most heartily recommend a separate program, taking, of course, under advisement, the necessity of the proper leadership and guidance."[17] In 1936 she advanced her philosophy even more succinctly to a conference of southern whites: "You white folks have your swimming pool if you think that best. Just give us one to enjoy too."[18] In regards to the NYA program, Bethune, in keeping with resolutions passed by several conferences of black leaders, interpreted separate but equal as meaning black supervisors for black projects; black participation in the policy-making phase of the program; and NYA activities for black youth which enhanced their training beyond traditional Negro jobs such as maids and janitors. She never waivered in her insistence upon these three principles in her private and public contacts with white and black administrators.[19]

Yet Bethune should not be harshly judged for her pragmatism, for scores of blacks who could hardly be termed conservative practiced, though without fanfare, the philosophy she openly preached. Throughout the tenure of the NYA, black leaders like the fiery Roscoe Dunjee, editor of the Oklahoma *Black Dispatch*, Dr. William Stuart Nelson, president of Dillard University in Louisiana, and Dr. Richard Grant, the president of a local Illinois branch of the NAACP, served on segregated NYA local advisory committees.[20] It should also be kept in mind that during the 1930s the NAACP, despite its idealistic integrationist position, tacitly bowed to southern segregation patterns. For example, after repeated, unsuccessful attempts to force integration of the southern school system, the organization adopted the tactic of demanding that black school facilities and teachers' salaries should be so nearly equal to those of whites that southern segregation would die from the weight of the financial expense. Thus, on what was perhaps the most important issue governing the conduct of NYA affairs, Bethune can safely be placed well within the mainstream of contemporary black thought and action.

1031

In my opinion, the greatest shortcoming of Bethune's tenure as NYA director of Negro Affairs was that in so many instances she was forced to accept not only separate but also less than equal consideration for her people. The root of the problem was the failure of national NYA administrators, even in the wake of demands of the director of the Division of Negro Affairs and the resolutions of black conferences, to apply fully the principle of federal auspices of racial equality at the state and local levels. A discussion of the role and activities of black NYA appointees on the state and local levels cannot be taken up at length in a study of this brevity. Suffice it to say that each state director was assisted in formulating NYA activities by a state advisory committee, which the national office dictated should be composed of representatives of predesignated occupational and minority groups—labor leaders, educators, welfare workers, Negroes, and civil leaders. In addition, each city or county within each state utilized a so-called local advisory committee, originally projected by the national office to be composed of the same occupational and racial categories as the state committees. The concept of integrated committees at both levels was implicit in this structure.[21]

The first major retreat of national executives from the policy of integrated committees came in 1935, when they failed to "press" Johnson about his insistence that whites in Texas would object to an integrated state committee. Aside from the Roosevelt administration's general reluctance to breach southern law and custom, national NYA administrators deliberately sought to foster local community participation and control out of consideration of the fact that the success of the NYA program largely depended upon the financial co-sponsorship of programs by community civic groups. The perennially destitute black race harbored little power in the realm of funding on a statewide basis, especially since Negroes were concentrated in only certain sections of the cities. The result was the paralleling of the white Texas state committee by an all-black Texas state advisory committee chaired by Dr. Joseph J. Rhoads, president of Bishop College.[22]

However, by the end of 1936, a series of factors had enhanced the existence of integrated NYA state advisory committees even in the states of the Confederacy. The actual functioning of the black Texas committee demonstrated that segregated committees created a duplication of expenses. A few months after the committee had been operating, Saddler complained that the white Texas committee was supplied stenographic and other assistance but that black committee members, despite their full-time personal professions, were expected

1032

to perform even routine chores personally. Richard R. Brown, the NYA deputy administrator, concluded that duplicate financing was one of the major drawbacks of segregated committees. Second, it should be noted that as a general trend, southern states looked first toward totally white administration of even the Negro phases of the NYA program, then preferred integrated administration, and only lastly agreed to totally segregated administration. Almost all of the southern states initially delayed in appointing Negroes to state committees, and a handful, the most notable of which was Tennessee, insisted that blacks had no objections to whites representing them. Even after constant, though subtle, pressure from the national office, Mississippi attempted to avoid the issue by permitting white state government officials, rather than black civic groups, to nominate the Negro candidate. Furthermore, it was a constant complaint of Bethune and participants at black NYA conferences that even when NYA work projects were comprised entirely of black youth, most southern states insisted upon white project supervisors. Nor would any southern state permit Negroes to supervise integrated work projects.[23]

1033

On the other hand, the majority of southern states appear to have considered affording Negroes separate and distinct administration of Negro activities an even greater evil. This contention is supported by the reluctance of all but a handful of southern states as well as some northern states to appoint black state directors of Negro activities. It was only after constant insistence by Bethune and black conference participants that national executives began, around the end of 1936, to pressure states to appoint Negro state directors because "Mrs. Bethune expects the office and Negro pressure demands it." In some states such as Alabama resistance seems to have been rooted in the intention not to provide any NYA activities whatsoever for Negroes. The fact that even after Negro state directors had been appointed the overwhelming majority enjoyed no official power and received extremely low salaries further suggests that whites did not wish to give the administration of NYA Negro activities to blacks.[24] It was undoubtedly for this reason that when national executives insisted upon Negro representation on NYA state committees, no southern state except Texas seriously pushed the idea of a parallel, all-black state advisory committee. The result was, ironically, that even die-hard southern states like Alabama, Arkansas, Mississippi, and Georgia had integrated state advisory committees, although segregated NYA activities. In the final analysis, less than a half dozen states utilized all-black state advisory committees. In the majority of these cases, such as

Oklahoma and California, the heavy geographical concentration of Negroes in certain areas, for example, Los Angeles, Oakland, and Oklahoma City, together with strong black community organization and aggressive leadership—Dunjee in Oklahoma and Augustus Hawkins and Vivian Osborne-Marsh in California—led blacks to seek voluntary control of Negro NYA activities as a reflex action to actual and potential white discrimination. The only states that were permitted by the national office not to appoint Negro state advisory committee members and Negro state directors were Wyoming, New Mexico, Vermont, and Montana, where the black percentage of the total population was infinitesimal. Some of these states appointed Indians to the state advisory committees since this racial group, rather than blacks, constituted the largest racial minority. But even in these states Negroes served on city and county local advisory committees wherever small residential pockets of blacks so warranted.[25] Consequently, though all states did not have Negro representatives on their state advisory committees, blacks were represented on at least some of the city and county local advisory committees of every state.

On the city and county levels the preferential order of segregation-integration was reversed. As has just been noted, all-black local advisory committees were common in both northern and southern states. Because the local advisory committees were expected to reflect and be knowledgeable of the problems of their particular community, the segregated residential patterns of both northern and southern cities favored all-black committees, which could relate the needs of the ghetto. There were also cases like those reported by Saddler in Buffalo, Poughkeepsie, and other sections of up-state New York in which Negroes gave up their positions on integrated local advisory committees to form segregated committees because whites deliberately sought to dominate the administration of Negro activities. Thus, both integrated and all-black local advisory committees existed simultaneously in New York, Delaware, Pennsylvania, and other northern states. Furthermore, that black community agencies—YMCAs, colleges, high schools, local branches of the Urban League, and others—financially co-sponsored many NYA projects gave blacks a major springboard for demanding administrative control of segregated neighborhood programs. Indeed, it was not at all unusual for Florida A. & M. College and Tuskegee Institute in Alabama to be given virtually complete supervision of projects that they sponsored on their campuses. NYA financial statistics demonstrate that blacks contributed more than 35 percent of the costs of NYA Negro activities on a nationwide average.

1034

This is not incompatible with our earlier contention that blacks did not harbor much financial clout in demanding representation on state advisory committees, for statistics also show that their financial contributions, though commendable, constituted less than 25 percent of total community-donated funds during the existence of the NYA.[26]

Hence, the shortcoming of Bethune's insistence upon equal, albeit separate, consideration of Negroes lay not in Negroes' failure to be represented on virtually all state and local advisory committees, but rather in the overwhelming majority of states in which blacks constituted an appreciable proportion of the total population but were not accorded representation on state advisory committees in proportion to their population percentage. Though the bulk of the black population was concentrated in southern states, Negroes usually were accorded no greater representation on southern state advisory committees than in states like Iowa, Ohio, and New Hampshire, where their percentage of the state population was relatively small. Though by 1938, some states, including North Carolina, Alabama, and Florida, had at least two Negro representatives on their state committees (North Carolina had six), other states with heavy concentrations of blacks, including Tennessee, Virginia, and South Carolina, each had only one black state representative. The degree of activism of the black community appears to have been the decisive factor in each case where Negroes approached equitable representation. North Carolina Negroes skirted the state director by nominating state advisory committee members during a personal visit by Bethune. She urged their selection of national executives. In Alabama the first Negro NYA project was initiated by Negroes alone in the wake of white apathy, and Tuskegee's president, F. D. Patterson (who served as one of Alabama's state committee members) became a trusted unofficial advisor on NYA Negro Affairs to the Alabama state director. In Miami, Tampa, and Pensacola, Negroes were organized into strong local advisory committees and chose even lower echelon black NYA personnel. In Omaha and Lincoln, Nebraska, the local branches of the Urban League sustained such agitation that they were virtually solely responsible for the appointment of a black to Nebraska's state advisory committee, despite the state's relatively small black population.[27] Nevertheless, despite Bethune's warnings that "token" Negro representation was not acceptable, only in rare instances did national officials, in the absence of black community pressure, voluntarily press states to appoint more than a minimum number of Negro representatives.

It should be remembered, however, that more blacks held impor-

1035

205

tant governmental posts on all levels during the New Deal than during any previous period since the Reconstruction era. But whereas historians are increasingly demonstrating that black officeholding during Reconstruction largely grew out of white initiative and white expediency, an in-depth study of the NYA suggests that black officeholding during the New Deal "Second Reconstruction" essentially was rooted in the growing political, economic, and numerical strength of Negroes.

The second most important failure of Bethune's avowed aim of totally equal consideration of Negroes lay in the realm of inequitable salaries for black NYA state officials. Positions on state and local advisory committees were totally without remuneration, but the office of state director of Negro Affairs, or the assistant to the state director in charge of Negro Affairs, was a full-time salaried position. The constant insistence of Bethune and NYA conferences of blacks that this office be instituted in the states already has been noted. In North Carolina, Alabama, and a handful of other states Negro members of the state advisory committees additionally pressured state directors to establish the office. By 1940 national NYA executives had devised a number of subtle ways to force state directors to appoint a Negro director: Indiana was told that Bethune and the black community demanded the office; Mississippi was told that if it did not wish to nominate a candidate, the national office would do so; Tennessee was informed that the national office had provided special funds in the state's budget for the office and that it was expected that an appointment would soon be made. Under this pressure all but those states with very small black populations had appointed Negro directors by 1940.

However, in no northern or southern state were the Negro directors afforded salaries commensurate with white assistants or assistant directors. Indeed, a comparison of state officials' salaries on a nationwide basis reveals that on the average the pay scale for Negro assistants was more nearly commensurate with that of low-ranking district supervisors and, in some states, common project foremen. As early as 1936 Bethune warned national executives that the major technical problem in the NYA program of Negro activities was the inability to secure competent black employees because of inadequate salaries. That this situation was never remedied is borne out by the complaint as late as 1942, by Bullock, one of the nation's most outstanding southern black NYA officials, that Negroes might withdraw from the NYA program completely if southern states did not accord them more equitable pay.

The pertinent files simply do not explicitly disclose why national executives responded so decisively to demands for the institution of the

1036

206

office of Negro state assistant, yet displayed no similar inclination to force more equitable pay scales. Their official authority to have made such demands upon the states was not in question, for all state budgets had to be approved by the national office and were subject to revisions. One of the most plausible explanations is that national officials were not fully convinced of the importance or necessity of the office of Negro state director. Shortly after the first of these positions was instituted, Gerald Barnes, the white NYA regional director of the northeast, complained to Brown, the NYA deputy executive director, that on several occasions Bethune had referred to the new officials as directors and questioned whether Brown wished "to take it up with her." Brown skirted the issue by noting that designation of titles was "no serious matter." It is also likely that Aubrey Williams, the NYA director, harbored reservations about the Negro directors, for he questioned the existence of even the national Division of Negro Affairs on the grounds that Negroes defeated their own purposes when they drew sharp racial distinctions in programs and activities. Whatever the case, the net result was that Bethune, time after time during her tenure as director, personally approved discriminatory salaries for black state directors.[28]

1037

Finally, the study of Bethune would not be complete without mention of her conception of her role as juxtaposed against the actual power relationship which accrued to her office and the Division of Negro Affairs. It is my conclusion that the Division of Negro Affairs, as a subunit of a larger agency, never attained the authority projected by Bethune because of (1) the NYA's failure to clarify and define the division's power relationship with other subunits of the agency or with the top echelon of the agency's administration, and (2) the extra-official means available to Bethune's subordinates and co-equals for potentially circumventing her division's authority. The net result was that the national Division of Negro Affairs never developed co-equal authority in the control of NYA Negro activities on the state and local levels, and Bethune, the division's director, never attained a power relationship with the agency's top administrative echelon beyond that of an advisor whose opinions were not officially binding.

It should be kept in mind that the NYA was a compound organization, having not only a central office in Washington, but also subordinate units in the form of state and local administration. Technically, the agency was predicated upon highly centralized authority, for although local officials were responsible to the state offices, and the state directors nominated members of the state advisory committees, the national office selected the state directors, approved or rejected nominees to the state advisory committees, formulated the budgets for the state offices, and laid down the broad parameters of the NYA activities that the state and local divisions could sponsor. It has already been suggested that the national office's desire to foster community financing and its reluctance to breach southern racial laws and customs significantly softened the national office's exercise of its full authority.

More important to the study of the Division of Negro Affairs is the fact that the national office sought to delegate authority and responsibility along geographical rather than functional lines. Geographical lines imply that the state offices handled all aspects of NYA activities and problems for a particular state, as opposed to functional delegation of authority whereby a given field office would handle, for example, only financial matters or other specific aspects of the total program of an area. Under a centralized arrangement, geographical delegation of authority almost always entails progressions of power relationships in which the lowest echelon of officials reports first to unit chiefs (in the case of NYA, the state directors) who, in turn, are responsible to the national top echelon or their designated intermediary representatives.[29]

One of the initial problems was that Bethune conceived of the national Division of Negro Affairs as exercising authority over Negro activities on all levels within a context of functional authority, although the NYA was predicated upon a geographical authority arrangement. According to Bethune's account, her division began operation in December 1935 with no clearly designated functions or procedures. After remaining in her office for two weeks without having any contacts with national executives, she unilaterally formulated a tentative outline of the division's potential work, which included the establishment of a national Negro NYA advisory committee (a projected parallel to the National Advisory Committee that was never inaugurated), the maintenance of satisfactory press relations, the compilation of files on the programs and philosophies of black organizations, and cooperation with black NYA appointees on the state and local levels. Obviously, this initial job description depicted the Division of Negro Affairs as largely a fact-finding and public relations agency and implied that it was to enjoy no significant power relationship vis à vis national executives or state directors. Bethune submitted the outline to Brown "in an endeavor to having him think with me in defining the job," but she later observed that "our interview did not net much that was definite however, in the way of establishing standards of procedures and work-

1038

ing out relationships here and in the field." Six months later Bethune reported that still no provisions had been made with national executives regarding the role and function of the Division of Negro Affairs.[30]

Undoubtedly the limbo in which the division began operation was partially because of its establishment after the structure and program of the NYA had been formalized. President Roosevelt invited Bethune and Mordecai Johnson to represent Negroes at the White House planning conference for launching the NYA; shortly afterward, the president, in recognition of their reputations as foremost educators of black youth, appointed both of them as the two black representatives on the National Advisory Committee. However, Roosevelt initially demurred in approving a distinct Negro unit largely because of the expressed fears of southern Congressmen that such a division would usurp authority over NYA Negro Affairs on the state level. Williams initially was hesitant because of the NYA's limited budget and his personal conviction that a separate Negro division would enhance, rather than diminish, the trend toward segregation. It was only in the wake of the demands of a 1935 conference of blacks, convened to discuss the participation of Negroes in the NYA, together with the sustained contention by the NAACP that the interests of blacks in the New Deal programs could not be adequately safeguarded by even the most well-intentioned white administrators, that Roosevelt approved the establishment of a distinct NYA Division of Negro Affairs. Nevertheless, Williams candidly informed the first NYA conference of blacks to be convened after the inauguration of the division that he still was not certain that a Division of Negro Affairs was not self-defeating for the best interests of blacks.[31]

1039

The most important consequence of the belated establishment of the Division of Negro Affairs was Bethune's concession, shortly after taking office, that because the broad parameters of the NYA program already had been formulated, the policy-making role of her division largely would be limited to "the adaptation of the [already established NYA] program to the needs of Negro people and the interpreting of the program to them." Yet she never wholly lived up to this initial statement. During her tenure as director she strongly urged national executives to approve a program of consumer education for blacks and a foundation for black crippled children similar to that at Warm Springs, Georgia, and she planned for the Division of Negro Affairs to compile studies of black workers' education councils, which were being newly debated and inaugurated by the NAACP and the Urban

League. Each of these proposed programs was outside of the realm of the NYA's project offerings; each was rejected by national officials on the grounds of inadequate funds and the fear of duplicating the work of other private and governmental agencies. A discussion of actual NYA Negro projects cannot be taken up in this study.[32] Suffice it to say that Bethune largely was confined during her tenure as director to efforts to insure equitable consideration of Negroes under the NYA program which existed at the time of her division's establishment.

It was not until 1936, after Bethune had conferred with black national leaders and NYA black state appointees, that she presented to national executives a forceful, three-point statement of the proposed power relationship between the Division of Negro Affairs and the NYA. The document, entitled "Relation of the Division of Negro Affairs to the General Program of the National Youth Association," partially was occasioned by the virtual ignoring of Bethune's division by white state officials and, to a certain extent, by national executives as well. Even where strictly Negro problems were concerned, northern and southern state directors almost always wrote directly to Williams and Brown or to the regional directors. Conversely, regional directors usually dealt with Negro problems and matters in direct consultation with national executives or state directors. Though national executives often requested Bethune's advice, there were numerous occasions on which they unilaterally dealt with Negro problems. Again, no guidelines had been established regarding the division's and the director's power relationship with national and state officials. Bethune also was informed by black state officials that because black state assistants were the subordinates of the state directors, the latter retained the authority to administer Negro programs as they saw fit, which portended discrimination, especially in the South.[33]

The document regarding the relationship of Bethune's division of the NYA was of major importance, because it called for the division to exercise authority over national Negro affairs along functional, rather than geographical, lines of administration. It requested (1) representation of the division at any meetings of the NYA national executives which concerned the division; (2) the handling of all correspondence pertaining to the Negro program "directly" by this office in cooperation with and with the approval of the deputy executive director; and (3) the referral of all complaints from Negroes (presumably on the state and local levels) "directly" to the Division of Negro Affairs, with the understanding that Bethune was to investigate and adjudicate

1040

210

them in consultation with national executives. In the same document Bethune set forth her main duties as interpreting the needs of blacks to NYA officials; reviewing and seeking to adjudicate Negroes' complaints; advising black state and local NYA officials; representing the NYA at all Negro conferences; and formulating new ideas and programs for black NYA activities, an aim she never realized fully.

In light of recognized principles of organization and administration this document contained both sound and unsound tenets. Bethune was correct in recognizing that no organization's divisions could be completely autonomous, because there must be at least one office—in the case of NYA, that of the executive director—which could unify command by taking ultimate responsibility. The insufficiency of her proposal is best illustrated through a comparison of the power relationship between other divisions of the NYA national office and the state offices. The predominant hierarchical line of authority seems to have favored the state director's right to channel initially all problems and complaints directly to the state office, followed by his option of referring these matters for final adjudication either directly to the executive director or directly to the division concerned. In the case of the former, the executive director's office usually either adjudicated the matter or referred it to the division immediately concerned. In other words, it was not standard procedure for employees or groups on the state level—for example, Negro officials or NYA participants in Mississippi—to bypass the state director, as Bethune was requesting, in lieu of communicating directly with a national division or the national executives of the agency.

1041

Neither national nor state NYA officials sustained the powers that Bethune requested for her division. When the state director of Mississippi found that the Negro state assistant was communicating directly with Bethune's office, he became the first of nearly a half dozen southern state directors to complain to national executives that the state directors' authority was being circumvented. He requested reaffirmation of their immediate jurisdiction over affairs within their respective states. Nor was the controversy confined to the South. For example, the state director of Connecticut complained to national executives that confusion had resulted form Bethune's informing Connecticut's black state assistant while he was visiting her in Washington that he was entitled to a higher salary when, according to the state director, no funds for a salary increase were available. In all of these cases, national executives overruled Bethune in recognition of the fact that the NYA was structured along geographical lines of administration, and that

211

state directors had prior authority first to review matters within their jurisdictions.[34]

Officially, therefore, Bethune had no direct relationship with Negro assistants or other black NYA officials on the state and local levels. National executives did request state directors to send her division copies of all correspondence pertaining to Negro affairs, but generally the overall absence of such correspondence in the official files of the division indicates that this request was not generally honored. Indeed, one of the most strikingly obvious features of the official files of the NYA is the relative paucity of material that comprises the files of the Division of Negro Affairs; the total of collected material for its nearly decade of existence consumes less than fifteen small boxes of correspondence and reports (out of a total of more than 1,200 file boxes for the entire NYA). Even when correspondence of the division, which is scattered throughout the general files of the agency, is taken into consideration, the division and its director appear to have amassed a total of less than thirty file boxes of material.

1042

This dearth of material offers an important, though indirect, commentary on the extent of the division's involvement, both officially and unofficially, in Negro affairs on the state and local levels. In addition to a paucity of correspondence from white state directors to the division, there is a lack of any sustained flow of correspondence between the division and black officials on the state and local levels. For example, there is nothing in the files to suggest that most Negro state assistants regularly corresponded, either officially or unofficially, with Bethune or her division. However, Bethune repeatedly urged Negro state assistants to send her division copies of their official reports to the state directors. These fairly complete reports comprise much of the division's files. The volume of the division's correspondence with black local advisory committee members and superintendents of projects was very small; in fact, she admitted that her office did not possess a complete roster of Negro state and local advisory committee members on a nationwide basis.[35] Finally, the files indirectly indicate that Bethune bowed to state directors' prior jurisdiction over Negro affairs. Official correspondence and documents from her division in reference to Negro affairs usually were sent first to state directors for their subsequent distribution to Negro state assistants and other black state officials.

The official and extra-official functions of the NYA regional directors, together with the appointment of so-called regional Negro affairs representatives after 1940, enhanced the tendency toward geographical rather than functional lines of administration, resulting in a further bifurcation of the autonomy which the Division of Negro Affairs hoped to exercise over Negro activities on the state and local levels. In addition to state and local organizations, the NYA initially divided the country into four regions, each consisting of approximately a dozen contiguous states, which corresponded to the regions of the Works Progress Administration. The regional directors were appointed by the national NYA director to serve as liaisons with state administrators and as field representatives who could provide the national office first-hand information regarding the actual operation of state programs. Officially the regional directors had virtually no administrative powers. They were observers and coordinators with no authority over state directors or the national NYA divisions. However, from the inception of the NYA, the regional directors functioned as unofficial, semi-autonomous administrative agents of the national executives, semi-independently approving and disallowing state budgets and programs, in general consultation with their superiors.[36]

1043

With the shift of the NYA to manpower training on the eve of World War II, the necessity of precise coordination of manpower led to the increase of the number of NYA regions and regional directors to twelve, together with the enhancement and formalization of the previous extra-official supervisory authority of the regional directors. Simultaneously, general recognition of Negroes' importance to the war effort, coupled with the pressure exerted by the NAACP, the Urban League, and other black groups, led to the appointment for the first time of black regional Negro affairs representatives. Nominated by the regional directors and approved by Bethune in consultation with national executives, the regional Negro affairs representatives usually were former state assistants of Negro activities whose experience and meritorious service as state officials easily warranted their promotions. They were subordinates of the regional directors and were charged with the responsibility of coordinating state Negro activities and advising the regional directors of the best utilization of black manpower resources. As coordinators and advisors, their opinions, like those of the Negro state assistants, were not binding upon either state directors or regional directors.[37]

The central point regarding the regional arrangement, both before and after 1940, was that this particular feature of the NYA's administrative structure afforded additional officials outside of Bethune and national executives a direct voice in Negro affairs. Sometimes, as in the case of Barnes's observations about Bethune's reference to Negro state assistants as "directors," the regional directors questioned policies of the Division of Negro Affairs. At other times, they pointed out factual errors in the information disseminated by Bethune's division. For example, Garth Akridge, director of the southern region, called to the attention of national executives in 1936 the fact that Bethune had requested additional NYA student aid funds for several black colleges, but that upon personally investigating he had found that the schools had not utilized already allocated funds. After the powers of the regional directors were increased after 1940, it became necessary for Bethune to lobby with them on behalf of blacks as much as with national executives. When Bullock, one of the most aggressive southern regional affairs representatives, complained to Bethune that the regional director could approve available funds for salary increases of blacks, but that he simply refused to do so, she proved powerless. National executives took the position that regional directors had general decision-making powers over budgetary allocations. Similarly, one of the northeastern regional directors, John N. Patterson, squashed the protests of Bethune and Philadelphia Negroes regarding NYA employment discrimination by informing her that his thorough personal investigation disclosed that there were no grounds for such charges.[38]

In the final analysis, Bethune can best be termed a coordinator and advisor on Negro affairs in the NYA throughout her tenure as director. Mordecai Johnson perhaps best summarized the meaning of her tenure during a telephone interview with the writer in July 1974. "I believe with all my heart that she sincerely worked on behalf of her people," said Johnson, "and had their best interests at heart. . . . She was not primarily an administrator; she was more a symbol of Negroes' aspirations, and she knew how to wield influence."

Notes

1. See, for example, Burke Marshall, *Federalism and Civil Rights* (New York: Columbia University Press, 1964); James C. Harvey, *Black Civil Rights during the Johnson Administration* (Jackson, Miss.: University and College Press, 1973); B. Joyce Ross, *J. E. Spingarn and the Rise of the NAACP* (New York: Atheneum, 1972); Charles Abrams, *Forbidden Neighbors: A Study of Prejudice in Housing* (New York: Harper, 1955).

2. For discussions of Bethune's rise from a poverty-stricken childhood in South Carolina to a role as advisor to presidents, see Catherine Owens Peare, *Mary McLeod Bethune* (New York: Vanguard Press, 1951), and Rackham Hold, *Mary McLeod Bethune* (Garden City, N.Y.: Doubleday, 1964).

3. Quoted in "Minutes of the Meeting of the National Advisory Committee," Aug. 1939, typescript, Files of the National Advisory Committee, Na-

1044

tional Youth Administration Archives, National Archives, Washington, D.C., hereafter cited as the NYA Archives.

4. Ibid.

5. Bethune, "Report of Field Trip to Nebraska, Kansas, Missouri," n.d. [1937], Files of the Division of Negro Affairs, NYA Archives.

6. Carter G. Woodson (head of Association for the Study of Negro Life and History) to W. E. B. Du Bois, Aug. 4, 1927, Papers of Carter G. Woodson, Library of Congress, Washington, D.C., and James Weldon Johnson to Walter White, Apr. 13, 1933, NAACP Administrative Files, Personal Correspondence, Library of Congress.

7. Quoted in Lucy Ficklin (admin. sec., National Advisory Comm.) to Richard R. Brown, May 25, 1937, NYA Administrative Files, NYA Archives.

8. See, for example, Bethune to Aubrey Williams, June 10, 1938, copy in Files of the Division of Negro Affairs, July 12, 1938, copy in NYA Administrative Files, to Juanita J. Saddler, Feb. 3, 1936, Apr. 12, 1936, Files of the Division of Negro Affairs, NYA Archives.

9. Bethune to Brown, Jan. 12, 1936, Apr. 7, 1936, Sept. 5, 1936, NYA Administrative Files, NYA Archives; to Jesse O. Thomas (exec. sec., National Urban League), Dec. 4, 1937, Dec. 20, 1938, Files of the National Urban League, Library of Congress; Daisy Lampkin (field sec., NAACP) to Bethune, Nov. 29, 1938, NAACP Administrative Files.

10. [Bethune], "Report for the Meeting of the [National] Advisory Committee," Mar. 17, 1937; Bethune to Williams, June 10, 1937, Jan. 15, 1938, to Brown, May 12, 1936, July 3, 1937, Files of the Division of Negro Affairs, NYA Archives.

11. For a summary of the function and composition of the National Advisory Committee, see NYA, *Information Exchange*, Bulletin no. 5, Apr. 1940, File of H. Dreiser, 1941–42, NYA Archives. Membership lists, minutes of meetings of the committee, and plans of reorganization are grouped in the Administrative Files, National Advisory Committee, NYA Archives.

12. Personal background material, correspondence, and personnel data regarding the administrative assistants to Bethune are scattered throughout the Files of the Division of Negro Affairs. However, for reasons that are not clear, very little information is extant in the files on Saddler. A small amount of personal data is also found in the Administrative, Budget, and Personnel Files, all in the NYA Archives. For statements of the assistants' duties, see "Relation of the Division of Negro Affairs to the General Program of the National Youth Administration" [1936], and "Need for an Assistant for Negro Press and Public in the Division of Negro Affairs National Youth Administration" [1935], Files of the Division of Negro Affairs, NYA Archives.

13. Saddler was born in Guthrie, Okla., in 1892. In 1915 she graduated from Fisk University, Nashville, Tenn., and received a master's degree in education from Teachers College of Columbia University in 1935. Between 1920 and 1933 her principal work was with the national student department of the YWCA. Widely recognized as an integrationist, she prepared a statement on the role of student YWCAs in integration that became the basis for the national organization's interracial charter adopted in 1946. In 1933 she interrupted her work with the YWCA to become dean of women at Fisk University and was called from the post to serve as Bethune's first assistant in the Division

1045

215

of Negro Affairs in 1935. In July 1936 Saddler resigned her post in the NYA, partially because of dissatisfaction with the pace of the organization's integration efforts, and returned largely to her YWCA work. Prior to her death in 1970, she organized and became executive director of the Cambridge (Mass.) Community Relations Committee, which integrated Boston nursing schools and offered other opportunities to young black women. Her last notable achievement was the operation of a pilot project for Church Women United during the 1960s in the Morningside area of New York to promote interracial and ecumenical activities among the churches of that area. New York *Times*, Jan. 13, 1970; Saddler to Bethune, June 14, 1936, to Brown, June 17, 1936, Files of the Division of Negro Affairs, NYA Archives.

14. For examples of Bethune's public statements on the NYA program, see her speech at the dedication of the center for Negro youth, Baltimore, Md., Sept. 1936; [Bethune], Statement [1937], Files of the Division of Negro Affairs; Bethune to Bullock, Dec. 3, 1941, Jan. 7, 1942, Files of the Regional Directors, NYA Archives. Cf. Saddler, Statement [Mar. 1936], with [Bethune], Statement on Need for Negro Assistants in the Division of Negro Affairs, n.d. [Apr. 1936]., Files of the Division of Negro Affairs, NYA Archives.

15. Saddler to Brown, Apr. 27, 1936 (copy), Dec. 16, 1935, Mar. 31, 1936, June 23, 1936, Mar. 28, 1936, to Bethune, July 13, 1936 (copy), Files of the Division of Negro Affairs; Saddler, "Report of Visits to Ithaca, Albany, Dutchess Junction and Buffalo, January 2–9, 1936," Administrative Correspondence Files, NYA Archives.

16. Saddler, "Report of Visits to Ithaca, Albany, Dutchess Junction and Buffalo, January 2–9, 1936"; Saddler to Johnson, Apr. 9, 1936 (copy), Administrative Correspondence Files; John J. Corson (NYA admin. asst.) to Williams, Sept. 25, 1935, Files of NYA Memorandums, 1935–38, NYA Archives.

17. "Minutes of the Meeting of the NYA National Advisory Committee," Apr. 1936, Administrative Files, NYA Archives.

18. Bethune, draft of speech in her handwriting, n.d. [1936], Files of the Division of Negro Affairs, NYA Archives.

19. See especially Bethune's remarks at the several conferences of black leaders and black NYA officials in the Files of the Division of Negro Affairs, NYA Archives. See also Bethune to Williams, May 5, 1936, July 14, 1938, to Brown, Feb. 12, 1938, Mar. 7, 1938, Administrative Correspondence Files, NYA Archives.

20. NYA of La., "Monthly Narrative Report," Mar. 1938, File of Administrative Reports; "Recommendations for NYA Advisory Committee: Winnebago County, Illinois, County District 1" [Dec. 1936], Administrative Correspondence Files; NYA of Okla., "Monthly Narrative Reports of Activities," 1937–39, File of Administrative Reports, NYA Archives.

21. Almost every aspect of state and local advisory committee composition and functions is grouped in data in the files of the National Advisory Committee, NYA Archives. Random material is scattered throughout the Administrative Correspondence Files, NYA Archives.

22. Corson to Williams, memo, Sept. 25, 1935, Files of Administrative Memorandums, NYA Archives. On the importance of community co-

sponsorship of programs, see, for example, John E. Bryan (state dir., Ala. NYA) to John Pritchard, Oct. 20, 1941, Files of the Regional Directors; "Preliminary Draft of Recommendations of the President of the United States Submitted by the National Advisory Committee," n.d. [1936], Files of the National Advisory Committee, NYA Archives.

23. See the narrative monthly reports of activities of the several states in the Administrative Reports Files. For data on Negro superintendents, see the Reports of State Directors of Negro Affairs (two boxes) in the Files of the Division of Negro Affairs, NYA Archives. See especially "Annual Report of the Division of Negro Affairs," 1938–39, ibid.; NYA of Ala., "Narrative Report of Negro Activities," Jan. 1939, State Director of Negro Affairs Reports in Files of the Division of Negro Affairs; D. B. Lasseter (state dir., Ga. NYA) to Garth Akridge (NYA regional field rep.), Feb. 28, 1938, Miscellaneous File; Bryan to Brown, July 5, 1938, Administrative, Budget, and Personnel Correspondence Files, NYA Archives.

1047

24. For examples of pressure upon states to appoint Negro state assistants, see Gerald Barnes (northeast regional field rep.) to Thomas J. Dodd (state dir., Conn. NYA), Mar. 15, 1937; Dodd to Barnes, Mar. 19, 1937, Field Reports of Barnes in Files of Regional Directors; Brown to Robert Richey (state dir., Ind. NYA), Jan. 11, 1938, Apr. 16, 1938, Administrative, Budget, and Personnel Correspondence Files, NYA Archives. On functions and appointments of Negro state assistants, see the Reports of State Directors of Negro Affairs in Files of the Division of Negro Affairs, NYA Archives. Additional data on these officials are scattered throughout the Administrative Files, NYA Archives. See also "Negro State Reports on NYA" [Sept. 1938], Files of the Division of Negro Affairs; Corson to Gladys J. Shamp (state dir., Nebr. NYA), Sept. 19, 1935, Files of the National Advisory Committee; Bethune to Brown [Oct. 1936]; Brown to J. C. Flowers (state dir., Miss. NYA), Oct. 15, 1936, Administrative, Budget, and Personnel Correspondence Files, NYA Archives.

25. Each state's summary of Negroes on state and local advisory committees as of 1941 is found in the File of H. Dreiser (NYA admin. asst.). See also Lucy Ficklin (as field rep. of the National Advisory Committee) to Pritchard, June 30, 1941, Files of the Regional Directors, NYA Archives. It should be noted that the majority of state advisory committees in the nation rarely met as a group because state directors experienced various problems in convening them. Negro members thus rendered the greatest service (as did white members) through individual contacts with state directors and the black community. By the time the national NYA office began urging regular convening of the committees around 1940, the NYA was on the verge of termination. Circular letter signed by Williams, Dec. 1940, Files of the National Advisory Committee; Margaret M. Griffin (state dir., Nev. NYA) to Brown, Oct. 15, 1937, File of Administrative Reports; telephone conversation between Bethune and Richey, Sept. 29, 1938, Files of the Division of Negro Affairs, NYA Archives. For an example of a state with virtually no Negro activities and personnel, see Nev. NYA, "Outline for State Youth Director's Monthly Reports," Dec. 28, 1935, Administrative Reports Files, NYA Archives. The number of Negroes on state advisory committees showed a sight decrease after 1940. The national

office could not provide an adequate explanation. "Summary of National, State, and Local Advisory Committees," Oct. 1940, Files of the National Advisory Committee, NYA Archives.

26. For examples of the participation of Negroes in local programs, see NYA of Ga., "Narrative Report on NYA Work Projects," Oct. 1938; "Report of the National Youth Administration of South Carolina for September 1936," File of Administrative Reports; "Suggestions for the Activities of the Coordinator of the National Youth Administration in the Southern Area," n.d.; "Minutes of the North Carolina State Advisory Committee on Negro Affairs," Mar. 31, 1939, Files of the Division of Negro Affairs, NYA Archives.

27. For examples of black pressure for more Negro officials on the state and local levels, see Saddler to Brown, Mar. 28, 1936, Files of the Division of Negro Affairs; Statement, n.n., n.d. [1938], Files of the National Advisory Committee; NYA Conn., "Report" [1937], File of Administrative Reports; Paul G. Prayer (exec. sec., Asbury Park, N.J., Urban League) to Williams, Sept. 5, 1936, Charles W. Washington (exec. sec., Minneapolis Urban League) to C. B. Lund (NYA adm. asst.), Apr. 28, 1941, S. Vincent Owens (exec. sec., St. Paul Urban League) to Lund, Feb. 11, 1942, Raymond R. Brown (exec. sec., Omaha, Nebr., Urban League) to Williams, Sept. 25, 1942, Files of the Regional Directors, NYA Archives. For Patterson's role, see, for example, Bryan (state dir., Ala. NYA) to Richard Brown, Aug. 5, 1936; Brown to Bryan, Aug. 11, 1936, Administrative, Budget, and Personnel Correspondence Files, NYA Archives.

28. See, for example, Richey to Brown, May 9, 1938, Brown to Richey, May 12, 1938, May 16, 1938, O. H. Lull (dep. exec. dir., NYA) to Richey, Sept. 30, 1938, Brown to John Bryan, Sept. 11, 1937, Brown to Flowers, Dec. 5, 1936, Administrative, Budget, and Personnel Correspondence Files, NYA Archives.

29. See Paul C. Bartholomew, *Public Administration*, 3rd ed. (Totowa, N.J.: Littlefield, Adams and Co., 1972); Catheryn Seckler-Hudson, *Organization and Management: Theory and Practice* (Washington, D.C.: American University Press, 1955).

30. "Report Covering First Six Months of the Work of the Office of the Negro Affairs National Youth Administration" [1935–36], Files of the Division of Negro Affairs, NYA Archives.

31. Ibid.; "Minutes of Meeting of Conference of Advisory Group on Negro Questions," Aug. 8, 1935, R. R. Brown File, NYA Archives. Participants at the conference included White, NAACP; Channing Tobias, National YMCA; Johnson, president of Howard University; Robert Weaver and William Hastie, advisors in Dept. of Interior. Roosevelt to Williams, Feb. 11, 1935, Administrative Files, NYA Archives.

32. "Report Covering First Six Months of the Work of the Office of the Negro Affairs National Youth Administration" [1935–36], Files of the Division of Negro Affairs; [Bethune], "Cooperatives," Sept. 1939, Administrative Files; Bethune to Brown, memo, Oct. 8, 1936, Files of the Division of Negro Affairs, NYA Archives.

33. "Relation of the Division of Negro Affairs to the National Youth Administration" [1936], Files of the Division of Negro Affairs, NYA Archives. For examples of the flow of correspondence between white officials regarding

1048

Negro affairs, see Barnes to Bankson T. Holcomb (state dir., Dela. NYA), Jan. 25, 1937 (copy), Barnes Field Reports in Files of the Regional Directors; William J. Campbell (state dir., Ill. NYA) to Brown, Nov. 5, 1936; Bryan to Brown, Sept. 9, 1937, Administrative, Budget, and Personnel Correspondence Files, NYA Archives. At times national executives overruled state directors on Bethune's advice. See, for example, Bethune to Brown, Nov. 11, 1936, Brown to Campbell, Nov. 17, 1936 (copy), Administrative, Budget, and Personnel Correspondence Files; record of telephone conversation between Dr. John M. Gandy and Bethune, Sept. 25, 1939, Files of the Regional Directors, NYA Archives.

34. Flowers to Brown, Feb. 9, 1937, Mar. 2, 1937, Brown to Williams, May 5, 1937, Dodd to Brown, Dec. 30, 1937, Brown to Dodd, Jan. 6, 1938, Administrative Correspondence Files, NYA Archives.

35. Bethune to Robert Brown, May 17, 1943, Files of the Regional Directors; Bethune to Brown, Sept. 3, 1936, Files of the Division of Negro Affairs, NYA Archives.

1049

36. For the role and functions of the regional directors, see Brown to Edward L. Casey (state dir., Mass. NYA), Sept. 8, 1937, Williams to Robert K. Salyers (dep. state dir., Ky. NYA), Oct. 22, 1938, Administrative Correspondence Files, NYA Archives.

37. See especially Bullock, "A Brief Resume of the Regional Office of Negro Affairs of the National Youth Administration . . .," 1941, Files of the Regional Directors, NYA Archives. For examples of the duties and activities of regional Negro affairs representatives, see Bullock to Bethune, Apr. 29, 1942, July 2, 1941, to Pritchard, June 8, 1942, May 14, 1942, to Charles G. Lavin (state dir., Fla. NYA), Apr. 30, 1942, Robert Brown to Bethune, Jan. 13, 1943, to Wilford Freischknecht (regional dir., Pacific states), May 31, 1943, June 25, 1943, Rufus Watson (regional Negro affairs rep., region III) to Bethune, June 8, 1943, Files of the Regional Directors, NYA Archives. For Negroes' importance to the war effort in relationship to the NYA, see, for example, "Summary of Conference on the Negro in New Jersey Defense Program," Trenton, Sept. 14, 1940; Bethune to Johnson, June 10, 1940, Harriett West (Johnson's sec.) to Bethune, June 26, 1940; "A Statement on the Negro's Participation in National Defense" [1940], Files of the Division of Negro Affairs, NYA Archives.

38. Bethune to Bullock, May 3, 1942, July 3, 1942, to Pritchard, May 1, 1941, Aug. 7, 1941, to John N. Patterson, Aug. 12, 1942, Files of the Regional Directors, NYA Archives.

Changes in the Status of Women During the Quarter Century (1955-1980)

by DELORIS M. SAUNDERS

On May 17, 1954, the United States Supreme Court rendered its most forceful decision affecting American Schools. The decision is undoubtedly the most celebrated, legal decision of all times. Cited in every major educational journal, state legal code, subsequent desegregation case: legal, administration and financial text; and every serious discussion of school desegregation, Brown versus the Board of Education, Topeka, Kansas has received the attention of more citizens than any other civil decision.

1051

The U.S. Supreme Court ruled and announced on May 17, 1954: "Racial discrimination in public education is unconstitutional; all provisions of Federal, State or Local Law requiring or permitting such discrimination must yield to this principle; the vitality of the principle can not be allowed to yield simply because of disagreement; the parties to these cases (Class Action Suits filed in behalf of Black Students) should be admitted to public schools on a non-discriminatory basis with all deliberate speed.[1]

On the twenty-fifth anniversary of that momentous decision, it seems most appropriate to engage in critical examination of its affects on Black Americans. From all outward appearances, the decision has significantly altered the educational attainment of Blacks thereby improving their economic and political status. Factual analysis suggest differently.

One could logically assume the intent of the Court decision was to insure equal educational opportunity to all Blacks. One could also logically infer opportunity to include access to quality academic programs, equal treatment of Black enrollees and undifferentiated, unbiased completion requirements. Further, one could logically accept these guarantees without examining true impact, particularly in a nation which espouses democracy as its foundation.

Many among us have been painfully forced to question the reality of democracy for Black Americans. On the one hand, the constitution guarantees the principles of democracy to all citizen. Thus, theoretically we have the right to speak freely, to join and assemble, and to pursue one's guarantees. On the other hand, though painfully true, the pursuits of one's rights in this nation through any means leads to unfair labeling, persecution and isolation. To simply question the absence of fairness, more often than not, leads to consequences which can be permanently detrimental. It appears that subscription to

---

[1] W.F. Mondale, et al., *Select Court Decisions Relating To Equal Employment Opportunity.* Washington, D.C., U.S. Government Printing Office, 1972, pp. 4,6.

Originally published in *The Negro Educational Review*, Vol. 32, No. 1 (January 1981).

democracy is more often rhetorical than functional. The search to experience "One nation indivisible" has too often resulted in greater divisiveness. R. Grann Lloyd states that "moral adequacy is based on action. Hence, the best democratic intentions and professions of belief are meaningless unless translated into action."[2]

Brown accepted the challenge of translating intentions into actions and rhetoric into practice. His suit against the school board was an attempt to make democracy functional for the whole of society. The Supreme Court responded to his (Brown's) and other challenges brought by other citizens. The Court affirmed the principles of democracy for education. Thus, equal educational opportunity became a guaranteed right of Black Americans. What has been the true impact of that decision? Did Brown (and class) achieve equality of educational opportunity? The answer can be predicated in large part on the educational attainment and current status of Blacks following two and one-half decades of implementation.

1052

At least one generation of Blacks has completed public schooling with guarantees of equal educational opportunities. In addition to this monumental judicial guarantee which amplified constitutional protection, the Civil Rights Movement of the 1950's and 1960's provided social and moral impetus. Black and white Americans experienced consciousness raising, value interrogation, and a radical change in the social order of schools during that era. An undeniable compensation to equality of opportunity was passage of the Civil Rights Act of 1964.

Again, what has all this meant to the current status of Blacks and what has been the impact on the status of women in our society?

Many of the problems experienced by women are manifested to a great degree in the attitudes which forced Brown to seek recourse to the Topeka Board of Education. Though not identical, by any means, racism and sexism result in similar denials, attainment limitations, requirements to struggle for a place in the hierarchy and seemingly insurmountable difficulty in developing hierarchies.

The framework for this paper centers around the principles of equal opportunity in general and its impact on the status of women specifically. Women have pursued universal equality of opportunity consistently since the beginning of the decade of the 1970's. Prior to the 1970's, women largely pursued isolated freedoms such as voting rights, dress codes, social practices, credit and abortion. Each issue was pursued separately. With the emergence of the 1970 sexism revolt came a combined focus toward total freedom for women. Much

---

[2] R.G. Lloyd, 'Democracy and Adequacy,' *The Negro Educational Review,* Jacksonville, Florida: April, 1980, p. 47.

to the dismay of advocates for women's rights, the grant of freedoms for women is as complicated as the struggle to achieve rights for Blacks. Perhaps, had women joined ambitiously in the struggle for civil rights, their rights may have been easily attainable. One fact is certain, the denials of civil rights for Blacks and the poor are perpetuated by the same members of society who deny women their rights, namely white males. If convinced of the immorality of denial of rights for the more seriously oppressed groups (i.e., Blacks and other poor Americans,) they are more likely to respond to the issue of women's rights.

Ottley and Weatherby suggest there are two realities in America, one for white and another for Blacks.[3] Such duality is keenly discernible when status data regarding employment categories, income and schooling are critically analyzed. Typically, employment data is reported in terms of gross population. Therefore, when one hears 6 to 9 percent unemployment for any given year, there appears to be no cause for alarm. When reported by age and color, the percentage disparity is alarming for Blacks on the whole and even more so for Black teenagers. A review of employment between 1948 and 1975 (see Figure 7) clearly illustrates this disparity. At no time during the twenty-seven year period did employment for Blacks parallel that of white. Thus, unemployment data reported on a total national scale in no way reflected the reality of Black unemployment.

1053

Vernon Jordan, Executive Director of the National Urban League reported 40 percent unemployment among Black youth in 1979. This statement was verified by the U.S. Department of Labor's statistics. For the same period, the Employment Training Report of the President (of the United States) cited 16.3 percent teenage unemployment among all teenagers.[4] The disparity results from averaging significantly lower unemployment rates among white teenagers with drastically higher rates among Black teenagers to arrive at a respectable median. The disparity between the status of Blacks and whites transcend age in employment categories and rates. White male adults were reported at 4 percent unemployment as compared to 16.3 percent for Black male adults.[5] Note that Black male adult unemployment in the Annual Report of the National Urban League for 1978 is indicated at 25 percent. The preceeding discrepancies indicated a need to analyze pertinent status data by age, race, and sex characteristics. These trends are clearly more acute for women in general and even more

---

[3] R. Ottley and W. Weatherby, 'The Depression,' *Justice Denied,* P. Colliers Editors. New York: Harcourt, Brace and World, Inc., 1970. p. 256.

[4] V. Jordan, "Annual Report on the Status of Black Americans, 1978", address to the National Urban League. January 1978.

[5] Employment and Training Administrations, U.S. Department of Labor, *Employment Training Report For The President,* Washington, D.C., 1979, p. 4.

for Black women. For example, when the employment of all females is compared to that of males, nearly 56 percent of all women work as compared to 81 percent of all men. Incomes for the two groups range from a median of $8,300 for women to $13,990 for men. When reviewed by color and sex Black women are significantly lower in employment rates levels and income. In 1978, 13.1 percent of all Black females were unemployed as compared to 6.2 percent of all white females. These data are highly significant when the employment of females in this country is traced back four or five decades. The labor force was, during the mid-century, populated most by Black females.

Blacks have lagged behind white in all categories of employment (i.e. income, occupational levels, numbers of positions held.) Such has been the

1054

FIGURE 7.

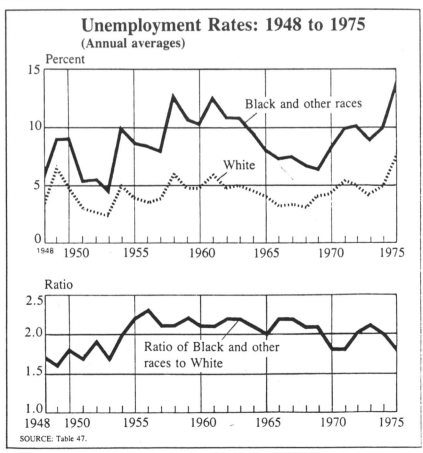

SOURCE: Table 47.

case for educational attainment. The followng table shows difference in levels of schooling between 1940 and 1975.

FIGURE 8.

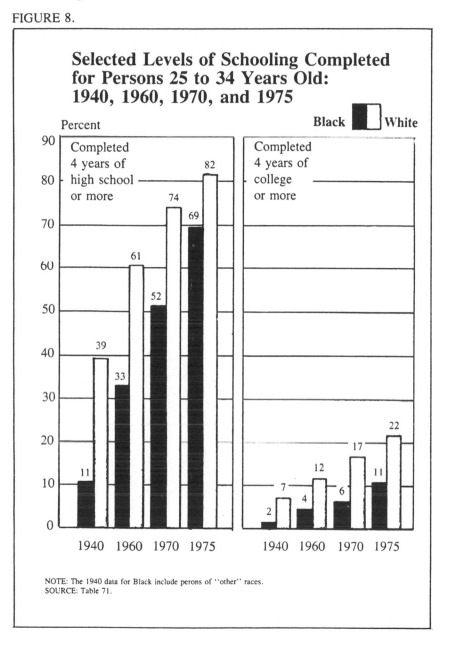

Selected Levels of Schooling Completed for Persons 25 to 34 Years Old: 1940, 1960, 1970, and 1975

Percent

Black ■ □ White

NOTE: The 1940 data for Black include perons of "other" races.
SOURCE: Table 71.

1055

Common belief among white Americans is that Blacks have low interest in educational attainment. The belief is mythical. The importance of education to Blacks is clearly documented in the rapid and constant incline in school enrollment. For example, enrollment for whites increased 43 percent between 1940 and 1975. For the comparable period, Black enrollment increased 60 percent (see Figure 8). The Census Bureau has noted that as members of a minority group that has suffered consistent cultural and economic disadvantages, Blacks have always placed special significance on acquiring higher education.[6]

1056

The proportion of Blacks enrolled in school has increased far more rapidly than that of whites, substantially narrowing the educational difference between the two population groups. The proportion of increase is far more drastic at the high school level than at the college level. Although there has been a gradual increase in the number of Blacks who have completed college between 1940 and 1975, Blacks lag considerably behind whites, particularly in 1975. The disparity is due largely to the critical gap in earnings among Black and white families and rising college tuition. Black families are not as likely to be able to afford the cost of a college education. In 1975, eleven percent of the Black population had completed college in comparison with 22 percent for whites.

According to the Department of Commerce, lower college enrollment among Blacks is attributed, in part, to fewer Blacks of college age finishing high school.[7] Such a dramatic difference must be embodied in less simplistic reasoning. An obvious demonstration of profound belief in education is suddenly eroding at the most critical level of academe. The alleged trend becomes highly suspect inasmuch as Blacks did complete high school during more conservative periods. Further, public schools are available to a near total Black population and attendance is now mandatory. What, then, are the underlying factors affecting the erosion of education for Blacks during an equality of education opportunity era?

To establish some further basis for this critical concern, a brief synopsis of academic attainment for Blacks since the turn of the century follows.

Although slavery was legally abolished prior to the turn of the century, few Blacks had access to education. Consequently Black enrollment was small. Limited access to schooling was imposed by meager wages, hard labor, long hours of work, insensitive employers, a lack of available and accessible schools, and a lack of equal protection under the law. It was often inadvisable, sometimes dangerous for Blacks to aspire to an education. The consequences

---

[6] Population Division, Bureau of the Census, *The Social and Economic Status Of The Black Population In The United States: An Historical Review,* 1790-1978, Washington, D.C., U.S. Government Printing Office, pp. 86, 87.

[7] Ibid, p. 86.

were painfully targeted at survival of the family in question. Schooling connoted an expanded exodus of Blacks from degradation, humiliation and entrapment (illegal slavery.) Klueger describes the story of a Black man who wanted simple justice for his children. He asked for a bus to transport Black kids to school. There were thirty buses for the white children. There was none for Blacks. He was run out of town.[8] Schools, when built for Blacks, were so poorly and sparsely situated, transportation prevented attendance by many.

Whitney Young recalled some of the consequences of the free choice for an education. He wrote: 'The negro who planned to go to school was often paid a nonscholarly visit from the Klan. Many were hung. Others were fired from their jobs, publicly humiliated, physically intimidated, while still others were denied credit and hounded from their homes.[9]

1057

It was not until the middle of the century that Blacks made impressive gains in school enrollment and educational attainment. The U.S. Department of Commerce, Bureau of the Census reported for 1940 (see Figure 8) a difference of 10.4 years of schooling for whites as compared to 6.9 years for Blacks. Grade equivalent data for women was reported in different measures but show 3 percent more white males in school than white females (52 and 49 percent, respectively) 2 percent more Black females in school than Black males (39 percent to 37 percent;) and 10 percent more white females in school than Black females (49 percent and 39 percent.)[10]

It should be noted that census data for Blacks in 1940 include 'other' races. Even where other races were combined with Blacks, they earned less and attained fewer years of schooling.

There were a number of appreciable gains in schooling among Blacks in the 1950's. This was the period which marked the onset of the Civil Rights Movement. Edmond Gordon cites the 1950's and 1960's as the civil rights period which impacted public education more than any other factor of our society.[11] It was during the mid-1950's when the barriers to public education for Blacks was challenged. The significance of Brown versus the School Board is embodied in the wide-spread, governmentally enforced segregated school systems throughout the nation. State and local governments legislated segregated schools which made integration unlawful. In the nine years following the decision, segregation increased rather than decreased. Gordon reports that the U.S. Commission on Civil Rights visited 100 city school systems to determine racial composition and found that racial isolation was extensive and had

---

[9] W. Young, Beyond Racism: Building An Open Society, New York: McGraw-Hill Book Company, 1969, p. 31.

[10] op. cit., p. 94.

[11] E.W. Gordon, *Equalizing Educational Opportunity In The Public School*, New York: AMS Press, Inc., 1974, p. 177.

increased since 1954. Seventy-five (75) percent of Black children that were studied attended schools which had 90 percent or more Black students. Eighty-three (83) percent of all white children were enrolled in schools which were 90 percent white. Contrary to common belief the practice was not different in Northern cities than in Southern ones.[12]

Enrollment in the decades of the 1950's and 1960's increased by more than 60 percent for both Blacks and whites, in spite of expanded racial isolation. The rapid growth was attributed, in part, to the Post War birth rate increases following World War II. The measure of attainment for Blacks, however, seemed to be equally related to (1) economic growth among Black families, (2) a proliferation of schools in Black neighborhoods and (3) busing of Black youngsters to achieve segregation.

1058

The median income for Black Families increased by 28 percent between 1947 and 1953 and another 20 percent by between 1959 and 1964. The most pronounced rate of economic growth occurred between 1964 and 1969 at the rate of 36 percent.[13]

The economic growth among Black families was by no means significant to raise the median income above the poverty level. Severe inflationary pressures and the recession of 1973 adversely affected Black income. The reported income for Blacks, though up between 1947 and 1973, was inflated with relatively higher incomes earned by 'other' races included in the data for Blacks. Additionally, the gap in earnings between Black and Americans increased during this period.

Black families earning a median income of $3,560 in 1947 earned a median $7,810 in 1974. This growth represented a 119 percent increase by 1974. Conversely, white families earned a median income of $7,500 in 1947 and $13,360 in 1974, representing a 92 percent increase.[14] Income increases for Black families have been disproportionate to whites, as evidenced by the expanding gap (see Figure 3.) While the percentage for Blacks was higher than that of whites, the gap in actual dollar amounts prior to the increase was so great, the gap remained significant following the increase. In other words, the family income gap in 1947 was $4,250 and in 1974 the gap was $5,550 (see Figure 3.)

The major contributing factor to economic growth among Black families between 1947 and 1974 was the increase in the number of women who entered the labor force. Typical employment for Black females prior to 1947 was non-institutional and therefore earnings were more meager. The trend toward

---

[12] E.W. Gordon, *Equality of Educational Opportunity In Public Schools*, p. 186.

[13] op. cit., p. 25.

[14] Ibid, pp. 22-26.

industrialized labor began during World War II and led to a gradual exodus from domestic employment. Coleman, Folger and other researchers report a correlation between income levels and educational attainment, thus some implied correlation between Black enrollment and income gains.[15],[16]

FIGURE 3.

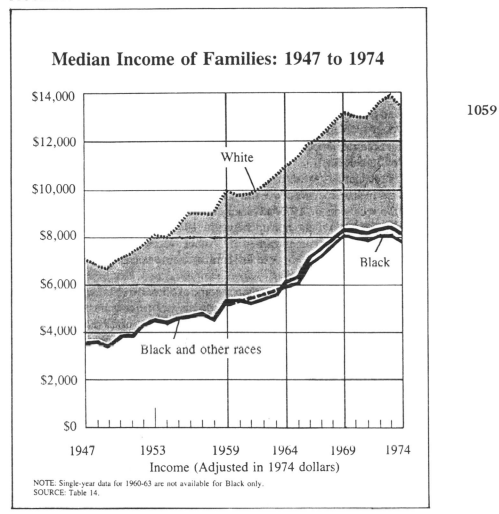

Median Income of Families: 1947 to 1974

NOTE: Single-year data for 1960-63 are not available for Black only.
SOURCE: Table 14.

1059

[15] J. Coleman, et al., *Equality of Educational Opportunity*, Washington, D.C.: U.S. Government Printing Office, 1966.

[16] J. Folger, et. al., *Education Of The American Population*, Washington, D.C.: U.S. Government Printing Office, 1967.

On the issue of neighborhood schools and busing, few schools districts had adequate schools within Black neighborhoods. Most schools, particularly senior high, required traveling great distances. For many youngsters, the ride began before dawn and often ended after dusk, as they traveled past white schools forbidden to them. There was a great surge of school construction between 1950 and 1970. The results were fewer Black youngsters being bused, a proliferation of segregated schools and non-compliance with the Supreme Court's decision of 1954.

1060

With the proliferation of neighborhood schools came constant growth in school enrollment. The Commerce Department reports a steady growth in Black enrollment since 1940. Since 1960, the increases have been marked. One out of 10 Blacks between the ages of 25 and 34 completed high school in 1940; three out of 10 in 1960; and 7 out of 10 by 1975.

It seems abundantly clear that Blacks have a genuine commitment to education. Against unparalleled obstacles, Blacks have pursued educational opportunities with vigor. At the high school level, attendance is verifiable and may be attributable largely to Brown. The neighborhood school in Black communities became an alternative for whites to desegregation by court order. They became a convenient means to an education for Blacks.

What remains unclear is the current discrepancy in the rate of increase in high school enrollment among Blacks as compared to the declining rate of completion of public high school. In an era of mandatory attendance and equality of educational opportunity this should not be true. Such was not the case prior to desegregation. Black youngsters are entering high schools but are failing to graduate and achieve expected competency levels. For those of us who maintain professional ties with public schooling, the causes are clear. Most public schools are administered by whites and the teaching staffs are likewise predominantly white. Most whites have low expectations for Blacks and teach accordingly. Numerous studies have verified the 'self-fulfilling prophecy' (low expectation yields low performance.) Such is the case for Black youth throughout America. The desegregated school has yielded negative results for many Black youth. Unfortunately, the results may be irreparable.

Levinsohn and Wright express optimism, however, in their shared belief in school desegregation. They write: 'Despite the impression we had gained that there was great divisiveness on this issue, all the responses we present strongly support continued desegregation of schools. Perhaps the effects of desegregation, if measured by other than test scores, would show positively and serve to encourage decision makers to implore imagination and foresight to improve educational offerings and make integrated classrooms which are comfortable for all kids.[17]

Not many scholars report significant gains for Black learners in desegregated schools. And, the trend of negative effects tend to be drastically different when presented by Blacks and whites. Blacks who record the impact of desegregation on Black learners appear to be concerned asbout those factors which insure the likelihood of success. Whites, on the other hand, tend to record factors which guarantee failure.

FIGURE 4.

1061

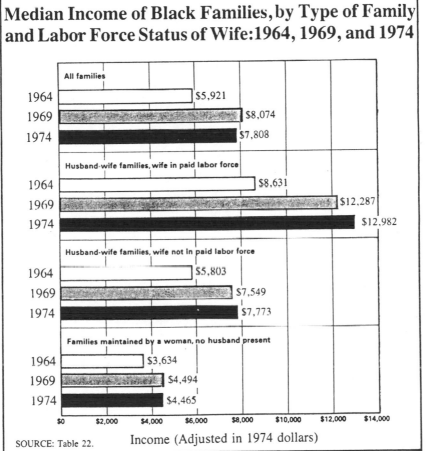

Median Income of Black Families, by Type of Family and Labor Force Status of Wife:1964, 1969, and 1974

All families

1964	$5,921
1969	$8,074
1974	$7,808

Husband-wife families, wife in paid labor force

1964	$8,631
1969	$12,287
1974	$12,982

Husband-wife families, wife not In paid labor force

1964	$5,803
1969	$7,549
1974	$7,773

Families maintained by a woman, no husband present

1964	$3,634
1969	$4,494
1974	$4,465

$0 $2,000 $4,000 $6,000 $8,000 $10,000 $12,000 $14,000

Income (Adjusted in 1974 dollars)

SOURCE: Table 22.

[17] F.H. Levinsohn, et al., *School Desegregation: Shadow and Substance*, Chicago: The University of Chicago Press, 1976, pp. 2-3.

These variations are displayed in various educational literature. For example, Webster, in EDUCATION OF BLACKS IN AMERICA, writes about administrative and teacher practices which have negative affects on learners and environments. He discusses negative interactions between white professionals and Black students, low expectations of learner achievement, disregard for appropriate language usage, tracking Black students into low level academic courses, high rates of suspension, unacceptable instructional practices and disregard for Black parents. [18] White writers such as St. John in School Desegregation, etc. details results of aptitude, intelligence and achievement measurement; student characteristics (racial attitudes, racial composition, and low self esteem among Black students,) and socioeconomic background. [19] The difference here is that one (St. John) talks of degree of failure while Webster describes the basic causes. What is not clearly understood in American Society is the need for consistent positive stimuli for Black learners that is accorded whites. In spite of rejection by whites and the coping ability of Blacks, Black learners as do white learners, also need positive environments and re-enforcement to achieve.

1062

What are the implications of this discussion for women? How has Brown affected the status and destiny of women in American society? Ironically, little attention is focused on school desegregation by sex. There are accounts which will attempt to verify greater tolerance of Black females than of males. One measure is in reported suspensions. Black males are suspended on an average of 4 to 1 compared to females. Academically, the issue of achievement is rarely addressed in relationship to Brown.

There have been significant changes in the status of women. These changes are reflected in the schooling and labor force in most categories of education and employment. Sexton believes that the sex segregated public school has almost vanished in the United States. [20] Though not in totality, females in modern schools do attend classes that are typically male oriented, participate in activities once prohibited to females and are as likely to complete high school.

In the labor force, there are increasing numbers of women in positions typically reserved for male and increasing numbers of women entering the labor force. However, the majority of women workers remain concentrated in lower paying, less technical and non-professional occupational groups. Of the 24.7 million persons below the poverty level in 1977 about 58 percent were women.

---

[18] S.W. Webster, *Education Of Blacks In America*, New York: Intext Educational Publishers, 1974.

[19] N.H. St. John, *School Desegregation Outcomes For Children*, New York: John Wiley and Sons, 1975.

[20] P. Sexton, *Women In Education*, Indiana: Phi Delta Kappa, 1976, p. 5.

Prior to 1955, revolutionary movements among females were uncommon and controlled. Activism through mass participation was resisted, particularly if the issue required sustained activity. Issues involving social participation of women had been addressed sufficiently, it seemed and there was little cause for activism in the interest of females.

Following the Brown versus School Board decision, demonstrations of many varieties spread throughout the nation. From the onset, Black women were involved, but had always been forerunners in the quest for equality. There was participation of white females on a limit scale, but often their participation made them suspect and subjected them to isolation in their communities. The Civil Rights Movement was an historical revolt against inequality and injustice and incorporated the basic issues of denial of the rights of all citizens. Women might have served their cause best by joining the Civil Rights Movement en masse. The attainment of rights inherent in the Civil Rights Movement included all oppressed groups. Women remained uninvolved in the total struggle, activated their own and is now experiencing the same dissolutionment as Blacks.

1063

The relationship of the Supreme Court's decision of 1954 to the women's movement of the 1970's and 1980's is not commonly documented. Though to advance the theory that the latter is a direct result of Brown does not seem illogical. The inception of wide scale activity in the interest of women's rights began during the late 1960's. The height of the movement occurred between 1970 and 1975. There are continued efforts to acquire and insure full participation of women in American society.

A search of the scholarly literature relating to women fixate the inception of the women's movement between 1968 and 1970. Unlike the clear, unalterable issue of equality of educational opportunity pursued by Brown in the interest of Blacks, the issues of the women's movement were multi-variant and sometimes confusing. Programs in women's studies began to surface in the colleges and universities around 1970. Sexual and personal awareness seminars, lectures and workshops became prolific around 1969. The issue of sex role stereotyping in curriculum and textbooks was confronted about 1970.[21]

The U.S. Department of Health, Education and Welfare reports that the concern for sex equality has been addressed in congressional hearings since the late 1960's. It further establishes some relationship to Brown and the Board of Education as it describes the concern for equality which dates back to the decision.[22]

---

[21] M. Guttentag, et al., *Undoing Sex Stereotypes*, New York: McGraw, Hill Book Company, 1976. p. 211.

[22] U.S. Department of Labor, *State Labor Laws In Transition: From Protection To Equal Status*, Washington, D.C.: U.S. Government Printing Office, 1976, p. 3.

A series of State and Federal anti-discrimination laws were enacted following the Supreme Court's Decision of 1954. The U.S. Department of Labor lauds the efforts of Governments in their enactment of laws applying specifically to women. Protections for women in the form of laws seemed to be the only means of achieving equity in the work place.[23] One needs only to review the history of protective legislation to be reminded that laws do not insure freedom or grant rights. Basically, protection for women in education became a legal requirement with passage of Title VI of the Civil Rights Act of 1964. Four additional anti-discrimination laws and a Federal Executive Order have been issued to insure sex equality requirements relevant to education. Yet, women have not attained equality of opportunity in employment or education. The chart below identifies the six major laws.

1064

FEDERAL ANTI-DISCRIMINATION LAWS

LAW	PASSAGE DATE	REQUIREMENTS
Title VI of the Civil Rights Act	1964	Prohibits discrimination against students on the ground of race, color or national origin. Prohibition include student admission, access to rourses and programs and student policies and their application. It also requires provision in bi-lingual instruction for limited English speaking people.
Title VII of the Civil Rights Act	1964	Prohibits discrimination in employment on the basis of race, color, religion, national origin or sex. All institutions and agencies with fifteen or more employees are covered. Prohibition include recruitment, selection, assignment, transfer, lay off, discharge, and recall; promotion, training opportunities, wages, leave, overtime, insurance, retirement, and other benefits.

---

[23] M. Matthew, et al., *Why Title IX?* Washington, D.C.: U.S. Department of HEW, 1977, p. 1,2.

The Equal Pay Act	1963	Prohibits discrimination in salaries and most fringe benefits for all employees of educational institutions and agencies. Prohibition covers equal pay for women doing essentially the same thing under similar conditions requiring substantially the same skills even when titles differ.	
Title IX of the Education Amendment	1972	Prohibits discrimination on the basis of sex against students and employees of education programs and activities receiving Federal funds. Practically all elementary, secondary and post secondary institutions are covered under this legislation. Prohibition covers admission to vocational, graduate, and professional and public undergraduate schools; access to courses and programs; counseling and guidance; physical education, financial assistance, student housing, extracurricular activities and employment.	1065
Executive Order 11246		Prohibits employment discrimination on the basis of color, religion, national origin, or sex in institutions or or agencies with Federal contracts over $10,000. Prohibition covers contracts and grants and requires observance in hiring, discharge, promotion, wages, benefits, training, and other conditions of employment.	

Many forms of sex discrimination still exist in spite of Federal legislation. One major obstacle to compliance with Federal laws is enforcement. Discrimination is so prevalent throughout society, Federal resources could be totally exhausted on enforcement if equality became a serious national priority. Typically, state and local governments enact some form of supporting legislation for major Federal laws. Enforcement to some degree at those levels offer greater assurances to victims of discrimination. Unfortunately, no discrimination proof remedy exist at this writing. Further, those who enact Federal legislation to protect groups from discrimination perpetuate discrimination on those same groups. The Congress of the Unitd States has failed to emply women, Blacks and other minorities in advanced level, higher paying positions. Equality of opportunity as a national priority seems unlikely. In spite of the handicaps women have made some advances.

1066

Throughout the 1970's, women were added to the labor force at the rate of over one million annually. Women 16 years of age and older increased by 11.5 million (41 percent) between 1967 and 1977.[24] The numerical increase was a climb from 28.4 million to 40 million. In a single, year, 1978, the female work force increased by 63 percent.[25]

The increase in labor force participation for women has highlighted the all too common practices which are discriminatory in all facets of employment. In decades prior to 1970, there was limited protection against sex discrimination. Increased work participation increased discrimination complaints thereby attracting attention and support of Federal and state agencies. The underlying message here is that there is safety and power in numbers.

When the female work force was significantly smaller, complaints of sex discrimination were threatening and hazardous to the complaining employee(s). Women suffered sexual harrassment, promotion and salary discrimination and unacceptable work environments. As the work force expanded, women banded together in collective efforts to eliminate discrimination. Complaints became common and the consistency of the nature of complaints disallowed cursory responses. As women pursued equality the momentum grew. The spillover effects of the quest for equality following Brown versus School Board and the demonstrations of the 1960's forced concrete consideration. Hence, the Federal protection laws and state protection laws.

---

[24] U.S. Department of Commerce, *A Statistical Portrait Of Women In The United States: 1978.* Washington, D.C.: U.S. Government Printing Office, 1978, p. 41.

[25] Employment and Training Administration of the U.S. Department of Labor, *Employment And Training Report Of The President, 1979.* Washington, D.C.: U.S. Government Printing Office, 1979, p. 14.

The Department of Labor disseminates pamphlets, newsletters and reports continuously which define protective laws for females. Additionally, material which describes the status of women in the labor force are disseminated to keep women informed of their new economic and social status. Broadcast and print media have given some attention to the issue of women's rights.

In spite of the fact that laws have done little to activate equality of opportunity for women, there are state laws which focus on their protection. The laws vary from state to state and not all states subscribe to the protection laws. The chart below summarizes state laws which were enacted to protect women from sex discrimination.

STATE LABOR LAWS[26]

LAW	REQUIREMENTS	1067
Minimum Wage	Minimum wage laws are of two varieties; (1) those which contain a minimum dollar amount in the law itself (statutory rate) and (2) those which empower wage boards to set minimum rates by occupation or industry. Only the legislature can change statutory wages. Wage boards may modify rates and issue wage orders for new occupations.	
Premium Pay for Overtime	Overtime laws provide pay at the premium rate. They are usually in minimum wage statues but are sometimes in hour laws. Typically, the provision require one and one-half times an employees regular pay after 40 hours.	
Equal Pay	Requires equal pay for women doing the same or holding jobs previously held by men.	
Fair Employment Practices	Prohibits against employment based on sex, race, color, religion, national origin, and often, age. In some states, the provision covers marital status and physical or mental handicap. All Federal Employment Practice (FEP) laws in include a provision specifically on sex discrimination.	
Maximum Hours	Establishes maximum daily or weekly hour provision for women with premium pay for volunteered overtime.	

---

[26] U.S. Department of Labor, *State Labor Laws In Transition: From Protection To Equal Status For Women*. Washington, D.C.: U.S. Government Printing Office.

Occupational Limitation	Prohibits exclusion of women from work which was deemed hazardous to their health and safety.

Weight-lifting Limitations	Places limitations on the amount of weight (expressed in pounds) that a woman can be required to lift or carry.

1068

Limitation on Employment Before and After Childbirth	Prohibits limitations on the exit of pregnant females and re-entry following childbirth. Pre and post pregnancy employment restrictions are no longer envorced except where hazard to mother and child are questionable.

Occupational Safety and Health	Requires, so far as possible, safe and healthful working conditions.

An analysis of employment trends clearly indicates a continuing denial of women in many employment categories and professions. Elizabeth Koontz reports that the Federal Government itself reflects the low opinion of women workers. In 1967, only 2 percent of the 849,000 Government women workers were in grades GS-12 and above compared to 21 percent of men. Some agencies had no females above GS-16 and the State Department and HEW had 49 and 47, respectively.[27] The data raise serious questions about the likelihood of America becoming an equality of opportunity society for women when the protectors of freedoms and rights (the Federal Government) deny women equal access.

In 1973, 644,000 women were full time white-collar (non-domestic) workers and comprised 47 percent of all Government Schedule (GS) and equivalent

---

[27] E. Koontz, *The Best Kept Secret Of The Past 5,000 Years*. Indiana: Phi Kappa Delta, 1972, p. 43.

grades. The following table illustrates the percentage of grade placement in grades below GS-13 as opposed to GS-13 and above.

GRADE	NUMBER	PERCENT
01	2,610	34.0
03	82,470	77.2
04	124,801	74.5
05	119,634	56.2
07	56,312	41.6
09	43,860	28.5
11	21,319	13.8
13	5,492	5.1
15	1,183	3.9
17	48	1.6
18	8	1.4

1069

Source: U.S. Department of Labor
1975 Handbook on Women Workers [28] (p. 117)

Department of Commerce data on women reveal that 39 million women were employed in 1978. They tended to be concentrated in four major occupational groups. The highest 935 percent) was clerical; second (21 percent) were service workers (food, cleaning, personal); third (16 percent) were professional with the highest number of jobs being teaching, social work, nurses and light craft; and fourth (11 percent) were equipment operators, excluding transport.

Occupational change occurs slowly and there are indications that women are slowly moving into many occupations traditionally held by men. Some occupational areas have barely been penetrated by women. Medicine engineering, physical sciences, judgeships, health administration, computer specialists and managers and highly skilled crafts are among those least populated by women.

It appears that educational attainment serves as no consistent criteria of measure for men being selected over women in most occupational groups. This would, of course, not apply to specialized professions such as law, medicine, engineering, etc. It does apply to admission opportunities for women. The Departments of Labor and Commerce verified that no appreciable difference exists between the number of males and females who compelte 4 years of high school (see Figure 3.) There is some disparity in the courses of study pursued. Males tend to select more technical courses (science, mathematics, etc.) than females in high school. A review of the years of school completed by 25 to 64

---

[28] U.S. Department of Labor, *1975 Handbook on Women Workers*, pp. 113-116.

year olds in some major occupational groups show a significantly higher percentage of women in white-collar positions to have completed 4 years of high school as compared to their male counterparts occupying identical positions.[29]

While women tend to have no less, and often more education than men, the gap in employment in advanced level positions is phenomenal. Women somehow, rarely seem to match promotional criteria. When women have the educational background, they need the experience. If they manage to have experience, they need to fulfill a host of non-job related and/or non-performance related social criteria. Affirmative action, at one time, seemed to be the answer. One only needs to study the qualifications of males selected for positions and qualifications of females who applied for those positions to know that affirmative action is a joke for women and Blacks. Even when women hold positions comparable to their male counterparts, the gap in employment widens as years progress (see Figure 8.) Women workers in essentially the same positions earned as average $6,380 less than men in 1978. Stated differently, male salaries exceeded women's by 68 percent during 1978 as compared to 64.5 percent in 1960; and 56.4 percent in 1955.

1070

One would presume that the protective legislation prohibiting sex discrimination would tend to narrow the gap in earning between males and females. The contrary seems to prevail. The gap has widened by 11.8 percent over the past twenty-five years. Thus, the fight for passage of the Equal Rights Amendment. Women are optimistically pursuing passage with strong faith in society's application of their Constitutional Rights.

It seems unlikely that additional freedoms will become reality as a result of Congressional action. The issue of enforcement by first the Congress and second other Governmental agencies makes application highly questionable. The Federal Government, including Congress, is the protector of freedom as stated earlier. When abridgment is the dominant model in employment by the Federal Government, other public and certainly private agencies and institutions are not likely to hasten into compliance.

Traditionally, status reports of a generalized nature rarely reflect the status of Blacks and other minorities. Statistical data up through the 1970 Census have grouped Blacks and other minorities. Accurate analysis of the Black population is not possible. The Department of Commerce, Bureau of the Census did, however, issue special subject reports for both women in Blacks. The Women's Report concentrates on 1978 data. The Report on Blacks covers the period between 1979 and 1978.

---

[29] U.S. Department of Commerce, *A Statistical Portrait Of Women In The United States: 1978.* Washington, D.C.: U.S. Government Printing Office, 1978, p. 65.

Women in general have made great advances in some selected categories of employment, education and wages (see Figure 16.) Almost equal numbers of women complete 4 years of high school as do men; sixty-two (62) percent of the labor force are female. Women's earnings are up considerably and they are increasingly holding job titles previously held by men. There are serious gaps in the wage levels of men and women. There are equally as serious gaps in access to technical careers. There is a need for continuous activity to insure application of the equalized society for women. Historically, rights are rarely granted de jure.

What has been the status of Black women throught this era? There have been advances in education, employment and wage increases. Nonetheless, Black women remain unemployed in extremely high rates. Black women ranked significantly higher than whites in unemployment, low paying jobs and on the job discrimination.

1071

Black women have continued to increase their educational attainment but have not achieved parity with white women. By 1978, 76 percent of Black women 25 to 29 years of age were college graduates. Eighty-six (86) percent of white women in this age group completed college.[30]

Economically, Black women regressed in the labor force. In 1970, fifty-eight (58) percent of Black women were in the work force while 49 percent of white women worked. By 1978, white women had increased their participation by 7 percentage points for a total of 56 percent employment. Blacks increased Their participation by only 4 percentage points so that 62 percent of Black women were in the labor force. The surge of white women who have entered the labor market during the past decade has been constant. Data to reflect the extent to which positions traditionally held by Black women are now being held by whites was unavailable. It may show displacement trends.

For those white women who are in the labor market, their earnings are an average $700 to $800 higher than Black women for comparable employment. The gap has been much wider (about $3,000 in 1970,) so that Black women have indeed progressed in wages, where they have managed to remain in the labor force.[31]

Education is one of the areas in which Black women have continued to make major advancements. During the 1970's, there has been a continuation of the trend for more Black women to be enrolled at the college level. In 1978, 569,000 Black women 14 to 34 years old were enrolled in college as compared

---

[30] Ibid, pp. 93-94.
[31] Ibid., p. 97.

to 269,000 in 1970, an increase of 112 percent. In fact, the proportion of Black women 14 to 34 years old enrolled in college in 1978 was not significantly different from the proportion of comparable white women.[32]

Although Black women have made strides in the 1970's toward achieving educational parity with white women, equality has not been reached. By 1978, the proportion of Black women 25 to 29 years old who were high school graduates (including those going on to college) reached 76 percent; this level was substantially above the 58 percent who were high school graduates in 1970. Yet in 1978, an educational gap still remained between Black and white women in that 86 percent of white women of this age group had completed high school.[33]

1072

There have been advances during the past twenty-five years. The rate of advancement was far more rapid between 1955 and 1975 than between 1975 and 1980. It appears that the past five years have resulted in regressive trends when compared with earlier trends. The regression includes education, economics and employment.

Unfortunately, many of the advances have been figurative rather than literal. The goal of the past 25 years was equality. That goal was established in relation to the advances and attainments of the oppressing groups in our society. As Blacks advanced, the advances of whites continued and at rates exceeding those of Blacks. What has occurred is regressive inasmuch as the gaps between Blacks and whites have widened in employment (positions held,) salaries and education (see Figure 3.)

Yes, Blacks no longer have a median income of $3,560, rather a median of $8,300. But whites no longer have a median income of $7,500. They now have a median income of over $14,000. Equality? Unfortunately no.

Given the reaction of white America over the past 25 years, the trends are not likely to be altered in favor of Blacks without a carefully planned agenda. Rights are legitimate assets, only when enjoyed fully. Blacks have yet to know that enjoyment.

All tables are reprints from U.S. Department of Commerce, Bureau of the Census.

---

[32] Ibid., p. 94.
[33] Ibid., p. 94.

William Seraile

Historians study the past with its emphasis on personalities and events. Sometimes the great doers of past decades are remembered. More often, men and women of achievement, while important in their own times, are overlooked by historians. Such a person is Henrietta Vinton Davis who made a name for herself not only as a major elocutionist but as a leading exponent of Marcus Garvey's "race first" concept.

1073

Davis, who was born in 1860, was the daughter of Mansfield Vinton Davis, a talented musician, and Mary Ann (Johnson) Davis. As a young woman, she studied under Marguerite E. Saxon of Washington, D.C., Edwin Lawrence of New York City, and Rachel Noah of Boston, where she attended the Boston School of Oratory. During her late teens she taught school in Maryland and Louisiana. In 1878 she became the first black woman to be employed by the Office of the Recorder of the Deeds in the nation's capital. It was in this capacity that she met Frederick Douglass who held the position of Recorder from 1881 to 1886.[1]

Davis' oratorical abilities, which proved valuable to the Garvey movement, were first developed in the nation's concert halls. A brief survey of her acting career is necessary before we examine her role in Garvey's Universal Negro Improvement Association. Frederick Douglass, a life time friend, introduced her to the audience in her first dramatic appearance on April 25, 1883. Davis' debut at Washington's Marine's Hall received a mixed review. "Our lady readers," commented the editor of The Washington Bee, "has found fault with Miss Davis' reading." "There are none in Washington," he added, "who can equal her in dramatic art."

The People's Advocate of Washington praised her for her talented

William Seraile is a faculty member of the Department of Black Studies, Herbert Lehman College of the City University of New York.

A shorter version of this paper was read at the 66th Annual Convention of the Association for the Study of Afro-American Life and History, October 30, 1981 in Philadelphia, Pennsylvania.

debut but indicated sadness that while one third of the audience was
white more blacks should have been in attendance to provide her with
moral support. John Edward Bruce, writing nearly forty years later,
provided this recollection: "I can recall the wild enthusiasm of the
audience which greeted [her] and the continuous applause that
followed each number. . . ." [2]

While Davis possessed a fine voice, her acting style was sometimes
criticized. Most papers, however, were quick to praise her for they
recognized her talents as being unique. Mr. Thomas T. Symmons, her
manager, and later her husband, sought in late April, 1884 to arrange
a testimonial for Davis in New York. On May 9, Philadelphia, as
reported by the **New York Globe**, provided Davis with "one of the
grandest receptions ever given to a colored lady in Philadelphia."
Despite her success in America's recital halls, critics still attacked
Davis' style. The **Bee** considered her performance of Lady Macbeth
at Ford's Opera House to be "a failure." She was accused of
"declaim[ing] her part like a school girl," and of lacking "harmony in
her voice." Defending herself, Davis complained about the "unkind
cut[s]." Nevertheless, the **Bee** replied that "we can not say that chalk
is cheese when chalk is chalk." [3]

1074

Praised more than criticized, Davis in 1884 resigned her copyist
position in the office of Recorder of Deeds to pursue her career full
time. In 1888 the Cleveland **Gazette** hailed her and Alice M. Franklin
as "two [black] females who give promise of a brilliant histronic
career." By 1893 she had established her own company which
produced "Dessalines." [4] Part of her success was due to her refusal to
desert the legitimate stage. Timothy Thomas Fortune, editor of the
New York **Age**, asserted in his overbearing way that Davis "could
achieve fame and fortune on the regular stage, if [she] . . . could get a
backer." Fortune argued that only "a manager with plenty of money
behind him" could achieve success for Davis or other talented
performers. Her attempt to dramatize Ignatius Donnelly's novel,
Doctor Huguet, the story of a white physician "whose soul and mind
occupied the body of an evil black man" was unsuccessful. By 1894,
Davis' career had shown remarkable improvement. This was noted
by the Cleveland **Gazette** which described her visit to Cincinatti as a
major improvement over her 1885 visit. [5]

As a reader, Davis was widely respected by many of the nineteenth
century's black leaders. In addition to Douglass, Bishop Henry M.
Turner, Booker T. Washington, and I.F. Aldridge thought highly of
her. [6] Their endorsements helped her to obtain church engagements
where "she [was] a great help to the ministers in raising money. . . ." [7]
Her delinations of Shakespear, which was a first for her race, and her
recitals of Paul Lawrence Dunbar's dialectic work won her praise
from many northern white newspapers. [8]

Due to missing records, little is known about her career during the years 1895 to 1911. Davis and Nonie Bailey Hardy, a contralto singer, toured in Jamaica in 1912. Later in the year, she managed Kingston's Convent Garden Theater. While in the island she introduced to Jamaicans the Loyal Knights and Ladies of Malachite, an Afro-American benevolent society.[9] In early 1913 the two returned to the United States after touring Central America.

Marcus Garvey, who came to the United States in 1916, managed to convince Henrietta Davis to forsake her stage career to become a missionary in the cause of African redemption. It may seem highly unusual that a popular dramatist would leave the concert hall for politics. After all, she was then close to sixty years of age. Yet, Davis had on earlier occasions shown an interest in politics.

A brief look at several episodes in her life would indicate that an activist role for her in 1919 was not out of character. In 1892, she wrote to Ignatius Donnelly, the Populist Party candidate for President, "I should like to take part in the present campaign. . . ." "I stand ready," she indicated, "to deliver speeches . . . in any part of the country where I could do the most good among my brethren." This plea to work with Donnelly was not just a passing thought because Davis apologized for writing him a second time. "But my eagerness," she indicated, "to serve my race and humanity must be my excuse."[10]

Her interest in her race is further revealed by a 1916 letter written from Bermuda to John Edward Bruce in which she revealed: "That is alright about the recital in Yonkers [N.Y.]. I know you did your best, but I am well acquainted with my people. I know their lack of cohesiveness—and it is that very lack that the whiteman takes advantage of. He knows the weakness of the Negro better than the Negro knows it himself."[11]

Garvey's emphasis on race love and self-reliance appealed to Davis. He probably reminded her of her step-father, George A. Hackett, a leader of blacks in Baltimore, who often entertained in his home prominent race leaders such as Frederick Douglass, Henry H. Garnet, Peter H. Clark, and the noted philanthropist, Stephen Smith. Douglass often conversed with Davis and undoubtedly shared with her many of his views on race questions. Garvey's ability to attract her to the U.N.I.A was a major coup for him because Davis, in 1918, had successfully avoided the vaudeville route, survived "radical shifts of popular taste," won the "praise of the press of both races," and was "doing the most brilliant work of her career."

It is not clear when Garvey and Davis first met. In 1921 Davis indicated that she met him in the West Indies. However, in 1923 she recalled that she first saw Garvey in Jamaica in 1910 but did not meet him until 1919 when, in her words, "I spoke at the [Harlem] Palace Casino on the invitation of Marcus Garvey." She immediately became one of the original thirteen members of the U.N.I.A. in New York City.[12] The two probably met in Jamaica and Garvey being impressed,

1075

renewed the acquaintance in 1919.

The association between the two became an important one personally and professionally. Garvey quickly awarded her with positions of both prestige and importance. By June 7, 1919, she was the international organizer, a director of the Black Star Shipping Company, as well as second vice-president of the shipping corporation. She was one of the signers of the Declaration of Rights for Negroes on August 13, 1920. During the next twelve years, Davis served as international organizer, first and fourth assistant president-general, delegate to Liberia, and secretary-general. [13]

1076

As an organizer, Davis had several advantages. Her oratorical skills certainly helped her to "reach" people because she kept her public statements eloquent but simple. Secondly, because of her previous travels throughout the Americas, many already knew her as an actress and undoubtedly came to see this new political woman out of curiosity. Upon hearing her, many became convinced of the soundness of the U.N.I.A.

As an organizer her dedication to the cause of African redemption was without question. John Edward Bruce described her as a useful and valuable asset because "she . . . put her whole soul into words." [14] Davis travelled widely in her role as the U.N.I.A. organizer. Her returns to Harlem's Star Casino and later Liberty Hall were spectacular successes, often similar to opening night on the stage. After Davis and Cyril V. Henry had returned from a Central and South American trip, Bruce wrote, "the demonstration . . . was the most successful public meeting of the organization. . . . The galleries and every available space was filled with people who had only been given two days notice. . . . Mr. Garvey was smiling from the crown of his head to the sole of his feet. . . ." Bruce added that the "eloquent and dramatic address of Miss Davis . . . [was one] of the notable features of a notable gathering of notable people." [15]

The year 1920 was very important for Garvey and the U.N.I.A. Branches mushroomed around the nation and the world, and many were not yet critical of his proposals for African liberation and self-reliance. On May 24, Garvey and Davis returned to New York after speaking in Baltimore and Washington. At Harlem's Liberty Hall, showpiece of the organization, Davis commented favorably on the display of hats manufactured by the U.N.I.A.'s newly opened Negro Factories Corporation. She urged the audience to buy hats and to tell their friends to purchase from the corporation where they would receive fair value for their money. Davis informed the enthusiastic crowd that they had to learn to share Garvey's greatness with the rest of America so that many would "know the great soul . . . purpose . . . ambition . . . hope of this man devinely sent to us." [16]

Davis' oratorical powers made her not only popular with the rank and file, but also with the U.N.I.A.s leadership. After returning from a trip to Cuba, Davis entered the Harlem meeting place admist "cheers and hand clapping."[17] At the organization's annual August convention, Garvey honored her by bestowing upon her the Order of Lady Commander of the Sublime Order of the Nile. The convention voted to pay her $6,000 in annual salary. Later, Garvey, who was to have problems with some of his executive staff, argued that only George A. McGuire, Chaplain-General, and Davis earned their pay. The others, according to him, were not worth more than $1,200 a year as an office boy or lackey.[18]

It is significant that Garvey thought highly of Davis because some of his contemporaries labeled him as a hater of mulattoes. Davis, a woman of fair complexion and an octoroon by race, certainly put to a misstatement Roi Ottley's assertion that only "one hundred percent Negroid [types] could hold office in the organization. . . ."[19] On a personal level, Garvey was very fond of the matronly Davis. She was one of the first to have his confidence when he decided to separate from his first wife, Amy Ashwood Garvey. Later he arranged for Davis to share a Harlem apartment with Amy Jacques, his future wife.[20]

1077

The year 1921 was a busy year for the international organizer as she travelled widely in the Americas. She spoke at rallies in Los Angeles on January 7 and 8, addressed an audience in San Francisco on January 11, and lectured in Oakland on February 6 and 7. At San Francisco's Bethel A.M.E. Church, Davis was introduced and "the audience went wild in their ovation, and it was some time before she was able to speak." The enthusiastic audience heard her preach that the Negro needed his own home so that lynching and discrimination would be things of the past. Reiterating her theme that Garvey was divinely sent, Davis indicated that she was happy to put aside her elocutionist talents to go "from the torrid to the frigid zones" on behalf of her race.[21]

At the end of February, Davis was back in New York exhorting the race to teach their children race love and pride so that they might redeem Africa. She urged them to become missionaries to reach the "lost" ones. Davis called for the putting out of the race the indifferent Negro who cannot accept the U.N.I.A. Shortly thereafter Davis and Garvey began an extensive recruiting drive throughout the West Indies, Central and South America.[22]

In early May, **Negro World** readers began to hear about the pair's successes. On April 14 Davis was in Moron, Cuba where the audience became agitated waiting for Davis to be introduced. While another was speaking and before being introduced, "there were thunderous applause, the windows and doors became darkened by the number who rushed from the outside to see and hear her." Four days later Davis spoke in Camaguey, Cuba where the local leaders called her Joan of Arc. On May 1 she witnessed the unveiling of the U.N.I.A.

charter at Santiago, Cuba. There she thrilled the crowd by telling them since they had fought to free Cuba they should fight to free Africa.[23]

Harlem became alive with excitement as Davis triumphantly returned on July 19. Speaking on behalf of the U.N.I.A. members and the High Executive Council, Fred A. Toote praised her in an address of welcome. Toote cited her as "an example of noble womanhood . . . [and as] a mother in [the] great work." He praised her for being to Garvey what "Miriam was to Moses."[24]

At the annual convention held in August, Davis was designated by Garvey as Lady Commander of the Nile. The gala celebration took on a liberating spirit as even the menu of shredded Liberian chicken, liberty special ice cream and Lady Vinton Black Cross Macaroons reminded the celebrants of the need to redeem Africa.[25] Davis' knighthood pleased the Lady President of the Philadelphia Division, Estelle Matthews, who wrote, "we now look for you for our standard of womanhood. H. stands for [your] honesty. . . . V. stands for your virtuous life. . . . D. stands for the devotion you have for the people."[26]

Throughout September and October of 1921 Davis spoke about the organization and Garvey's leadership. On September 4, after returning from Washington, she told the Liberty Hall audience that people were tired of so-called leaders like Robert R. Morton, principal of Tuskegee Institute, telling veterans to "take the inferior place we had before. God gave . . . Marcus Garvey to redeem Africa or die." Boston audiences heard her refer to Garvey as "a man chosen by God to lead his people." Davis described the month of recruiting efforts in the Boston area as a place where blacks were "hungry and thirsting for the truth. . . ." Speaking for Garvey and often like him, Davis attacked those who preferred to address themselves as colored which she said meant "something dyed." Like her leader she found the word Negro to be "a strong . . . virile word . . . full of life." Those blacks who sought petty political appointments and who were contented in cleaning white men's cuspidores were castigated by Davis for seeking so little when they could "be President of Africa."[27]

Davis' popularity as a speaker knew no bounds. On October 28 thousands paraded through the streets of Newark, New Jersey but were disappointed when Davis was unable to keep a speaking engagement. Many, according to the **Negro World**, "felt like leaving" when they heard that she was not coming.[28]

Lady Davis closed out 1921 by storming Kansas City, Kansas where she organized the Universal African Legion and Black Cross Nurses. **The Negro World** reported on December 31 that Davis, in Okmulgee, Oklahoma, converted many of her critics to the cause of African redemption.[29]

In 1922 Garvey was arrested and indicted for allegedly using the mails to commit fraud. His leadership was challenged by J.W. Eason who was eventually expelled from the U.N.I.A. Eason's

1078

assassination in New Orleans was cited as an example of Garvey's machinations.[30]

A great portion of Davis' time was used to defend Garvey against the mail fraud charges. She had a difficult assignment because many had bought shares in the Black Star Shipping Line, perhaps, because of her eloquence on behalf of the organization's economic programs. At the beginning of the year, Davis, despite suffering from a severe cold, told a New York audience that women had to "stand by this noble man." She pledged that "the woman militant [would] continue to fight by [his] side. . . ."[31]

While Davis did not seek to compete with Garvey, she was a forceful speaker in her own right and a person who spoke her mind. After a recent trip to California, she told New Yorkers that "as long as we depend upon the white man for a job, so long we will be his football."[32] At the end of January, Garvey and Davis addressed hundreds at Wilmington, Delaware's Bethel A.M.E. Church. Davis was so eloquent in her presentation that a skeptical minister said, "Lady Davis is not only a wonderful elocutionist, but she is a perfect angel." From February 1 3, the two spoke at Baltimore's Trinity Baptist Church. The F.B.I. quickly sought the services of a "competent and reliable negro [sic] informant . . . to spy on them." Baltimore's audience heard Davis say that blacks in Tulsa were afraid to be on the streets because of recent Klan activity. She urged them to follow the teachings of Garvey and to emigrate to Africa where they would have a country to protect them.[33]

1079

Garvey and his international organizer spoke in Philadelphia on February 4, in Rochester, New York on the 17th and 18th, and in Buffalo the following day. The two arrived in St. Louis on March 1 and remained there for three days. In St. Louis several hundred attended St. Paul's Baptist Church where, according to the F.B.I., Davis spoke about the aims of the organization and urged blacks not to "bow down in suppression and segregation." She told them that they were superior to whites. She ended her speech dramatically by shouting "Beware! Ye Stumbling blacks, for Marcus is coming."[34]

As was previously stated, Davis speaking ability was legendary. **The Negro World** edition of February 18 contained correspondence from Guatemala pledging support for the organization because that Central American nation had "hundreds of Vinton Davises ready to go out into the world. . . ." While speaking in Fort Wayne, Davis' eloquence caused a correspondent to write that she so bewitched people "that even the very stones would rise to pledge there must be a redeemed Africa."[35]

August in New York is usually a time of rising temperatures and high humidity. The 1922 U.N.I.A. August convention raised the temperature a few degrees as Garvey fought to maintain the loyalty of his followers. Realizing that his authority was being challenged because of the federal indictment and because of his contact with the Imperial Wizard of the Ku Klux Klan, Garvey sought to dominate the convention. He accused many on the Executive Council of being incompetent. In an exagerrated report, a F.B.I. informant indicated that the American delegates who were not on salary to Garvey were opposed to him because he had created "strife amongst the American Negroes and the white man."

The delegates were shocked as they witnessed the wheeling and dealing of Garvey and others. Sensing that some of his followers were wavering in their support for him, Garvey astutely resigned as President-General and Provisional President of Africa effective August 31, 1922. His resignation was followed by that of Davis and F.W. Elligor, Auditor-General. Confusion reigned as J.W. Eason, the American Leader, and Garvey became engaged in a bitter fight over charges and counter-chargers of fiscal mismanagement and collusion with the Klan. Although impeachment charges were brought against both, only Eason was found guilty and expelled from the U.N.I.A.[36]

1080

Out of the confusion surrounding Garvey's resignation and Eason's expulsion, officers were elected. As expected Garvey was returned to his leadership role. It was decided that the fourth assistant president-general would be a woman. Henrietta Davis easily defeated two candidates for the position. In her acceptance speech she declared her loyalty: "I have sworn that should he go up, I will go up, and should he fall, I shall fall by his side."[37]

Despite Garvey's triumph at the convention, some of the women delegates were not happy with their lack of influence. On August 31 a number of resolutions concerning their grievances were presented. One in particular called for Lady Davis to make plans, with Garvey's approval, so that women could function without restrictions from men. Garvey's reply was that the U.N.I.A.'s constitution protected women's rights. He suggested that the resolution be reworded so that it would not be interpreted that the men were not to be involved equally with women in the organization's work.[38] No one protested against Garvey's sugary answer.

Garvey's tribulations at the August convention was only a prelude to the problems that confronted him in 1923. His black critics increased their pressure against the government to prosecute him. On January 3, the U.N.I.A. issued a press release describing how Garvey, William Ferris, editor of the **The Negro World**, and Davis were going on a one year tour around the United States and the world. Garvey expressed a desire to take his message to white America to offset the negative feelings that his critics presented about him and the U.N.I.A. A special F.B.I. report noted that Garvey could not obtain a passport because of his legal difficulties, and that he was only trying to create sympathy from a future white jury.[39]

Internal arguments over salaries caused some to leave the

organization.   Others began to question whether Garvey was
emphasizing the race question too much.[40]Agent Battle of the F.B.I.
reported on March 1 that Sidney De Bourg, leader of the Negroes of
the Western Provinces of the West Indies, Central and South
America, believed that several officials including Fred A. Toote and
Davis, "are all waiting for the Government to call them so they can
give evidence as will convict Marcus Garvey." De Bourg added that
they had remained silent because Garvey would put them out of
office. Therefore, they would not be re-elected and would be unable
to take over after Garvey's death.[41]

The charge against Davis in not supported by any concrete evidence.
One would not expect a woman, who was then sixty-three, to wait for
a man twenty-seven years younger to die. More importantly, she
continued to speak on behalf of Garveyism. On May 28, she told
Garveyites in New York that Garvey had support around the
country. She believed the answer to the black man's problem was
migration to Africa where they could exist "under their own flag of
Red, the Black and the Green."[42]

1081

Garvey was brought to trial in the spring of 1923, and charged with
using the mails to commit fraud in the selling of shares to the Black
Star Shipping Line. Acting as his own lawyer, Garvey called many
witnesses, including Henrietta Davis. Testifying as a former member
of the Board of Directors of the shipping corporation, Davis reported
that she never saw Garvey receive money at meetings when
donations were given or when stock was sold for the steamship line.
She embarrased him by describing how in Jamaica his funds were so
low that she loaned him five dollars. More damaging to Garvey's case
was her numerous "I don't know," and her "I don't remember" replies
to many of his questions.[43]

Garvey, according to the F.B.I., was furious at Davis' "failure to
give proper testimony." According to the report for June 24, Garvey
"ordered the discharge of Miss Davis" and others. William Ferris
reported that the discharge involved only salaries, and that Garvey
had no objection if they went out into the field "and raise money for
the U.N.I.A." If they did, "they could take 15 percent of the all the
money they raised." On June 26, Rudolph Smith confirmed that G.L.
Gaines, G.O. Marke, Davis and himself "had received word their
salary had stop. . . , and when they received their letters [of
confirmation] they would split . . . and call a convention . . . of all the
[branch] presidents so they could vote against Garvey managing the
organization while in prison." Agent Battle reported on July 1 that
Davis revealed that Garvey was "still insulting the government."
She thought that he should stop writing for **The Negro World** so that
race relations between whites and blacks and between West Indians
and Afro-Americans could improve. Davis indicated that she would
travel to try to save the organization.[44]

While Garvey was incarcerated in New York City's Tombs Prison, after being convicted and sentenced to five years imprisonment, Davis, despite the F.B.I. insinuation of disloyalty, maintained public support for her leader. Prior to departing New York, Davis spoke in Harlem and told Garvey's followers on July 1, that "they cannot imprison that grand soul. . . ." She indicated that the organization could not be destroyed "while the love of liberty remains in the Negro's heart." **The Negro World**, recognizing Davis' extraordinary efforts on behalf of her imprisoned leader, reported in the July 28 issue that people were being tested. They were happy to grade "favorable" in regards to Lady Davis.

After traveling around the country drumming up support for Garvey, Davis returned to New York. In late August she spoke in Harlem where, according to Agent James W. Amos, Davis said, "we want to let him know that we live . . . [and] die by him. We will give up our last drop of blood for him." While some were willing to die for Garvey, few were willing to contribute towards the goal of raising five hundred dollars to purchase a loving cup for his birthday. The plea yielded only twenty-seven dollars.[45]

After staying in the Tombs for several months, Garvey managed to get out on bail while his sentence was being appealed. With the possibility of still spending five years in prison, Garvey saw 1924 as an important year in his effort to recoup the psychological damage of his conviction. Not one to mourn his setbacks, Garvey quickly organized the Black Cross Navigation and Trading Company to take the place of the dissolved Black Cross Shipping Line. Garvey sought also to gain a foothold in Liberia to begin his African colonization scheme. Davis was to have major responsibilities in both endeavors.

Lady Davis was the only woman sent by Garvey to Liberia on December 11, 1923. The delegation arrived in Liberia on February 1, 1924, and after initial promises from the government, met with disappointments in their colonization scheme. The setbacks of that venture will be highlighted later in this paper.

On June 25 Davis left New York for Panama, Colon, Costa Rica, Jamaica, British Hondurus and Guatamala. Garvey praised her after the ship had departed by saying, "on the high seas we have Lady Davis . . . carrying the message of good will. . . . ."[46] Davis' voyage was taking her to familiar territory where undoubtedly she sought to keep support for the organization alive.

A major purpose for blacks owning a ship was to eliminate the humiliating Jim Crow experience of second-class treatment. Although the voyage was her thirteenth, it was difficult for her to accept the inferior accommodations and discriminations. Davis and her travel companion, S.A. Haynes, were forced to bunk in the annex, and eat their meals after the whites had theirs. These embarrasing incidents not only occurred to them with their first-class tickets but within sight of the Statute of Liberty.[47]

In Panama and Central America, Davis won many converts and successfully solicited funds for the shipping line. Haynes described Davis as being treated like "the queen of some foreign nation. . . ."[48]

1082

The pair arrived in Jamaica on July 19 where Davis referred to Africa as being the "brightest" rather than the "darkest" continent. In Spanish Town, listeners were impressed with her comments about Liberia's potential for settlement.[49]

On August 24, Davis returned to New York to catch the end of the annual U.N.I.A. Convention. During her absence, she was chosen with six others to present on September 3 a petition to President Coolidge asking for his cooperation in helping to establish a homeland for Afro-Americans.[50] After describing her trip to the Caribbean, Davis urged the delegates to raise funds to purchase a ship so that the world could witness black people willing to sacrifice for a noble cause of African redemption.[51]

1083

On August 27, Davis and others presented the Liberian Delegation Report which indicated that despite the enthusiasm of both the "civilized people . . . [and] the Aborigines," President King reneged on his earlier agreement to let the U.N.I.A. colonize part of Liberia. Garvey bitterly accused the Liberian officials of selling out to British and French pressures. The Liberians in return advised the United States Department of State that it was "opposed, both in principle and in fact, to the policy of the [U.N.I.A.]." Davis urged the delegates to have hope of settling in Liberia for she intended until death came to "knock at the door of liberty. . . ."[52]

After the convention ended, Davis traveled to Bermuda. On November 9, she told New York's Liberty Hall audience that Garvey had support from that Atlantic island. The following week she provided Liberty Hall with a magnificient oratorical account of African redemption. She mentioned how some had forsaken Garvey while others had remained true and "are working towards an opportunity that a race has waited for thousands of years." She urged the membership to support the shipping venture so they could emigrate to Africa where the strength of the black man would be on display after the world has learned of the birth of a new nation.[53]

Shortly before Christmas, Davis informed Garveyites in New York that African redemption was ordained because "it is the call of the blood in our veins." Prophetically, she stated that one day Africa would be under black rule.[54] As 1924 came to an end, this Ethiopian Amazon urged the membership to "rectify the mistakes of the past year, [and] strengthen the weak points. . . ." They were urged to make 1925 "the banner year for the Negro. . . ."[55]

The year 1925 was pivotal for the U.N.I.A. The Black Cross Navigation and Trading Company acquired a ship. More importantly, Marcus Garvey, the reigning spirit of the organization, lost his right of appeal and began serving his sentence at Atlanta prison.

On January 4, Davis, speaking at Liberty Hall in Harlem, stated that the organization was close to having its own ship. A week later she prematurely announced that the last payment had been made to purchase "The Booker T. Washington." She exhorted them to carry on race progress because they were showing the world the stamina of the New Negro.[56]

On January 18, approximately two or three thousand paid one dollar each to board the pride of the Black Cross Navigation and Trading Company. The maiden voyage to the Caribbean left amidst a cheering multitude. Aboard the ship were fourteen passengers, including Davis, and six white officers led by the Norwegian Captain, J. DeRotter Hiorth. The crew as Garvey proudly proclaimed were black men. The enthusiastic crowd proudly watched as Garvey launched the ship and remarked, "she also carries that person that is always aboard, Lady Henrietta Vinton Davis."[57]

The scheduled three week voyage turned into a fiasco as it took four months for "The Booker T. Washington" to return. Speaking in 1929, Davis recollected how the Klan had attacked the ship in Norfolk while she was the only person aboard. She did not mention if they attempted to board the vessel. In Cuba, officials confiscated the vessel for payment of the defunct Black Star Line debts. The crew's salary was stolen in Jamaica. The ship with about one hundred aboard was docked in Jacksonville, Florida from May 8 to May 15, while Davis and others gave lectures. Some of the crew requested police intervention so that they could receive their back pay and leave the ship. The F.B.I. became involved when the local authorities wanted the vessel out of the harbor before Will Douglass, a fugitive, was to be extradicted from New York. They feared trouble if Douglass was returned and managed to get on the ship. The F.B.I. used its influence to get "The Booker T. Washington" out of Jacksonville because clearance was being held up since the Chief Engineer was an alien.[58]

In early June, Davis made her first appearance in New York since her exit nearly six months earlier. Garvey was in prison, the shipping line was in jeapody and Liberty Hall in Harlem was threatened with sale by auction. Davis gallantly sought to rally the troops. She reminded them that "Africa is waiting for Marcus Garvey." To show her loyalty to the organization she joined others on the Roll of Negro Patriots by donating ten dollars to the U.N.I.A.[59]

Garvey's troubles increased in 1926 as dissidents turned against him and sought to reform the image of the U.N.I.A. Supporters of the Jamaican held a special emergency meeting in March where Garvey and Davis were reelected to their respective positions. Critics of Garvey, however, met in New York on August 1 to attack their former leader.[60] Six hundred delegates heard Garvey denounced for his impractical schemes, for his machinations that forced men of character and vision to leave the organization. The dissidents urged that the organization's motto should be "build from the ground up and not from the air down."[61]

Garvey's supporters held their own convention on August 15 but the damage had been done. The dissidents elected George A. Weston president. Significantly they held title to the incorporation papers

1084

and controlled Harlem's Liberty Hall. Garvey's supporters still maintained control over the newspaper.[62]

Garvey's luck changed for the better in 1927 when President Calvin Coolidge pardoned him and had him deported to Jamaica. His friend and associate Henrietta Davis joined him there where she handled the "Foreign Headquarters" throughout much of 1928 while Garvey was in Europe. By 1929, when the U.N.I.A. held its annual convention in Jamaica, the organization had no constitutional leadership except for Garvey and Davis.[63]

Garvey, back in his native land, minced no words as the convention opened. He warned his followers that a coalition of whites and "cheap, brainless . . . treacherous . . . Negro[es]. . . ." were out to destroy the organization. Chaos broke out as Garvey indicated that the convention's purpose was to "create a new organization" because the name U.N.I.A. was bankrupt. Many in attendance were alienated by Garvey's comment that while he was in prison "wicked . . vicious . . . greedy men" cheated the organization. Even Davis, one of his most devout associates, was not spared Garvey's wrath. He accused her of doing "nothing to give new life to the organization" during his prison stay. He chastised her for asking for back salary when he had personally paid salaries and bills out of his own pocket. His attack on her was malicious in view of her support for him during the chaotic years of his imprisonment, particularly when in 1926 only Davis and Bishop McGuire did not sue for back salaries.[64]

Davis made no effort to publicly defend herself. She continued to take part in the convention but was "conservative during most of the deliberations." Despite Garvey's vicious attack, delegates unanimously elected her to the office of secretary-general.[65]

In 1930 Davis returned to the United States on vacation and spoke on behalf of Garvey's organization now known as the U.N.I.A. (August, 1929) of the World, to distinguish it from the dissident U.N.I.A. Inc. Garvey apparently forgiving her, indicated that while men were often disloyal, two women, Davis and Madame M.L.T. DeMena, International Organizer, were loyal to the organization. Still devoted to Garvey, Davis, while in Chicago, promised to stick with her leader "until Shiloh comes, till Africa is redeemed."[66]

Despite a comment of loyalty, Davis and Garvey drifted apart in 1931. During the first half of the year she managed to speak around the country, but ill health kept her confined to bed for weeks at a time.[67]

On August 15 a bombshell exploded off the pages of **The Negro World**. Editor H.G. Mudgal attacked the American leadership and urged Garvey to appoint a capable leader because the job was too difficult for "feminine hands." Davis remained silent while Madame DeMena replied in a forceful manner.[68] Sometime after the editorial

was published, Davis, whether saddened at the implications against
her, or Garvey's silence, or other reasons drifted away from the
organization and joined the rival faction headed by Dr. Lionel A.
Francis, a former leader of the Philadelphia branch of the original
U.N.I.A.[69] Neither Garvey or **The Negro World** commented on her
defection.

After serving as first assistant president-general in the U.N.I.A.
Inc., Davis, in 1934, became acting president after Dr. Francis was
expelled for conduct unbecoming an officer.   The position became
hers in August when she was elected president after George
LeMond declined the position.   She made it clear that the
organization was "upholding" Garvey's principles because of his
"contribution to Negro progress . . . despite his mistakes and
shortcomings." Under her leadership the organization continued to
insist upon civil rights for blacks. The depression hit blacks hard
economically, and in the fall of 1934, the U.N.I.A. Inc., developed
plans for the creation of "a national employment exchange" to notify
blacks about the available job market.[70]

This effort at finding employment for her people might have been
her last major effort on behalf of the U.N.I.A. Inc., as no other news
items have been located mentioning her association with the
organization. By 1940, Dr. Francis was once again the leader of the
U.N.I.A. Incorporated. The organization, long known for its efforts
on behalf of African redemption, was reduced by then to aiding
"Negroes to get the benefits of the various forms of public
assistance."[71]

Henrietta Vinton Davis, the "queen of [Garvey's] royal court," died
on November 23, 1941, eighteen months after the death of Marcus
Garvey. The woman that urged African redemption, race pride and
self-reliance died in total obscurity.   A survey of leading black
newspapers, as well as **The Washington Post** and **The New York
Times** failed to turn up an editorial or even a death announcement.[72]

How do we honor this majestic woman with the golden voice? Not
a single **Who's Who in the Theater** mentioned her dramatic career.
Historians of the Garvey movement have either ignored her or at
best granted her one or two lines in passing. To honor her we must
go back to those who observed this grand lady in action.   In
recognition of her unceasing fight for racial uplift, Crummell Lambert
wrote in 1925:

> I went to hear a lady Sunday night.
> A lady who is foremost in the fight.
>   . . .
> I sat enraptured as I heard her speak.
> Condemn the mighty and defend the weak.
> Tell how we've suffered in this alien land.
> Ruled by the white man with an iron hand.[73]

1086

Her ability as an African freedom fighter was recognized by **The California Eagle**, a Los Angeles newspaper. After hearing Davis speak, a reporter wrote in 1921, "she is by sentiment and deed a genuine African pàtriot, full-fledged, sincere, uncompromising, ready to do, dare and die for her convictions." The reporter added that her oratorical abilities easily approach that of Eugene Victor Debs. Although "her skin is fairer and whiter than [others] she is entirely oblivious to her own Ethiopian-Caucasianized pulchritude and prefers . . . the true . . . beauty of her original black sisters."[74]

Also in 1921, Fred A. Toote, in praise of her organizing skills told her, "when the history of this giant movement shall have been written, [your name] shall be written emblazoned in letters of gold as the lady, the stateswoman and the diplomat."[75]

1087

Henrietta Vinton Davis has been dead for over forty years. All over the Americas there are people who still recall her majestic figure walking down the street.[76] Let this paper be a start in telling to the world the contributions of this amazing woman who faithfully served Marcus Garvey for twelve years, and who assisted Garvey in making the Universal Negro Improvement Association the largest mass organization in the African world.

NOTES

1 **Who's Who of the Colored Race, 1915. A General Biographical Dictionary of Men and Women of African Descent**, Vol., 1, 87. Annotation to Vol 1, The Marcus Garvey Papers (to be published). Robert A. Hill, editor, to William Seraile, December 10, 1980.

2 **The Washington Bee**, April 28, 1883, 3; May 5, 1883, 3. **The People's Advocate** (Washington), April 28, 1883, 3. John E. Bruce Papers, Schomburg Collection, New York Public Library, Group D, BMS 11-21, Bruce Grit's column, n.d.

3 New York **Globe**, April 26, 1884, 3, May 3, 1884, 3; May 10, 1884, 4; May 17, 1884, 4. The Washington **Bee**, May 10, 1884, 2; May 24, 1884, 2. For other criticisms see New York **Globe**, November 22, 1884, 3.

4 Hill to Seraile, December 10, 1980 (Annotation). Cleveland **Gazette**, May 12, 1888, 1. New York **Age**, September 19, 1891, p. 2.

5 Henrietta V. Davis to Ignatius Donnelly, July 12, 1892 in Ignatius Donnelly Papers, Archives/Manuscripts Division of the Minnesota Historical Society, St. Paul. Microfilm reel 104, frame 74-75. Cleveland **Gazette**, April 28, 1894, 2.

6 Frederick Douglass to [unknown], November 18, 1883, Henry M. Turner to [unknown], January 21, 1891, I.F. Aldridge to [unknown], January 21, 1891 in Donnelly Papers, roll 158, frame 630-631.

7 Aldridge to [unknown], January 21, 1891, **Ibid.**

8 **Who's Who of the Colored Race**, 1915, 87. Donnelly Papers, roll 158, frame 630-631.

9 **The Daily Gleaner** (Kingston, Jamaica), May 2, 1912, 10. Hill to Seraile, December 10, 1980 (Annotation).

10 Davis to Donnelly, July 12, 1892, roll 104, frame 74-75.

11 Davis to Bruce, April 30, 1916, Group A, MSS 155, Bruce Papers.

12 **Negro World**, October 8, 1921, 10; June 16, 1923, 5. I am grateful to a former Garveyite, Reverend Hilton R. Jordan for his personal recollections of Davis. See the Baltimore **Afro-American**, February 24, 1917, p. 6 for Davis' views on Frederick Douglass. The Washington **Bee**, March 9, 1918, p. 4; April 16, 1918, p. 5.

13 Hill to Seraile, December 10, 1980 (Annotation). **Negro World**, October 29, 1921, 4. Davis claimed that her great grandfather signed the Declaration of Independence.

14 Bruce Papers, B MS 11-21, Group D-Miscellaneous Manuscript-Bruce Grit's Column, n.d.

15 **Ibid**, B 9-57, un-identified letter, n.d. [1920-1923?].

16 **Negro World**, June 5, 1920 in Marcus Garvey Clipping File, 1925-1974, Schomburg Collection, NYPL.

17 **Ibid**.

18 Elton Fax, **Garvey The Story of a Pioneer Black Nationalist**. Forward by John Henrik Clark. (New York: Dodd, Mead & Co., 1922), 125, 175.

19 Roi Ottley, **Inside Black America**. (London, Eyre & Spottiswoode, Ltd., 1948), 58. George Padmore, **Pan-Africanism or Communism**. Forward by Richard Wright. Introduction by Azinna Nwafor. (Garden City, New York: Doubleday & Co., 1971), 68.

20 Amy Jacques Garvey, **Garvey & Garveyism**. Introduction by John Henrik Clarke. (London: Collier Books, 1963), 43.

21 **Negro World**, February 12, 1921, 9, 10.

22 **Ibid**., February 26, 1921, 3; March 5, 1921, 3; March 12, 1921, 4.

23 **ibid**., May 7, 1921, 8; June 4, 1921, 8; July 2, 1921, 4.

24 **ibid**., July 30, 1921, 3; August 20, 1921, 12.

25 **Ibid**., September 3, 1921, 3, 12, in Marcus Garvey Movement, Schomburg Collection Clipping File, 1925-1974.

26 **Negro World**, September 17, 1921, 4.

27 **Ibid**., September 10, 1921, 3; October 8, 1921, 10; October 15, 1921, 5.

28 **Ibid**., November 12, 1921, 10.

29 **Ibid**., December 10, 1921, 11; December 24, 1921, 10; December 31, 1921, 7.

30 Garvey was arrested on mail fraud charges on January 12, 1922.

31 **Negro World**, January 21, 1922, 5 ; January 28, 1922, 2. For Davis' reiteration that Garvey was heavenly sent see February 25, 1922, 11 and April 1, 1922, 9.

32 **Ibid**., February 4, 1922, 3.

33 **Ibid**., February 10, 1922, 9. Report of Harold Nathan February 8, 1922 for the period February 1-3 in Henrietta Vinton Davis FBI File in author's personal collection.

34 **Negro World**, February 25, 1922, 8. Report of W.L. Buchanan February 20, 1922 for the period February 19-24; Report of M.F. Blackman, February 20, 1922, for period February 19; Report of Emil A. Solanka March 6, 1922 for period March 1-3 in Davis FBI File.

35 Letter to the Editor, n.d. from women of Guatemala, Puerto Barios Division No. 34, Los Amates Division No. 212 signed by Amy Boaster, Emily Chandler and Caroline Gray. **Negro World**, February 18, 1922, 8; July 22, 1922, 5. For similar comments see April 22, 1922, 8; May 6, 1922, 22; May 20, 1922, 3; July 15, 1922, 12.

36 Report of Andrew M. Battle, August 29, 1922 for period August 18 in Davis FBI File. **Negro World**, August 26, 1922, 9.

1088

37 **Negro World**, September 2, 1922, 2, 11, 12. Others who were elected were Dr. Leroy N. Bundy, 1st assistant president-general; William Sherrill, 2nd assistant president-general; Rudolph Smith, 3rd assistnat president-general. Davis received 107 votes to A.I. Robertson 50 votes and Lillian Wills 5 votes. For Davis additional support for Garvey see September 30, 1922, 2, and January 6, 1923, 2.

38 **Ibid.**, September 9, 1922, 5, 6.

39 **Ibid.**, January 6, 1923, 2. Special Report from William E. Dunn, Jr., January 13, 1923 in Davis FBI File. The proposed trip scheduled a five month tour of the U.S., with one month each in Canada, West Indies, Africa, and Japan, and two months each in South and Central America and Europe. For views of Garvey's critics see Marcus Garvey, **The Philosophy and Opinions of Marcus Garvey or Africa for the Africans.** Compiled by Amy Jacques Garvey with a new introduction by E.U. Essien-Udom. 2 vols., in one. (London: Frank Cass& Co., 1925), II: 293-309.

40 Fax, **Garvey The Story of a Pioneer,** p. 178.

41 Report of Andrew M. Battle, March 1, 1923 for period February 28 in Marcus Garvey FBI File in author's personal collection.

42 **Negro World**, June 2, 1923, 3.

43 **Ibid.**, June 16, 1923, 5.

44 **Ibid.**, July 7, 1923, 10. Report of Mortimer J. Davis, July 2, 1923, for period June 28-29 in Garvey FBI File. Report of Andrew M. Battle July 1, 1923 for period June 24-26 in Davis FBI File. Report of Battle July 5, 1923 for period July 2 in Garvey FBI File.

45 Report of James W. Amos August 20, 1923 for period August 20 in Davis FBI File. **Negro World**, July 28, 1923, 7; August 25, 1923, 8.

46 June 21, 1924, 2; July 5, 1924, 3, 16.

47 **Ibid.**, July 19, 1924, 7.

48 **Ibid.**, August 2, 1924, 5.

49 **Jamaican Times**, July 26, 1924 as cited in **Negro World**, August 16, 1924, 7.

50 **Ibid.**, August 16, 1924, 3; August 23, 1924, 11; September 13, 1924, 3.

51 **Ibid.**, August 30, 1924, 5; September 6, 1924, 11.

52 **Ibid.**, September 6, 1924, 3, 10. **New York Times**, August 27, 1924, 10; August 28, 1924, 10, 16.

53 **Negro World**, November 15, 1924, 3; November 22, 1924, 5.

54 **Ibid.**, December 27, 1924, 3.

55 **Ibid.**, January 10, 1925, 2.

56 **Ibid.**, January 10, 1925, 3; January 17, 1925, 3.

57 **New York Times**, January 19, 1925, 18. **New York Age**, January 24, 1925, 3; **Negro World**, January 24, 1925, 2.

58 **Negro World**, August 31, 1929, 3. Report of H.P. Wright, May 15, 1925 for May 14, 1925 in Davis FBI File.

59 **Negro World**, June 13, 1925, 3.

60 **New York Times**, August 2, 1926, 7. **Negro World**, March 28, 1926, 2. Marcus Garvey, **The Black Man: A Monthly Magazine of Negro Thought and Opinion**. Compiled with an introductory essay by Robert Hill (Millwood, New York: Kraus-Thomson Organization Limited, 1975), 8, 9. Others elected include Fred A. Toote, 1st assistant president-general; Dr. J.J. Peters, 2nd assistant president-general, William A. Wallace, secretary-general and J.S. St. Clair Drake as international organizer.

61 **New York Times**, August 2, 1926, 7. **New York Age**, August 7, 1926, 3.

62 **New York Times**, August 30, 1926, 17. **New York Age**, August 21, 1926, 3; September 11, 1926, 3.

63 Garvey, **The Black Man,**, p. 9 (introduction).

64 **Negro World**, July 20, 1929, 4; July 27, 1929; August 17, 1929, 1; August 24, 1929, 1, 3. Garvey, **Garvey & Garveyism**, 170.

65 **Ibid.**, September 7, 1929, 3; September 14, 1929, 3; September 21, 1929, 1.

66 For Garvey's comment see **Ibid.**, June 7, 1930, 1. For Davis' comment see **Ibid.**, January 31, 1931, 3.

67 **Ibid.**, July 11, 1931, 3, July 18, 1931, 3.

68 **ibid.**, August 15, 1931, 1, 4; September 19, 1931, 3.

69 Tony Martin suggested that Davis might have left because of the Isaiah Morter estate that the two groups were contesting. The U.N.I.A., Inc., had a better legal claim to the fortune which they eventually received in 1939. Tony Martin to William Seraile, January 9, 1981.

70 **New York Age**, August 13, 1932, 1; August 20, 1932, 1; August 27, 1932, 1; May 5, 1934, 1; August 18, 1934, 9; October 13, 1934, 3. **Norfolk Journal & Guide**, September 1, 1934, 5.

71 **Memorandum of the Progress, Ideologies, Tactics and Achievements of Negro Betterment and Interracial Organizations,** June 7, 1940, reel 1 in the Carnegie-Myrdal Study The Negro in America Research Memoranda for use in preparation of Dr. Gunnar Myrdal's **An American Delemma.** (Interview with Dr. Lionel A. Francis, January 3, 1940 by Ralph Bunche(. 419, 422, Schomburg Collection, NYPL.

72 **New york Post**, May 17, 1940 in Marcus Garvey FBI File. Hill to Seraile, December 10, 1980 (Annotation).

73 **Negro World**, January 3, 1925, 4.

74**California Eagle** (Los Angeles), n.d. [1921] as quoted in **Negro World**, March 19, 1921, 3.

75 **Negro World**, August 20, 1921, 12.

76 Hilton R. Jordan, known as "Young Marcus," is one of many who remembered Davis' triumphal marches through Harlem. Jordan to William Seraile, January 28, 1981.

April 28, 1941

Mr. Orren H. Lull
Regional Director, Region IV
Colorado

Mary McLeod Bethune
Director, Division of Negro Affairs
National Office

Negro Adviser in Omaha, Nebraska

I have read your letter and the report of Miss Risher concerning Bennie Brown.

There is only one thing to say. If Bennie Brown does not measure up to the needs of the position, please, by all means, let us get someone else. If you cannot find a good man, then get a good, strong woman. Do not keep anyone in the position if he cannot deliver.

MMB:THOMAS:ADMINISTON

Memo from Mary McLeod Bethune. The force of Bethune's personality as well as her administrative methods can be seen in the few lines of this memorandum. She pressed for the appointment of blacks to NYA staff positions and to the agency's advisory councils at the local, state, regional, and national level, but her ultimate goal was an effective program for Negro youth.

(Bethune to Orren H. Lull, April 28, 1941, Miscellaneous Alphabetic-Name Correspondence, 1935-41, Records of the Deputy Executive Director, Records of the National Youth Administration, RG 119.)

MARY MCLEOD BETHUNE AND THE NATIONAL YOUTH ADMINISTRATION

Elaine M. Smith

"If I were a young woman," declared a short, stout black woman in 1937, "I would go to Congress." This was about three decades before a black female went to the United States Congress and two years before such a person sat in a legislative assembly at even the state level. Nevertheless, when the sixty-two-year-old Mary McLeod Bethune flung out this idea to the New York City Association of Women's Clubs, she electrified the Negro women with the "mightiness of her enthusiasm."[1] As the president of the National Council of Negro Women and a former president of the National Association of Colored Women, she characteristically promoted the cause of black women in this way. She once commented, "Next to God, we are indebted to women, first for life itself, and then for making it worth having."[2] She was well aware that the "work of men is heralded and adored while that of women is given last place or entirely overlooked." But regardless of society's attitude she told women, "We must go to the front and take our rightful place; fight our battles and claim our victories!"[3]

Throughout her life Mary McLeod Bethune symbolized what she preached. Born in 1875 near Mayesville, South Carolina, to Samuel and Patsy McLeod, ex-slaves who ran a small farm, Bethune became educated through a local school, a girls' seminary, and a Bible institute. She married a fellow teacher, Albertus Bethune, and became the mother of a son. She could not conform to the restricted role of most women in American life, however, because she chose to pattern

This article is based in part on research supported by a Graduate Fellowship for Black Americans administered by the National Fellowships Fund. I wish, also, to acknowledge the assistance of Beauford J. Moore, former director of the Bethune Foundation and Richard V. Moore, former president of Bethune-Cookman College, for facilitating my use of the Mary McLeod Bethune Papers, Bethune Foundation at Bethune-Cookman College, Daytona Beach, Florida.

Originally published in *Clio Was a Woman: Studies in the History of American Women*, Mabel E. Deutrich and Virginia C. Purdy, eds. (Washington, D.C.: Howard University Press, 1980).

herself after two of the most outstanding black women in the South, Emma Wilson, her first teacher, and Lucy Laney, principal of the first school in which she worked as a young adult. Both of these women had established their own boarding schools; and in 1904 in Daytona Beach, Florida, she followed suit with an institution which developed into Bethune-Cookman College.

When the eminent sociologist and journalist, W.E.B. Du Bois, visited this college in 1929, he noted it had been created by "the indomitable energy of one black woman and her enthusiastic spirit inspires it and makes it live."[4] Agreeing with this evaluation and recognizing that despite insuperable difficulties, Bethune made the school into a standard junior college, and in 1935 the National Association of Colored People presented her its Spingarn Medal, an annual award signifying meritorious service to the Negro race. Within six weeks after receiving this round, gold medallion on a black, red, and gold sash, Bethune started down a different road toward a career in the National Youth Administration (NYA).

The National Youth Administration existed from 1935 to 1944 primarily to assist young people aged sixteen to twenty-four in getting work. During the middle of the Great Depression with its unprecedented and staggering unemployment in America, this age group justified a special agency in constituting about one-third of all the unemployed and in lacking work experience and work habits vis-a-vis other workers. Even when defense spending began to turn the economy around, many youths still needed the NYA services to get a job.

The NYA's major objective was to find employment for jobless youths in private industry. In line with this, all youth in the out-of-school work program maintained active registration with their State Employment Services. The NYA placed some young people in private employment during the late thirties but even more in the early forties. In the war projects of 1942-43, it virtually guaranteed jobs through its inter-state transfer plans.[5]

Besides placement, two other objectives of the agency were to provide employment through work-relief projects and vocational training projects. In the 1930s, the NYA required all youth who participated in these programs to come from families certified as eligible for relief services. It paid them approximately $15 or $16 per month for about forty-four hours of work. Most early projects centered around public-service activities, but after the first year the agency placed increasing emphasis upon vocational training. In 1937 it initiated a resident training center program through which youth were trained for employment near to or in cooperation with educational institutions. The first centers were oriented toward agriculture, but beginning in 1938 with the resident center in Quoddy, Maine, the NYA emphasized industrial training. Later, it created standardized workshops throughout the country to prepare young people for jobs in areas such as aviation mechanics, sheet metal welding, pattern making, electrical work, radio, forge, foundry, and industrial sewing.

The NYA training projects in 1942 concentrated solely upon enabling persons to develop a single skill necessary for a war production job such as operating a lathe, drill press, or a welder. In addition to placement and developing projects, the

1094

Youth Administration was directed to provide part-time employment for needy high-school and college students. The rationale for this was to keep youth usefully occupied and off the saturated labor market. At the secondary level, the agency supplied school authorities with funds to pay some students from relief families between $3 and $6 per month for educationally valuable work. Without any relief strings, it allotted college and university officials funds to enable them to pay from $10 to $25 to undergraduates and $30 to graduate students for hours in the NYA student work program.[6]

The number of youths the NYA assisted through placement services, work-relief, and vocational training projects, and the school program fluctuated. For example, in 1936-37, with $51,156,505, it helped 450,000 persons; in 1940-41, with $157,159,000, it reached 758,000.[7] The agency was created through Executive Order Number 7086 on June 16, 1935, under the Emergency Relief Appropriation Act of that year and resided within different larger organizations beginning with the Works Progress Administration, then the Federal Security Administration, and finally the War Manpower Commission. Throughout it all, however, the NYA administrator maintained much autonomy while he directed the program through a state system and then a regional one.

1095

Both blacks and whites dubbed the NYA one of the more liberal New Deal agencies in its relationship to Negro people. Its most influential policy-makers cast it in this mold. Among these were Eleanor Roosevelt, wife of the United States president, and Aubrey Williams, the NYA's sole administrator. Along with the U.S. Office of Education and the Children's Bureau, Mrs. Roosevelt was among the chief sponsors of the NYA. During the early years, she provided critical support and continued thereafter to identify actively with the program.[8] Williams, an outstanding social worker, had come to head the NYA via his position as assistant administrator to Harry Hopkins in the Federal Emergency Relief Administration and later in the Works Progress Administration. His attitude toward minorities was akin to the well-known liberal attitude of Mrs. Roosevelt. Although as a native of Alabama he may have occasionally used the word "nigger," nevertheless, he wanted the NYA to make at least a small beginning toward alleviating Negro problems. This type of sentiment and the hope that eventually the NYA would become a permanent program reflecting the idealism of American democracy led to the agency's recognition of blacks.[9]

Initially, this recognition was manifested by having two blacks on the National Advisory Committee, a group consisting of thirty-five persons representing business, agriculture, education, and youth. The NYA formulators probably selected Mordecai Johnson and Mary McLeod Bethune because of their status as educators and their high visibility. As president of Howard University, a distinguished black institution in Washington, D.C., relying heavily upon federal funding, Johnson was known to the NYA inner circle and had been among the select informal advisers on the youth program immediately after its creation.[10] Bethune came to the inner circle's attention through Josephine Roche, assistant secretary of the treasury and chairman of the NYA's six-member executive committee. A few weeks before advisory members were selected, Mrs. Roche had been caught up in Bethune's oratory, personality, and achievement as Bethune received the Spingarn Award in St. Louis, Missouri. No doubt, Eleanor Roosevelt, who had met Bethune about eight years earlier, endorsed Roche's proposal to have Bethune on the committee, for she personally asked her to represent Negro youth.[11]

Of all youth reeling from the depression, Negro youth suffered most because of the earlier marginal existence of their families. Bewildered, frustrated, and defeated, they had reason to lose hope for a better life. They constituted roughly 13 percent of all youth in America but about 15 percent of youth on relief. Most had received grossly inferior education in the segregated schools of the South. With southern states denying them a proportionate share of federal funds for vocational education in addition to other injustices, their vocational training was "scarcely more than crude instruction in obsolete crafts and skills."[12] Regardless of education, black youth were hampered on the job market by the general conditions of Negro occupational life. When they could find work, it was usually in agriculture or domestic and personal service which employed nearly two-thirds of all Negro workers. But their chances of finding work even in traditionally Negro jobs were somewhat diminished because white workers were taking employment in these.[13]

Sensitive to this distressed status of Negro youth and oriented toward public service, Mary McLeod Bethune jumped at the opportunity to serve on the NYA's National Advisory Committee. Although the position demanded primarily attendance at committee meetings scheduled once or twice a year, the aggressive Bethune immediately transcended this limited role. Seeing in the NYA the best potential aid for Negro youth, she publicized the program among blacks all over the country. Concentrating on Florida, however, her home base, she worked closely with state officials to ensure black youth a proportionate share of benefits and helped to get two Negroes appointed to the NYA Florida advisory committee at a time when all other states except Alabama had appointed either one or none. By working with farmers, Bethune assisted in developing an extensive rural recreation project. She also obtained NYA programs at her own Bethune-Cookman College.[14]

At the national level, Bethune endeavored to have the NYA adopt policies that would extend its benefits to more blacks. Thus, she advocated that the agency drop the requirement of relief certification before allowing out-of-school youth to receive aid. She and other blacks emphasized that in many areas, especially the South, the Works Progress Administration, which determined whether youth were qualified for relief, would not declare some Negroes eligible regardless of the evidence. Nevertheless, Aubrey Williams believed that the southern states were doing a good job with certification, and throughout the depression-oriented program Bethune went unheeded.[15] She was persuasive, however, on the point of a special fund for Negro college and university students. Negro students who could not receive part-time aid from their institutions' regular NYA funds — even after the institution had given Negroes a fair share of this aid — could apply through the school for special fund assistance. Black students needed the extra help because

1096

most came from families that lacked sufficient incomes for higher education. And, too, they needed it for the increased costs of going to school in states other than their own because southern and border states generally denied them training opportunities at the graduate and professional levels and in some areas of under-graduate work.[16]

For Mary McLeod Bethune, however, the burning issue for extending NYA benefits to more blacks focused on neither certification nor the special fund. It was Negro leadership within all components of the program. She believed as she once said, "The white man has been thinking for us too long; we want him to think with us now instead of for us."[17] Arguing that blacks needed opportunities for leader-ship if they were to become effective citizens and if democratic values were to be realized in race relations, she urged the National Advisory Committee and NYA officials to permit black leadership over the youth program as it affected blacks. In doing this, her primary concern was not the segregation-integration issue but a greater measure of equality for Negroes within the existing contours of American society. She explained that where there was no need for dual programs she "heartily recommended" a single integrated program; but where racism made this impossible, she recommended two, provided proper leadership existed. This meant Negro leaders, she said, for they had greater understanding and sympathy for the problems of Negro youth than whites.[18]

Bethune proposed a permanent national advisory committee on Negro affairs and later, she advocated simply adding another Negro to the existing National Advisory Committee. She also suggested that the NYA administrator and his deputy should each employ a Negro assistant. At the state level, Bethune cam-paigned for hiring black assistants to state directors to interpret their own needs. Locally, she wanted the leaders to determine the nature of black projects and black supervisors employed who would receive compensation equal to that of their white counterparts.[19]

The NYA responded positively to two aspects of Bethune's agenda for black leadership. With the prodding of the black press, it employed in the Washington office one Negro specialist. Also, in states with concentrated numbers of blacks, it advised the state director to employ a black assistant. In 1936 this was about as far as the agency would go in the interest of in-house black advancement, for when Aubrey Williams proposed to his Executive Committee that the NYA place three or four Negroes in regular staff positions, the committee refused to take it seriously.[20]

Mary Bethune's status as a mere NYA adviser changed primarily as a result of her encounter with President Franklin Roosevelt on April 28, 1936. As a climax for the second meeting of the National Advisory Committee, she and other advisory members went to the White House to present resolutions adopted on major issues in the youth program. They had made no specific reference to Negro participation but permitted Bethune to compensate for this through an oral report.[21] In meeting the president for the first time, Bethune hoped to reinforce his support for the agency. As was her custom, she spoke positively and optimistically.

1097

Basically, she said, "We are bringing light and spirit to these many thousands who for so long have been in darkness." When she finished, Roosevelt grasped her hands as he pledged his best efforts to improve the status of the Negro people.[22] Within two months after this initial meeting, Roosevelt had her back at the White House offering her the top position in the NYA Office for Negro Affairs. Like thousands of other educated whites who had heard Bethune, the president probably had been struck by her sincerity, fearlessness, and zeal for social justice.[23] He believed that she was a leader possessing the tact, common sense, and courage to obtain more benefits for blacks through the NYA than anybody else. Roosevelt said of Bethune, "I believe in her because she has her feet on the ground; not only on the ground, but deep down in the ploughed soil."[24] No doubt, the chief NYA officials influenced the president's attitude. They were pleased with Bethune's work and wanted to give her latitude in continuing it. Both Charles Taussig, the chairman of the Advisory Committee, and Richard Brown, the NYA assistant administrator, had commended Bethune for her contributions. She had been one of the most active advisory members, and Brown declared that she could not have done more for the NYA had she been on the payroll in Washington. Perhaps they respected her most for establishing clear goals, then working persistently but patiently for their realization.[25]

Believing that it was important to have talented black women such as herself working in responsible federal jobs just as white women did, Bethune started work in June 1936. In doing so, she displaced the competent Juanita Saddler, the NYA's "Administrative Assistant in charge of Negro Affairs" who had been previously the student field secretary for the Young Women's Christian Association in New York City. With Bethune's laudatory recommendation, the NYA had employed her in December 1935 because of the keen interest she had shown in the agency from its inception and more importantly, because she had been the best qualified candidate for the Negro job.[26] Initially, however, it had failed to define her role and was slow in providing a secretary and suitable office space. Saddler had seen her major responsibility as fostering Negro leadership in every phase of the program affecting Negroes. She believed that as long as society sanctioned a dual system, the provisions for whites and blacks had to be equalized regardless of the inherent duplication, economic waste, and division.[27] Thus, Saddler and Bethune shared a basic philosophical outlook on how to promote adequate Negro participation in the NYA. And too, they worked closely when Bethune was only an advisory person. Nevertheless, within three weeks after Bethune's arrival in Washington, Saddler submitted a curt resignation. She was uncomfortable in seeing Bethune in her former position as the chief Negro specialist.[28]

Bethune began work in Washington ostensibly as the director of the Division of Minority Affairs, which the agency soon changed to Division of Negro Affairs. She later recalled that she occupied the first federal position in the history of the country created for a black woman. Yet the news media did not immediately publicize her new status. For example, the *Pittsburgh Courier,* a leading black weekly, omitted mentioning it for about six weeks and the Democratic party failed to list her among "Roosevelt's Negro Appointees" advertised in the *Courier* to win black votes in the 1936 presidential election.[29] The most reasonable explanation for this curious development was that Bethune's appointment could not bear close scrutiny. The Civil Service Commission did not recognize a Negro division within the NYA nor Bethune as a division director. Instead, Bethune's official title was the same as Saddler's had been "Administrative Assistant in Charge of Negro Affairs." Characteristically, however, Bethune lived her hopes. After acting for two and a half years, the commission made her official director on January 16, 1939.[30] With this new reality, Bethune observed that her division paralleled the six others in the NYA regarding salary schedules, grade levels, and other matters.[31] Regardless of title, the black lady administrator was typical of directors who firmly controlled their divisions. For example, when her assistant director once submitted a site visit report directly to one of their administrative superiors while she was out of the office, she wrote him: "Our procedure is that all field reports be made to my desk and together we will study them and send such part of them we deem wise to Mr. Lasseter over my signature."[32]

Mary Bethune was able to employ in her office several individuals. In the first year she employed three. When sixty-seven persons constituted the entire NYA national office force in the next year, she still had three workers. By 1941, however, when the agency had shifted from a depression orientation to national defense, the number had increased to seven and included an assistant director, an administrative assistant, a section chief for Negro Relations, two stenographers, and two secretaries. In the course of her seven years with the Youth Administration, she had four capable assistant directors. The first two, Frank Horne and R. O'Hara Lanier, came from academic backgrounds; the next, T. Arnold Hill, from the National Urban League in New York City; and the last, Charles P. Browning, from the NYA staff based in Chicago.[33] Bethune's right hand, however, was another competent and out-going black woman, Arabella Denniston. She had graduated from Bethune-Cookman College and had worked in the Urban League and such organizations in New York before joining the NYA as a secretary. In the Office of Negro Affairs, she became involved in all phases of Bethune's professional activities. She consistently offered her basic support as both an employee and friend. In one Denniston-to-Bethune letter, for example, she expressed concern for Bethune's well-being; reminded her to send a card of sympathy to her friend Bishop Reverdy C. Ransom, whose wife had just died; delivered messages that had come to the office during her absence; indicated Bethune's pending travel arrangements; passed on news of the NYA operations; and reported on the Washington visit of the Liberian President Barclay whom Roosevelt had entertained at dinner with two black Americans present, Dr. Mordecai Johnson and Gen. Benjamin O. Davis.[34]

As a recognized black leader, Mary McLeod Bethune's importance to the administration transcended her activities in the NYA. She was an administration representative to blacks. As Gunnar Myrdal noted in *An American Dilemma*, politically, blacks and whites dealt with each other through the medium of

1099

plenipotentiaries. Only their leaders normally interacted across racial lines. Therefore, the white power structure needed black leaders, for through them it could
indirectly influence the Negro people.[35] As a sagacious leader, Bethune was
mindful of this aspect of her position. She ardently worked to build support for the
administration and judging from her popularity among blacks in the late thirties
and early forties, she did this job well. Bethune was careful in what she said about
President Roosevelt so as not to cause embarrassment. When the Associated Negro
Press, for example, pressured her for a formal statement on how the president
received recommendations from the 1937 NYA-sponsored Conference on the
Negro, she high-lighted his sympathetic attitude: "The President was most interested and cooperative in his consideration of the problems confronting us. He
was deeply interested in the forward steps that Negroes were taking toward a more
definite integration into the American program. The Negroes of America may
depend upon the interest and the sincerity of our President in his efforts to justify
their confidence in him and his program." Despite this innocuous tone, Bethune
waited for approval from Stephen Early, the assistant secretary to the president,
before releasing her comment.[36]

1100

   As an administration official, Mary Bethune publicly cast the New Deal program in the most favorable light possible. Her article, "I'll Never Turn Back No
More" in a 1938 issue of *Opportunity* magazine summarized the points she made
time and time again. She emphasized that blacks could not afford to turn back to
the times before the New Deal. In every respect they were "the real sick people of
America in need of every liberal program to benefit the masses." The programs
she referred to included the NYA, the large-scale relief efforts, adult education,
social security, the Housing Authority, resettlement projects, farm loans, credit
unions, cooperatives, soil reclamation, rural electrification, and long time purchase plans. She claimed that although the doors of opportunity were not open
wide enough, it was still the dawn of a new day for Negroes.[37]

   As national defense became the primary political concern, Bethune promoted
ideas favorable to the war effort. In February 1941 she spoke briefly on the
Columbia Broadcasting System radio network for the Committee to Defend
America by Aiding the Allies to generate support for Lend-Lease. In June 1942 she
went to the War Department for about five days to help select candidates for the
Woman's Army Auxiliary Corps officers training school in Fort Des Moines,
Iowa, and from that beginning she continued to identify publicly with this new
camp.[38] More importantly, she preached a "Close Ranks" message: "These are
not the days to consider from whence one came, nor the traditional customs of
social standing, caste and privilege. These are the days for a united front with a
united purpose to fight for that victory which we must have, or regardless of caste,
creed or position, we will all sink together."[39] In addition, she attributed transcen-
dent moral purposes to the war in statements such as: "We are fighting for a
baptism in that spiritual understanding that all mankind has been created in the
image of God" and "We are fighting for the perfection of the democracy of our

own beloved America, and the extension of that perfected democracy to the ends of the world.''[40]

In whipping up Negro support for the war effort, she observed that the Roosevelt administration had recognized Negroes as an integral part of American life. She recited the New Deal programs that offered benefits to blacks and pointed out the Negroes who were in responsible positions in the federal government such as Robert Weaver, William Pickens, Hobart Taylor, William Hastie, and Crystal Byrd Faucett. She hailed Roosevelt's Executive Order 8802 that banned racial discrimination in government and defense industries as a big step forward, yet she warned that it would not immediately solve the problems for which it was designed. Blacks, themselves, had to be the constant aggressors: ''We must not be content to sit and wait for someone to bring the opportunities of today to us. . . . [You must] organize into groups and ask to be heard and insist that you be considered.''[41]

1101

Bethune's activities for the administration were rooted in personal loyalty and respect for Franklin and Eleanor Roosevelt. Mentally, she separated Roosevelt from his Democratic party, especially its flagrantly racist southern wing and clung fervently to his idealism. In the midst of escalating black criticism of the administration, she emphasized that ''FDR is fair at heart in his attitude toward the Negro, and regularly inquires of the New Deal agencies as to what is being done for the Negro.''[42] She saw his greatest contribution to blacks as bringing hope through sponsorship of such programs as the NYA.[43] Bethune was especially devoted to the president's wife and proclaimed her a ''great humanitarian,'' ''a grand and charming personality,'' ''a symbol of true unadulterated democracy,'' and a friend.[44] She had good reasons for these attitudes. Eleanor Roosevelt publicly identified with all of Bethune's interests. In the 1940s she visited Bethune's school and participated in a series of its fund-raising activities that included a small meeting of potential donors at the White House. She regularly appeared at conferences of the National Council of Negro Women, arranged for the organization to use government facilities for its meetings, and entertained council women at teas in the White House. She assisted Bethune in her NYA work most visibly by supporting and addressing the two Negro conferences over which Bethune presided. In addition, Mrs. Roosevelt solicited Mrs. Bethune's opinions and advice, invited her to social functions at the White House, contacted the president and government officials on her behalf, and arranged for her to see the president.[45]

In an era of plenipotentiaries for racial blocs, blacks potentially gained from the black-white leadership contact just as whites did. Their leaders not only represented the white establishment to blacks but also expressed to it the concerns they had as black people. More specifically, Negro leaders influenced the establishment to act favorably on Negro-related issues.[46] Bethune conceived of herself primarily in this role as a Negro leader. She frequently declared that this was her purpose for being in Washington. For example, after one White House affair she remarked, ''It is for me a sacred trust so to touch these fine people as to interpret to them the dreams and the hopes and the problems of my long-suffering people.''[47]

Understandably, confrontation with government officials was not her style and she was pleased that President Roosevelt partially acquiesced to the demands of the black March on Washington movement in June 1941 without the march having taken place.[48] In attempting to influence whites, she usually dealt with them on an individual basis. She appealed to a person's noble instinct and usually expressed confidence in her or him regardless of what she actually thought. This was the case with Paul V. McNutt, chairman of the Fair Employment Practices Committee and governor of the War Manpower Commission. In January 1943 she told him: "I want you to understand that I have the utmost confidence in you and your relationship to my people and the deepest appreciation for what you have done in the past and what you will do in the future."[49] Yet in a cautiously worded letter to a black editor she revealed a different attitude: "The President has placed the entire Fair Employment Practice Committee under the directing hand of Mr. McNutt. I think political pressure has brought this about. In my mind, it seems that the whole thing will not be as active, yet we cannot tell how things will work out."[50] Though unquestionably championing Negro causes, Mary Bethune's success in influencing the administration outside of the NYA was centered upon getting particular exceptions to generally discriminatory policies and procedures.

1102

Bethune had the support of the black masses, for they perceived her as a "symbol of greatness without ostentation; of action without subservience, and of thorough sympathy and understanding" of their problems.[51] In order to further enhance her capabilities and credibility as a black spokesperson, she organized several groups of Negro leaders in the center of the political spectrum, most notably the National Council of Negro Women, the Federal Council on Negro Affairs, and the National Conferences on the Problems of the Negro and Negro Youth. She listened carefully to the participants in each and then tried to harmonize divergent viewpoints within a group because she believed ardently in a black united front.

The National Council of Negro Women grew out of Bethune's yearning for an organization to represent black women forcefully in public affairs. On December 5, 1935, at the 137th Street Branch of the Young Women's Christian Association in New York City, Bethune had thirty representatives of national women's organizations listen to her reiterate her philosophy and goals:

> I am interested in women and believe in their possibilities. . . . We need vision for larger things, for the unfolding and reviewing of worthwhile things . . . through necessity we have been forced into organization. . . . We need a united organization to open doors for our young women so that when it speaks, its power will be felt.[52]

Responding to the Bethune charisma and a motion made by Addie Hunton of Alpha Kappa Alpha Sorority and seconded by Mabel Staupers of the National Association of Colored Graduate Nurses, the women voted to create the National Council of Negro Women. When Mary Church Terrell of the National Association of Colored Women moved that Bethune become president, the women then unanimously voted approval.[53] A few months later President Bethune stood before the NYA National Advisory Committee explaining the nature of the National Council and the assistance it would give to the NYA programs throughout the country.[54] Though individual council women may have backed the NYA locally, the council itself lacked the resources to do it. In the early forties, however, it was becoming established and demanding recognition. In October 1941, for example, when the Public Relations Bureau of the War Department failed to invite any black women to participate in a conference to organize the women behind the national defense effort, Mary Bethune, in the name of the council, protested to Secretary of War Stimson; Brigadier General Surles, chief of the Public Relations Bureau; William Hastie, civilian aide to the secretary of war; Mrs. William Hobby, president of the women's group which the Public Relations Bureau organized; and Eleanor Roosevelt. In a widely publicized letter she wrote:

1103

> We cannot accept any excuse that the exclusion of Negro representation was an oversight. We are anxious for you to know that we want to be, and insist upon being considered a part of our American democracy, not something apart from it. We know from experience that our interests are too often neglected, ignored, or scuttled unless we have effective representation in the formative stages of these projects and proposals. We are not blind to what is happening. We are not humiliated. We are incensed. We believe what we have asked is what we all desire — unity of action, thought and spirit.[55]

The same belief in the efficacy of black cooperation which inspired Mary McLeod Bethune to establish the National Council of Negro Women also led her to organize the Federal Council on Negro Affairs, an informal group which was popularly dubbed the "Black Cabinet." Though the term cabinet was inaccurate because the group was not the president's council, nevertheless, it did influence some patterns of thinking within the government. Its primary concerns included nondiscrimination in government-sponsored facilities such as cafeterias, expansion of opportunities especially in government jobs, prevention of government actions potentially harmful to Negroes, and promotion of Negro support for the New Deal.[56]

In August 1936 less than two months after Bethune arrived in Washington to work for the NYA, she assembled in her home at 316 T Street Northwest seven other prominent blacks in government who were all male and college-trained. At that time, she set the tone for the group she was organizing with: "Let us forget the particular office each one of us holds and think how we might, in a cooperative way, get over to the masses the things that are being done and the things that need to be done. We must think in terms as a 'whole' for the greatest service of our people."[57] Throughout her NYA tenure, she tended to hold this informal and somewhat elusive council together and was critical to its operations because of her access to the White House. The council's membership fluctuated over this period, but in September 1939, thirty individuals belonged to it.[58] Jane R. Motz, who studied this Black Cabinet, identified its inner circle as including William Hastie of the Department of the Interior and the War Department; Robert Weaver of Interior, Housing, and several manpower agencies; Henry Lee Moon and Booker T. McGraw, two of Weaver's assistants; Frank Horne of the NYA and Housing; William Trent, Jr., of Interior and the Federal Works Agency; Ted Poston of the Office of War Information; Campbell Johnson of the Selective Service System; Alfred E. Smith of the Federal Emergency Relief Administration and the Works Project Administration; and Lawrence Oxley of the Labor Department.[59]

1104   The federal council helped Bethune in planning and arranging for the National Conference on the Problems of the Negro and Negro Youth which also strengthened her position as a black spokesperson to the administration. The striking virtues of the conferences were that they focused the government's attention on the inferior status of blacks in American life, and they constituted a forum through which Negroes spoke for themselves about the problems they wanted the government to address. Bethune personally presented the conference reports to the president and had her office distribute thousands of copies to government officials and interested citizens. The first meeting was held at the Labor Department January 6-8, 1937. Though Aubrey Williams was reluctant to have the NYA sponsor this gathering because a comprehensive consideration of Negro problems was beyond the scope of his agency, nevertheless, Bethune prevailed upon him.[60]

The conference was not national in terms of the geographical homes of the participants, for very few of the eighty-three conferees and twenty consultants resided west of the Mississippi. However, it was national in terms of the interests it represented. The federal government, six major newspapers, eighteen civic, fraternal, and professional organizations, five religious denominations, and numerous educational institutions and organizations sent participants. The delegates categorized the basic problems of the Negro into four areas: unemployment and lack of economic security, inadequate educational and recreational facilities, poor health and housing conditions, and fear of mob violence and lack of protection under the law. They gave overwhelming attention to the economic problem with fourteen specific recommendations. In terms of general policy, they urged the government to offer leadership in abolishing de facto segregation but where legally mandated, they wanted it to provide more opportunities and facilities.[61] The second conference held two years later was convened to evaluate the status of the Negro since the last meeting, highlight problems which the government could help alleviate, and consider the possible effect of more recent legislation. It was on a grander scale in that two hundred and twenty-five delegates, approximately fifty visitors, and thirty-five consultants participated. Yet, the conference organization, the problems, and the solutions were similar to the first.[62]

Though very proud of the conference proceedings, Bethune was disappointed that they had not noticeably stimulated the government to act in behalf of the Negro. For this reason, she privately turned thumbs down on another such gathering. In relation to the conference recommendations, she cataloged the most obvious government failures in this way: insufficient Negro personnel in policy-making positions in key federal agencies affecting Negro life, the absence of Negroes on important emergency committees, neglect in integrating Negroes into army and navy active combat units and providing equal opportunities for advancement in the military, and a steady decline in Negro employment in the permanent government agencies.[63]

Backed by the National Council of Negro Women, the Federal Council on Negro Affairs, and the National Conferences on the Problems of the Negro and Negro Youth, Mary Bethune urged President Roosevelt to lead the civil rights struggle on several fronts such as antilynching and voting, but most frequently, she seemingly called on him to appoint blacks to top-level jobs. Though Bethune was more interested in programs and policies designed to reach millions of blacks than in the "token" employment of a Negro here and there, she viewed getting blacks in major positions as an essential step toward elevating the Negro people.[64] Sometimes she requested that a specific individual be given a certain office: for example, that Charles Houston, the NAACP attorney who in 1938 successfully argued the Lloyd Gaines case before the Supreme Court, be appointed to that Court.[65] Usually, however, she did not recommend specific individuals but concentrated only on the positions. She asked the president to appoint a Negro to either a federal district court or a circuit court noting that while it was encouraging to have a Negro federal judge in the Virgin Islands, he did not have indefinite tenure as federal judges do in the continental United States. She requested that in the military establishment he name a Negro to the Office of War Information, a Negro special assistant to the secretary of war, and twenty Negroes to the Military Academy at West Point and the Naval Academy at Annapolis. She petitioned for more blacks in the New Deal agencies, especially the Civilian Conservation Corps, the Social Security Board, the Federal Housing Authority, and the Home Owners Loan Corporation. In addition, she called for blacks on various other staffs: the Board of Appeals of the Civil Service Commission, the Labor and Agriculture Departments, the Office of Education, and the White House. Though pushing primarily for new jobs, Bethune also requested that positions blacks had previously occupied be restored to them such as the register of the treasury, minister to Haiti, auditor of the navy, and collector of customs at several ports.[66] Roosevelt made a few black appointments but Bethune's role in these cannot be assessed. Although the president listened to her, he did not act upon most requests. In January 1942 she was really concerned about this and probably pressed the issue by asking that he appoint blacks to positions other than those related exclusively to race problems.[67]

The emphasis on appointments did not preclude Mary Bethune from making other requests in behalf of blacks. Noting that Negroes North and South were irked by the president's periodic visits to the segregated Warm Springs, Georgia, when no comparable black rehabilitation center existed, at least twice she tried to interest the NYA in rectifying the situation. She suggested that it create a special fund to train unemployed, physically incapacitated Negro youth for work careers, but the agency vetoed it.[68] Going outside of the NYA framework, Bethune turned to Eleanor Roosevelt to help improve the status of blacks by facilitating the approval

1105

of certain projects. Usually, Mrs. Roosevelt obliged. Frequently, her intervention did not mean immediate approval, but Bethune always gained from it a better understanding of a given situation. This was the case with the Community Colored Hospital in Wilmington, North Carolina. In September 1941 Bethune pointed out that the expansion of this hospital was essential because Negroes were flocking to Wilmington. They were lured by the two recently established army camps and defense jobs in the shipyard that was constructing thirty-seven steel freighters weighing ten thousand tons each. Bethune asked Mrs. Roosevelt to "take a moment and see to it that this one project is brought to the attention of the proper persons with your personal emphasis." She complied and reported that the Federal Works Agency was making every effort to expedite the project.[69] Sometimes when Bethune turned to Eleanor Roosevelt the results were immediate. This happened in 1939 when Bethune asked her by telephone to facilitate the approval of a 167-unit Negro housing project in Daytona Beach, which had been stalled for some time. After Mrs. Roosevelt contacted Nathan Strauss, head of the Federal Housing Authority, things moved smoothly for the $500,000 project.[70]

Though frequently working outside of the NYA framework, Mary McLeod Bethune was always mindful of her NYA responsibilities. As the top Negro specialist, she continued to strive for greater Negro leadership within the agency. This involved getting blacks named to all the advisory committees in southern states, and she accomplished this in 1941. Also, it meant having blacks hired in the NYA professional jobs outside of her division. By 1941 the Youth Administration had employed six blacks in such positions, four of whom were women.[71] Bethune concentrated, however, on placing black administrative assistants in the offices of the state youth directors. She had first proposed this on August 8, 1935, before the NYA had crystallized. She quickly won an endorsement for the idea from the National Advisory Committee and her persistence in pursuing it led to its realization. When she became the agency's chief Negro specialist, there were about fourteen states with assistants. The number employing them gradually increased to twenty-seven and in 1941 included all southern states except Mississippi. In addition, New York City and the District of Columbia each had a black administrative assistant.[72] The assistants' monthly pay varied from state to state. In 1939, Robert J. Elsy, the assistant for New York City received $333.34, the highest salary among them, and Venice Spraggs of Alabama received $140.00, the lowest.[73] William H. Shell of Georgia, who in 1940 headed a state Negro staff of eleven, was the outstanding assistant in the South as Charles Browning of Illinois was in the North. Their success stemmed from their own capabilities and the leeway and support they obtained from their state directors. Most state directors, however, denied black assistants such substantive opportunities for leadership. Some were plainly prejudiced, insensitive to Negro needs, or unwilling to improve black-white relations. They prohibited black assistants from attending meetings with the regular staff, failed to make needed materials available for their work, provided inferior office arrangements and paid them lower salaries than they did whites.[74]

Early, Bethune advised assistants to convert unsympathetic directors, be patient, use common sense, and glorify their work and not themselves.[75] Behind the scenes, she endeavored to eliminate black-white salary differentials and to improve working conditions. In addition, she tried to bring the assistants together for periodic national or regional conferences as one method of keeping them informed of the changing policies and programs of the agency and to better prepare them to promote the interest of Negro youth. Seeing the assistants as agents of her division, she also attempted to strengthen their ties with her office. It was always an uphill battle because the Youth Administration frowned upon any administrative framework wherein Bethune could develop a closely knit relationship with the assistants. Williams promoted state autonomy and emphasized to the black personnel that their purpose was to assist the state directors in allotting a proper share of the NYA program to Negroes.[76] Consequently, Negro assistants made reports to the national office usually through the state directors, and comprehensive and accurate data on Negro activities were difficult for Bethune to obtain. Some state directors even intimidated assistants for communicating with Bethune's division because they interpreted it as disloyalty to their own offices. Despite these obstacles, Bethune persevered in her efforts until 1942 when the NYA completely ended the state programs in favor of a regional one. Within the new structure, the program employed nine regional Negro Affairs Representatives, and Bethune tried to help them cope with problems similar to those experienced by the former state assistants.[77]

1107

As director of the Negro Division, Bethune sometimes got caught in the middle of disputes involving blacks who expected her support and whites who did likewise. On the one hand, she had to champion Negro rights to be a creditable leader; on the other, she had to maintain white support to be an effective employee. In one such case, Bethune attempted to fudge the issues but nevertheless veered toward the white establishment. This was in the summer of 1940 after George R. Vaughns, president of the Dumas League in Oakland, California, protested the abolishment of the Office of Negro Affairs and dismissal of the Negro administrative assistant, Vivian Osborne Marsh by the California NYA. Believing that the state office was insensitive to Negro needs, Vaughns contacted Eleanor Roosevelt to facilitate a satisfactory adjustment of the problem. In doing so, he referred her to Mary McLeod Bethune for "all the facts in the case." In response to Roosevelt's inquiry, Bethune, who personally knew Mrs. Marsh, noted that Marsh had done an excellent job in California. Then her facts became: "The policies, activities, and records of the NYA show definitely that discrimination because of race will not be, and has not been tolerated. . . . There would be evidence of discrimination if the State Administration refused to employ Negroes in any capacity." She understood, however, that the state administrator was willing to hire blacks in clerical and supervisory positions and Marsh could apply. Stating that the administrator was doing all he could to adjust the matter satisfactorily, Bethune also endorsed his right to abolish the Negro office. He should know whether such a scattered California youth population could justify a state office. Furthermore, she claimed, even some of the state's black leaders were opposed to the Negro office because "they felt that it would bring about a form of segregation." The records failed to reveal why Bethune emphasized the general integrity of the NYA when she knew so well its shortcomings at the state and local levels. Maybe this was only a public stance, for Mrs. Roosevelt had asked for a statement that she could give to Mr. Vaughns, and Bethune exerted constructive pressure within the agency. Maybe she believed that black visibility in California was a losing battle and she needed to conserve her moral weight for more promising ones. Whatever the truth, the situation illustrated the dilemma of a black leader in government.[78]

1108

Bethune spent much time interpreting the NYA to Negro groups so as to encourage them to become involved in the program either as youth participants or project sponsors. In doing this, she naturally publicized notable projects. One was Camp John Hope in Macon, Georgia, a rural recreational center consisting of twenty-four cabins, a dining room and assembly hall, and other buildings which NYA Negro youth had constructed. Another, involving the Civilian Conservation Corps and the Works Progress Administration as well as the NYA, was the National Park Service project in San Francisco, California, which employed youths under competent supervision for work in photography, blueprinting, woodworking, and art.[79] Even more than substantive projects, however, Bethune publicized the psychological impact and the potential of the NYA. During the depression, she stressed this in order to buoy the spirit of black youth. She never claimed that the NYA was meeting their needs adequately but more modestly that it was "indicating the path along which lies increased opportunity" for education, job training, employment, and recreation. The NYA was a priority agency for blacks, Bethune broadcast, because its administration was characterized by a spirit of justice and fair play. She repeated this message from the beginning to the end of her association with the agency. After President Roosevelt's Executive Order 8802, she specifically publicized Aubrey Williams's immediate affirmation of the antidiscrimination order to the NYA staff.[80] Bethune got this message across in several ways. She used letters, the NYA booklets, magazines, and newspapers. In 1937 and 1938, she even wrote a column, "From Day to Day," for the *Pittsburgh Courier*. Her most effective means of publicizing the NYA, however, was personal contact with groups of people, of which she had a great deal. During her first year as a specialist, she traveled forty thousand miles through twenty-one states. She generally kept up this pace until 1940 when Negro regional representatives were employed. Her most extensive single tour was a swing through the central and western part of the United States from April 5 to May 18, 1938.[81]

In addition to publicizing the NYA, Mary McLeod Bethune's primary responsibility as specialist was to insure equitable black participation in each of the major program components. Although this was an ideal that was not generally realized, especially in terms of proportionate expenditures for black youth vis-a-vis white, nevertheless, Bethune enjoyed considerable success in the student aid program. From the very beginning of the NYA until 1942 when the student program was curtailed, it was the most satisfactory component of the program for blacks. In July

1939 the NYA even acquiesced to longstanding requests from Negroes for an official statement banning discrimination in student aid. It adopted a policy regarding the distribution of school aid funds to a minority racial group which specified that it could "not represent a smaller proportion of the total school aid fund quota than the ratio which this racial group bears to the total population of the school, district or state."[82]

Probably, Bethune's most striking contribution toward an equitable program at the secondary level related to the training of teachers for rural Mississippi. Though she characteristically saw something positive in every situation, when she visited Mississippi in 1937 she reported that the problems were so grave she could not publicly discuss them but she would continue to work toward their alleviation.[83] In doing this, she helped to influence the agency to approve a plan whereby some funds allocated for Negro high school youth in Mississippi were diverted into the employment and training of teachers for Negro rural schools in that state. Prior to this, rural Negro youth had received few NYA school funds because with so few high schools available to them, they simply were not in school. Under the new plan, the NYA made available a yearly average of one hundred and twenty-five teachers for rural schools in an intensive nine-month training program that the State Department of Education approved. The training was conducted in five high school centers located at Brookhaven, Clarksdale, Edwards, Greenwood, and West Point. Such a program was in line with Bethune's suggestions for rural areas when she initially joined the NYA staff.[84]

1109

Bethune did even more toward assuring blacks equitable participation in the college and graduate programs even though relatively few blacks benefited from them. She worked, for example, to include Negro institutions in the Civilian Pilot Training Program that the NYA administered from 1939 to 1941. As a result, it became the major avenue through which blacks entered aviation and paved the way for black pilots in the military. Six black colleges participated: Howard University, Washington, D.C.; Tuskegee Institute, Tuskegee Institute, Alabama; Delaware State College, Dover, Delaware; Hampton Institute, Hampton, Virginia; North Carolina Agricultural and Technical State University, Greensboro, North Carolina; and West Virginia State College, Institute, West Virginia. West Virginia State was the first black institution to win approval for the aviation program and in addition to training black male pilots, it also trained black female pilots and white male pilots. Tuskegee Institute operated the largest program among the black schools in that it offered advanced as well as primary training.[85]

Bethune's greatest contribution in promoting more equitable benefits in the higher education program, however, revolved around administering the special fund for Negroes. It began as a fund for Negro graduate students but was expanded in 1938 to include Negro colleges as well. Since black students also benefited from regular NYA higher education work-relief, this fund was justifiable in terms of the greater needs of Negroes and as a means through which the NYA could somewhat approximate the aid it gave to white students. In its first year, the fund accounted for black students receiving 7.4 percent of higher education aid as compared to 2.5

percent in the previous year.[86] During the seven years of the fund, four thousand one hundred eighteen students participated in a total of $609,930. From a beginning of $75,060 in 1936-37, the fund reached its highest level in 1940-41 with $111,105. This was below the $200,000 annual allotment which Bethune wanted, but she was still encouraged.[87] With the fund, she supported two notable programs. The first was graduate training to make available one hundred librarians for high schools that needed them in order to become accredited. Participating institutions were Atlanta University, Atlanta, Georgia; Fisk University, Nashville, Tennessee; Prairie View College, Prairie View, Texas; and Hampton Institute, Hampton, Virginia. The other was commercial dietetics training to prepare students for positions as dieticians, chefs, and waiters. Tuskegee Institute offered this program.[88]

1110

Mary McLeod Bethune was unable to influence the out-of-work work-relief and training program for Negroes as she did the student-aid program. Her division did not administer any funds for these projects, and it had neither an approval role nor a regular feedback regarding Negro participation in them. Nevertheless, through various actions and recommendations, Bethune had some success in broadening the base of Negro participation in this component, as in the others.

Initially, her concern was getting projects into immediate operation. The easiest projects to start for Negroes were those relating to their unskilled occupational status. This was especially true since projects required organizational sponsorship and Negro communities possessed relatively few financial resources for advanced training. Cognizant of this reality and a believer in industrial education somewhat in the Booker T. Washington mold, Bethune promoted training in domestic service, cooking, sewing, beauty culture, laundering, truck gardening, chicken raising, and other such areas.[89] In 1937 she saw the establishment of resident training projects in twenty-five southern communities as a major step forward in the Negro program. These centers were located on or near black college campuses and recruited trainees from nearby rural areas. They continued to train youth in agriculture and domestic and personal service occupations.

After a year's experience with the resident projects, Bethune reported to Aubrey Williams that this type of training was entirely too narrow, and black youth needed opportunities in other areas. In addition, she sharply criticized black projects across the board. They were poorly organized, they were not the equivalent of projects for whites, and they did not begin to approach needs. With uncharacteristic bluntness, Bethune told Williams, "There is no really outstanding NYA project for Negroes in the country."[90] At a time when the NYA was beginning to invest in showcase projects for whites, Bethune requested that it do the same for blacks. She believed that it was not enough to have some black youth participate in these projects in places such as Charleston, West Virginia, and Quoddy, Maine. If, despite Negro protests, whites could conduct a segregated regional project in metal arts and crafts, auto mechanics, and aeronautical mechanics in Algiers, Louisiana, blacks needed something superior also. In June 1938 one among her several ideas for a superior Negro project was a permanent and imposing building in

Washington, D.C., to house a Little Theater and Arts Center. It would provide for stage productions, choral concerts, exhibits of African art, and other such activities. In making the recommendation, she noted the limited platforms blacks possessed for such artistic expressions despite their talents in these areas. In the next year she proposed expanding the existing aviation-oriented black project in Chicago into a Negro-supervised national resident program for machine shop practice, aviation ground mechanics, metal crafts, and specialized woodwork.[91]

Bethune's hopes for a truly superior Negro project along these lines were unfulfilled in the NYA's depression-oriented program but realized in its War Production Training Project at Wilberforce, Ohio. This project was so outstanding that it became the symbol for expanding Negro youth participation in the war training phase of the NYA. Several agencies sponsored it: the Army Ordnance, Fairfield Air Depot, Wilberforce University, Cedarville High School, and the NYA programs in both Wilberforce and Columbus, Ohio. From relatively small beginnings in September 1938, by 1942 the project had developed into one employing 350 youth in residence and twenty-three staff persons and containing twelve modern prefabricated buildings for living, working, recreation, and health. It offered training in machine shop, sheet metal, radio, arc welding, and auto mechanics.[92]

In addition to Bethune's emphasis upon a few superior projects, around 1938 she placed even greater priority upon getting NYA black youth out of the service-oriented projects into those offering construction and mechanical and metal working activities. In that year, the NYA decided as a matter of policy to train youth in such skills because shortages were apparent or expected. The agency, at that time had neglected to hire black youth because industry in general had refused to hire them in construction and mechanical jobs, and there were few immediately available jobs for blacks in 1940 and 1941 when it undertook the training program in earnest. In light of this, Bethune worked hard to see that black youths were not ignored in manpower training for vital war industries. She exhorted Negro young people to "Prepare Today for Tomorrow's Jobs" and successfully pressured the agency to expand Negro opportunities.[93] In February 1941 the number of black youth in out-of-school projects reached 63,622 which represented 13.2 percent of all such youth employed.[94] In April 1943 though the number had decreased to 10,742, they constituted roughly 20 percent of all youth in work projects. Certainly, not all of these Negro youth were given advanced training but a large proportion were.[95]

During the depression, Mary McLeod Bethune was least successful in facilitating equitable Negro participation in the placement component of the NYA, but her persistent efforts toward this end led to some achievements during World War II. In the 1930s there was a continuing scarcity of youth jobs, and many of the existing few were closed to blacks. The State Employment Services that were associated with the NYA program made no systematic effort to place blacks. The NYA employed few Negro junior placement counselors — for example, in 1937, it had only four in the whole country — and its white counselors generally found their hands full trying to get white youth employed without addressing the more difficult problems of black youth unemployment. Bethune believed that the crux and the culmination of the NYA was the placement of blacks into viable employment and that the agency would aggravate an already serious problem by supporting education and training without conscientiously assisting blacks in finding jobs. She argued further that this was so important that, if necessary, it should be promoted at the expense of school-aid and work-projects. In 1937 she recommended the employment of a national field representative to promote guidance and placement among Negroes, the publication and dissemination of materials on vocational opportunities, and the employment of more junior placement counselors.[96]

1112

Over the next few years, the agency moved toward implementing these recommendations, but major changes did not occur until its defense and war-training phases. Then the NYA provided "the crack in the door" which led to the employment of Negroes on assembly lines in plants such as Bell Aircraft, Buffalo, New York; Sun Shipbuilding in Chester, Pennsylvania; Radio Corporation of America in Camden, New Jersey; and Kane Manufacturing Company in Louisville, Kentucky. One of its guiding principles was that "Negro youth should, if feasible, be introduced along with other NYA workers when a plant is just being opened or is expanding, and like in NYA both white and colored employees should be permitted to progress in their jobs together."[97] In 1942-43 the agency placed more than three thousand Negro youth in jobs through its interstate transfer plan. After training individuals, the plan involved transferring them to labor-shortage areas and introducing them to jobs through the medium of the NYA resident induction projects to industrial sites. Between May 1, 1942, and January 30, 1943, in Rocky Mount, North Carolina, 963 males participated in the largest induction project for blacks. From there they received jobs in the Norfolk Navy Yard.[98]

In July 1943 when Congress terminated the services of the National Youth Administration, black people, in particular, had reason to mourn its passing. Black newspapers had consistently given the agency a good press.[99] In the early program, blacks seemed to have appreciated most its school-aid component as indicated in an editorial comment from the *Pittsburgh Courier:* "Perhaps one reason why nothing but good is said of the NYA is because it has been doing a so obviously necessary work in aiding young people to complete their schooling and to adjust themselves to the developing social order."[100] In the later program, they valued most the training component. In December 1941 Walter White, executive director of the National Association for the Advancement of Colored People made this point clearly: "The N.Y.A. has offered the best opportunity for shop training and work experience according to modern industrial procedures which Negro youth could obtain."[101] Blacks knew that Mary Bethune was a significant force within the NYA and regretted seeing her lose her job with the agency's demise. Whether in Durant, Mississippi, or Detroit, Michigan, they had hailed her as a great leader.[102] Such leadership involved "will power, sensitivity to the age, clear thinking rather than profound thinking, the ability to experience the emotions of a group and to voice their aspirations, joined with control over those emotions in oneself [and] a sense of the dramatic.''[103] When Consuelo Young-Megahy of the *Chicago Defender* met her in 1937, she publicized that Bethune was "the angel" in the black NYA.[104] Most people were more restrained and there was reason to be because Bethune tended to monopolize situations unduly, dominate others, and exaggerate the truth.[105]

Mary McLeod Bethune managed to build a record of substantive achievement within the NYA despite great obstacles within the agency, an extended workload (for she was still president of Bethune-Cookman College until late 1942), recurring illnesses, and harassment from the House Committee on Un-American Activities.[106] She was able to use a relatively minor advisory position as a springboard to power on the NYA staff. She persuaded the agency to recognize Negro leadership through an expanded Office of Negro Affairs and the employment of black administrative assistants in more than twenty-five states. She guided it toward addressing the special needs of black people notably through the Special Graduate and Negro College Fund. She also promoted a somewhat "color-blind" approach to blacks by assuring them the same defense training and placement opportunities as whites. Records, publications, and correspondence fail to provide evidence of the same substantive achievement for Bethune as a black leader or a representative to the Roosevelt administration. In this capacity, which was intricately meshed with her NYA activities, instead of obtaining general policies geared toward antidiscrimination and a recognition of special black needs, Bethune got specific exceptions to unfavorable policies or procedures. This reflected no lack of zeal on her part in advocating black equality within government but rather the administration's unwillingness to give civil rights any priority. Bethune knew that the deeply rooted racism in American life dwarfed her best efforts toward improving the status of the race. She said that faith alone sustained her as it did oppressed peoples everywhere. She looked to the future noting that "It may take a long time, but because enough of us are willing to work for a better world, we will finally attain it.''[107] A division directorship in the NYA was a low echelon position for an individual of Bethune's leadership capability. But then, she was both black and female and encountered the difficulties of belonging to both minorities. In the 1930s and 40s, a little niche in a temporary agency was the best that the government could offer a luminous black woman.

1113

NOTES

1. *Chicago Defender,* 27 November 1937, in scrapbook, Mary McLeod Bethune Papers, Bethune Foundation, Daytona Beach, Florida. Since only the Mary McLeod Bethune Collection at Bethune Foundation and the Amistad Research Center were used, papers from these repositories will be referred to by repository name only after the first citation. All references to "Williams" are to Aubrey Williams except where otherwise indicated.
2. *National Notes,* July 1928, p. 3. This was the periodical of the National Association of Colored Women.
3. *California Eagle* (Los Angeles), 20 August 1926, p. 1.
4. Du Bois's statement found in Sadie Iola Daniel, *Women Builders* (Washington, D.C.: Associated Publishers, 1931), p. 79. Bethune's recollections are contained in "Interview with Dr. Johnson," typescript, undated, Bethune Foundation. Book-length biographies are Catherine Owen Peare, *Mary McLeod Bethune* (New York: Vanguard Press, 1951); Emma Gelders Sterne, *Mary McLeod Bethune* (New York: Alfred A. Knopf, 1957); and Rackham Holt, *Mary McLeod Bethune* (Garden City: Doubleday, 1964).
5. Published accounts of the NYA from a national perspective are found in Betty Lindley and Ernest K. Lindley, *A New Deal for Youth* (New York: The Viking Press, 1938); Palmer O. Johnson and Oswald L. Harvey, *The National Youth Administration* (Washington, D.C.: Government Printing Office, 1938); and National Youth Administration, *Final Report* (Washington, D.C.: Government Printing Office, 1943).
6. The defense orientation of the NYA was highlighted in the following: Aubrey Williams, *The Role of the NYA in the Nation's War Training Program,* undated; and *Youth, Jobs and Defense,* a NYA booklet, July 1941, both located at the Bethune Foundation. The rationale for the school-aid program was offered in Lindley, *A New Deal for Youth,* pp. 33-34.
7. NYA, *Youth, Jobs, and Defense,* p. 23.
8. Minutes, Conference of the National Youth Administration, 10 July 1935, File "Conferences, Aubrey Williams," File of Agenda, Stenographic Transcripts, and Proceedings of Conferences Called by the Executive Director and the Administrator, 1935-39, Records of the Executive Director and Administrator, Records of the Office of the Administrator (hereafter referred to as Proceedings of Conferences, Records of the Administrator), Records of the National Youth Administration, Record Group 119, National Archives (the Record Group will hereafter be referred to as RG 119, NA); Proceedings, Conference of State Youth Director, 19-21 May 1936, p. 13, Publications Issued by the Central Office, NYA File of Processed and Printed Materials, 1935-42, NYA Publications File (hereafter referred to as NYA Publications File), ibid. Mrs. Roosevelt's interest in the NYA is most apparent in the Charles Taussig Papers and the Aubrey Williams Papers, Franklin D. Roosevelt Library, Hyde Park, New York (hereafter referred to as FDRL).
9. Proceedings, National Advisory Committee Meeting, 28-29 April 1936, and Proceedings, Conference of State Youth Directors, 19-21 May 1936, NYA Publications File, RG 119, NA. In the report of another State Directors' Meeting, 26 October 1937, Williams used the word "niggers" (p. 8). On a transmittal slip, Bethune called this to the attention of Richard R. Brown, the assistant director, and asked that it be deleted on 24 November 1937. (Quasi-official Correspondence and Data File of the Deputy

1114

Executive Director, 1935-38. Records of the Deputy Executive Director and Deputy Administrator, Records of the Office of the Administrator, RG 119, NA.)

10. Minutes, Conference of the National Youth Administration, 10 July 1935, File "Conferences, Aubrey Williams," Proceedings of Conferences, Records of the Administrator, RG 119, NA.

11. Rackham Holt, *Mary McLeod Bethune*, pp. 191-92; Mary McLeod Bethune, "My Secret Talks with FDR," in *The Negro in Depression and War*, ed. Bernard Sternsher (Chicago: Quadrangle Books, 1969), p. 57, reprinted from *Ebony*, April 1949, pp. 42-51. Florence Roane was with Mrs. Bethune when Mrs. Roosevelt called her in Daytona Beach to ask her to serve on the Advisory Committee in 1935. Interview, Florence Roane, 9 June 1972. Mrs. Bethune first met Mrs. Roosevelt in December 1927 when she attended the buffet luncheon for presidents that Mrs. Roosevelt gave as a part of the biennial meeting of the National Council of Women of the United States in New York City.

1115

12. In 1935, Negro youth constituted 12.8 percent of the youth population but 15.3 percent of youth on relief. Marian T. Wright, "Negro Youth and the Federal Emergency Programs: CCC and NYA," *Journal of Negro Education* (July 1940), p. 405; and Final Report of the Division of Negro Affairs, 31 December 1943, pp. 12 and 22, Bethune Foundation.

13. Final Report of Negro Division, 31 December 1943, pp. 2-3 and 7-8.

14. Bethune to John J. Corson, 24 August 1935, and Corson to Bethune, 27 August 1935, File "Executive Committee," Correspondence and Reference File of Thelma McKelvey, Secretary to the Chairman, Records of the Chairman, Records of the National Advisory Committee (hereafter referred to as File of Thelma McKelvey); National Advisory Committee Meeting, 28-29 April 1936, pp. 143 and 153, NYA Publications File; and Report of the NYA State Advisory Committees, 14 April 1936, Inactive Correspondence, Negro Affairs, RG 119, NA.

15. Report of Conference on Negro Activities, 8 August 1935, File of Early "Inactive" Correspondence, 1935-38, Records of the Director, Records of the Office of Negro Affairs (hereafter referred to as Inactive Correspondence, Negro Affairs); and Conference of State Youth Directors, 19-21 May 1936, p. 4, NYA Publications File, RG 119, NA.

16. National Advisory Committee Meeting, 28-29 April 1936, pp. 167-71, ibid.

17. *Pittsburgh Courier*, 30 November 1940, p. 3.

18. National Advisory Committee Meeting, 28-29 April 1936, pp. 167-71, NYA Publications File, RG 119, NA.

19. Conference on Negro Activities, 8 August 1935; Juanita Saddler to Brown, 17 June 1936, Inactive Correspondence, Negro Affairs; National Advisory Committee Meeting, 28-29 April 1936, pp. 167-71, NYA Publications File; Bethune to Corson, 24 August 1935, File "Executive Committee," File of Thelma McKelvey, ibid.

20. Unofficial Minutes of Executive Committee Meeting, 2 December 1936, File "Meetings of the Executive Committee, August 1935 to the present," File of Thelma McKelvey, ibid.

21. National Advisory Committee Meeting, 28-29 April 1936, pp. 219, NYA Publications File, RG 119, NA.

22. Mary Bethune, "Secret Talks," pp. 57-58. Here, Bethune placed the meeting in 1934. Since it was the first committee meeting to report on the accomplishments of the agency, it took place in April 1936.

23. *Boston Chronicle*, 10 December 1938, scrapbook, Bethune Foundation; *New York Times*, 18 February 1931, Mary McLeod Bethune Papers, Amistad Research Center, Dillard University, New Orleans, Louisiana.

24. Bethune, "Secret Talks," p. 59.

25. National Advisory Committee Meeting, 28-29 April 1936, pp. 153, NYA Publications File, RG 119, NA.

26. Brown to Williams, 21 November 1935; Saddler to Carl A. Jessen [*sic* for Karl E. Jensen], 12 July 1935, File "Juanita Saddler," File of Copies of Letters Sent by Officials in the NYA Central Office and Accumulated in the Office of the Deputy Executive Director and the Deputy Administrator, 1935-40, Records of the Deputy Executive Director and Deputy Administrator, Records of the Office of the Administrator (hereafter referred to as Correspondence, Office of the Deputy Administrator), ibid.

27. Report Covering First Six Months, 15 July 1936, Inactive Correspondence, Negro Affairs, RG 119, NA.

28. During the Conference of Negro Administrative Assistants, 2-3 June 1936, Bethune even urged the assistants to cooperate with Saddler. (Report of the Conference, File "Negro Administrative Assistants, June 1936," Inactive Correspondence, Negro Affairs, RG 119, NA). Saddler submitted her resignation on 11 July 1936, and it became effective July 15. (Brown to Saddler, 18 July 1936, ibid.) Saddler's uneasiness with having Bethune in the NYA Office was confirmed to me in interviews with Lawrence Oxley, 3 November 1972, and Edward Rodriquez, 9 June 1972, both of whom were familiar with this situation.

Historian B. Joyce Ross presented a warped view of Saddler, Bethune, and the Office of Negro Affairs during the early period of the NYA in "Mary McLeod Bethune and the National Youth Administration: A case Study of Power Relationships in the Black Cabinet of Franklin D. Roosevelt," *Journal of Negro History* 60 (January 1975): 1-28. Her misunderstanding of the early Negro Affairs Office damages the credibility of a major segment of her article. In attempting to delineate Saddler's and Bethune's racial philosophies and to analyze Bethune's actions and problems during the agency's formative period, she misconstrued the relationship of Saddler and Bethune to the NYA. She saw Bethune as director of the Negro Office from 1935 to 1943 and Saddler as Bethune's assistant who "served for less than two years." Bethune, however, did not become an NYA employee until 24 June 1936. See copy of Bethune's record from the Civil Service Commission, Bethune Foundation. Saddler was employed only for about six and a half months. She was offered the job on 25 November 1935, reported to work on 2 December 1935, and left on 15 July 1936. See telegram, Brown to Saddler, 25 November 1935, ibid., and Report Covering First Six Months [July 1936], Inactive Correspondence, Negro Affairs, RG 119, NA. She was not Bethune's assistant except for twenty-two days. When Saddler began work, Brown notified twenty Negro leaders that she was the NYA "Negro Liaison Officer," a title early discarded in favor of "Administrative Assistant in Charge of Negro Affairs." Letters announcing her appointment were dated either 2 December 1935 or 3 December 1935. Regarding Saddler's title, see memo, Elizabeth S. Sanders to Mrs. Holmes, 24 February 1936, File "Juanita Saddler," Correspondence, Office of the Deputy Administrator, RG 119, NA. Therefore, for about six months Juanita Saddler was the only staff member in the Office of Negro Affairs.

1116

Yet, during this period, Joyce Ross attributed to Bethune ideas, actions, and problems that belonged to Saddler. In this respect she ascribed authorship of the "Report Covering First Six Months of the Work of the Office of Negro Affairs" to Bethune instead of Saddler. Using this source she wrote: "According to Mrs. Bethune's account, her division began operation in December 1935, with no clearly designated functions or procedures. After remaining in her office for two weeks without having any contacts with national executives, she unilaterally formulated a tentative outline of the division's potential work. . . . " (Ross, "Mary McLeod Bethune," p. 21). This key report consisting of four pages was both undated and unsigned. Nevertheless, Saddler's authorship can be determined by an analysis of the document. The report included the following: the Negro Office began on 2 December 1935; the author submitted an outline to Brown two weeks later regarding the Negro program; very soon after the author arrived she visited Pennsylvania, New Jersey, and New York; and the author had been interested in evaluating projects. Saddler started work at the NYA the day the Negro Office began. She wrote the outline (Saddler to Brown, 16 December 1935, File "Juanita Saddler," Correspondence, Office of the Deputy Administrator, RG 119, NA). She made the visits and wrote reports about them. See for example, Report of Visits to Ithaca, Albany, Dutchess Junction, and Buffalo, 2-4 January 1936, Inactive Correspondence, Negro Affairs, RG 119, NA. And Saddler, not Bethune, characteristically made critical written evaluations of projects. In the report just noted, she observed that in some projects exclusively for Negroes, paternalistic whites had pre-empted all the staff positions.

1117

29. Bethune, "Secret Talks," p. 58; *Pittsburgh Courier,* 1 August 1936, p. 9, and 17 October 1936, p. 9.
30. Copy of Civil Service Commission Record of Mary McLeod Bethune, Bethune Foundation.
31. Statement undated [1940], Bethune Foundation. R. O'Hara Lanier is listed as the assistant director in the statement.
32. Bethune to T. Arnold Hill, December 1940, Bethune Foundation.
33. Lindley, *A New Deal for Youth;* Annual Report of the Division of Negro Affairs, 1 July 1936-30 June 1937, File "Administration, Miscellaneous," General Subject File of the Director, Records of the Division of Negro Affairs, RG 119, NA (hereafter referred to as Annual Report, 1936-37, File "Administration, Miscellaneous," General Subject File of the Director, Negro Affairs, RG 119, NA); Annual Reports, 1936-38 and 1940-41, Negro Division Bethune Foundation.
34. Arabella Denniston to Bethune, 27 May 1943. Denniston's background was related to me in an interview with James C. Evans, 10 November 1972.
35. Gunnar Myrdal, *An American Dilemma* (New York: Harper, 1944), pp. 721-26.
36. Bethune to Stephen Early, 16 February 1937, President's Personal File, Number 4266, FDRL. Handwritten O.K. on letter, 17 February 1937.
37. Bethune, "I'll Never Turn Back No More," *Opportunity,* November 1938, pp. 324-26.
38. *Pittsburgh Courier,* 15 February 1941, p. 9; Aubrey Williams to Henry L. Stimson, 13 June 1942, Aubrey Williams Papers, FDRL.
39. Bethune, "What Are We Fighting For?" speech, The Southern Conference on Human Welfare, undated, Amistad Research Center, Dillard University, New Orleans, Louisiana.
40. Ibid.

41. Bethune, "The Negro and the National Defense," speech, patriotic demonstration, Detroit, Michigan, 3 August 1941, Bethune Foundation.

42. *Pittsburgh Courier,* 22 June 1939, p. 4; *Tampa Bulletin,* undated, scrapbook, Bethune Foundation.

43. Statement on the Blue Radio Network after the death of FDR, 13 April 1945, Bethune Foundation; *Pittsburgh Courier,* 2 October 1937, p. 14.

44. Introduction of Eleanor Roosevelt, Conference on the Problems of the Negro and Negro Youth, 12 January 1939, NYA News Release; radio script on Kathryn Craven's Program, Station WNEW, New York City, 30 April 1943, Bethune Foundation; and *Pittsburgh Courier,* 1 January 1938, p. 2.

45. Evidence of these activities is found in the Bethune Papers, Bethune Foundation, and Eleanor Roosevelt Papers, FDRL.

46. Myrdal, *An American Dilemma,* pp. 721-26.

47. *Pittsburgh Courier,* 5 June 1937, p. 8.

48. Bethune to Eleanor Roosevelt, 10 July 1941, Eleanor Roosevelt Papers, FDRL.

49. Bethune to McNutt, 22 January 1943, Bethune Foundation.

50. Bethune to Robert Durr, 5 August 1942, Bethune Foundation.

51. *Boston Chronicle,* 10 December 1938, scrapbook, Bethune Foundation.

52. Ruth Caston Mueller, ed., *Women United: Souvenir Year Book* (Washington, D.C.: National Council of Negro Women, 1951), p. 16.

53. Ibid.

54. National Advisory Committee Meeting, 28-29 April 1936, p. 171, NYA Publications File, RG 119, NA.

55. *Pittsburgh Courier,* 25 October 1941, p. 1.

56. Jane R. Motz, "The Black Cabinet: Negroes in the Administration of Franklin D. Roosevelt," (M.A. Thesis, University of Delaware, June 1964). My thanks to Mr. DeWitt Dykes for bringing this thesis to my attention.

57. Federal Council on Negro Affairs, 7 August 1936, Bethune Foundation.

58. Dutton Ferguson to Bethune, 23 September 1939, Bethune Foundation.

59. Motz, "The Black Cabinet," pp. 23-24.

60. Minutes, Executive Committee, 30 November 1936, File "Executive Committee," File of Thelma McKelvey, RG 119, NA.

61. Report of the National Conference on the Problems of the Negro and Negro Youth, 6-8 January 1937, NYA Publications File, ibid.

62. Proceedings of the Second National Conference on the Problems of the Negro and Negro Youth, 12-14 January 1939, Bethune Foundation.

63. Bethune to Williams, 17 October 1939, Bethune Foundation.

64. Bethune to James L. Fieser, 16 October 1943, Bethune Foundation.

65. Bethune made the suggestion in this manner: "It is interesting to notice that the press generally and Negro newspapers particularly are featuring the recent suggestion that Charles H. Houston of Washington be appointed to the United States Supreme Court bench." Bethune to Franklin D. Roosevelt, 27 November 1939, Bethune Foundation.

66. Ibid.; Bethune to Franklin D. Roosevelt, undated, Bethune Foundation; Bethune to Eleanor Roosevelt, 8 April 1941, Eleanor Roosevelt Papers, FDRL; Bethune to Eleanor Roosevelt, 4 February 1943, Bethune Foundation. Correspondence relating to the Federal Council on Negro Affairs also reveals an emphasis on appointments.

67. T. Arnold Hill to Bethune, 6 January 1942, and "Motions Passed at Conference" to reflect the wishes of the Negro people, statement, 7 January 1941, Bethune Foundation.

68. "Project on Crippled Youth," Bethune to Brown, 17 September 1936, File "Negro Administrative Assistants, June 1936," Inactive Correspondence, Negro Affairs, and "Negro Participation in NYA," Bethune to Williams, 6 June 1938, General Subject File of the Director, 1936-41, Negro Affairs, RG 119, NA.

69. Bethune to Eleanor Roosevelt, 26 September 1941, and John M. Carmody to Secretary to Mrs. Roosevelt, 8 October 1941, Eleanor Roosevelt Papers, FDRL.

70. Bethune to Eleanor Roosevelt, 25 May 1939, Eleanor Roosevelt Papers, FDRL; and *Sentinel Star* (Orlando, Florida), 25 June 1939, scrapbook, Bethune Foundation.

71. Annual Report, 1940-41, Negro Division; Karl Borders to Bethune, 20 October 1939, Bethune Foundation.

72. Conference on Negro Activities, 8 August 1935, Report of Conference of Negro Administrative Assistants, 2-3 June 1936, and Report of Activities with Special Reference to Negro Youth, undated [April 1936], File "Negro Administrative Assistants, June 1936," Inactive Correspondence; Negro Affairs, RG 119, NA; Annual Report, Negro Division, 1940-41, Bethune Foundation.

73. List of Negro Personnel on State Staffs, statement, 31 July 1939, Bethune Foundation.

74. Confidential Report on the Negro Program, undated [1938], Inactive Correspondence, Negro Affairs, RG 119, NA; Annual Report of the Negro Divison, 1936-37, File "Administration, Miscellaneous," General Subject File of the Director, Negro Affairs, RG 119, NA; Annual Report, 1938-39, Negro Division, Bethune Foundation.

75. Conference of the Negro Administrative Assistants, 2-3 June 1936, File "Negro Administrative Assistants, June 1936," Inactive Correspondence, Negro Affairs, RG 119, NA.

76. Ibid. See for examples, letter, J.P. Bond to Bethune, 28 July 1939, Bethune Foundation; notes of a telephone conversation, Brown to Garth Akridge, 14 October 1936, File "Field Reports General, Garth Akridge, July '36 thru July '37," Reports Received from Field Representatives and Regional Directors, 1935-1938, Records of the Office of the Deputy Administrator, RG 119, NA.

77. Annual Report, 1936-37, File "Administration, Miscellaneous," General Subject File of the Director, Negro Affairs, RG 119, NA, and Bob Brown to Bethune, 27 February 1943, Bethune Foundation.

78. George R. Vaughns to Eleanor Roosevelt, 11 July 1940; Secretary to Mrs. Roosevelt to Bethune, 22 July 1940; Bethune to Eleanor Roosevelt, 1 August 1940; and Secretary to Mrs. Roosevelt to Vaughns, 9 August 1940, Eleanor Roosevelt Papers, FDRL.

79. Annual Report, 1938-39, Negro Division, Bethune Foundation; *Pittsburgh Courier,* 2 April 1938, p. 14 and 7 May 1938, p. 15; and Final Report of Negro Division, 31 December 1943, pp. 187-88, Bethune Foundation.

80. "The Contribution of the National Youth Administration to the Development of Youth," speech, Kentucky Negro Education Association, Louisville, Kentucky, 15 April 1937, and "The Negro and the National Defense," speech, Patriotic Demonstration, Detroit, Michigan, 3 August 1941, Bethune Foundation; *Pittsburgh Courier,* 21 August 1937, p. 14 and 29 January 1938, p. 14.

1119

81. Annual Report, 1936-37; File "Administration, Miscellaneous," General Subject File of the Director, Negro Affairs, RG 119, NA, and Annual Report, 1938-39, Negro Division, Bethune Foundation. Bethune's column which began on 23 January 1937, was originally labeled "Weekly Chats" but was changed on 20 March 1937 to "From Day to Day."

82. Report of Activities with Special Reference to Negro Youth, undated [April 1936], Inactive Correspondence Negro Affairs, RG 119, NA; and Policy prohibiting discrimination, adopted 25 July 1939, NYA letter, Bethune Foundation.

83. *Pittsburgh Courier,* 4 December 1937, p. 14.

84. Final Report of Negro Division, 31 December 1943, pp. 109-10, Bethune Foundation.

85. The Negro and the National Youth Administration, statement, undated [1944], p. 10; Patricia Strickland, *The Putt-Putt Air Force: The Story of the Civilian Pilot Training Program and the War Training Service* (Washington, D.C.: Department of Transportation, n.d.), pp. 39-47. My thanks to Mr. James C. Evans for giving me this book and emphasizing the role of the NYA in the development of Negro aviation.

86. Annual Report, 1936-37, File, "Administration, Miscellaneous," General Subject File of the Director, Negro Affairs, RG 119, NA.

87. Final Report of Negro Divison, 31 December 1943, p. 102; Bethune Foundation; and Annual Report, 1940-41.

88. Final Report of Negro Division, 31 December 1943, pp. 107-8, Bethune Foundation.

89. Bethune to Arthur Williams, 20 August 1936, Inactive Correspondence, Negro Affairs, RG 119, NA.

90. Confidential Report, undated [1938], and "Negro Participation in NYA," 6 June 1938, General Subject File of the Director, Records of the Division of Negro Affairs, RG 119, NA.

91. Ibid.; and Annual Report, 1938-39, Negro Division, Bethune Foundation.

92. Final Report of Negro Division, 31 December 1943, pp. 165-68, Bethune Foundation.

93. Ibid., pp. 116-20; *Pittsburgh Courier,* 14 May 1938, p. 14.

94. Final Report of Negro Division, 31 December 1943, p. 125, Bethune Foundation.

95. Aubrey Williams, Participation of Negroes in the War Program of the NYA, statement, undated [June 1943], Bethune Foundation.

96. Annual Report, 1936-37, Negro Affairs File "Administration, Miscellaneous," General Subject File of the Director, RG 119 NA; *Pittsburgh Courier,* 7 March 1937, p. 8.

97. The Negro and the National Youth Administration, statement, undated [1944], pp. 16-17, Bethune Foundation.

98. Final Report of Negro Division, 31 December 1943, pp. 149-50, Bethune Foundation.

99. See, for example, Annual Report, 1938-39, Negro Division, Bethune Foundation.

100. Ibid.

101. Circular letter, Walter White to members of Congress, 29 December 1941, Bethune Foundation.

102. *Pittsburgh Courier,* 8 May 1937, p. 8 and 4 December 1937, p. 14.

103. This description of leadership qualities given in "In Quest of Leadership," *Time,* 17 July 1974, pp. 21-34.

104. *Chicago Defender,* 25 September 1937, scrapbook, Bethune Foundation.

105. An example of Bethune monopolizing a situation was her keeping her presidential position at Bethune-Cookman while she also served as NYA Negro specialist; an example of stretching the truth was her saying that she was a division director before it became a fact. Several writers mention her domineering trait. See, for example, Motz, *The Black Cabinet,* p. 22.

106. Bethune was also investigated by the Federal Bureau of Investigation. Benjamin Davis, Jr., to Bethune, 27 September 1942, and Bethune to Benjamin Davis, Jr., 6 October 1942, Bethune Foundation. Bethune was named under H.R. 105, 78th Cong., 1st sess., as one of the government employees to be investigated on charges of subversive activities by the Dies Committee. Bethune was also investigated by the Federal Bureau of Investigation acting under the authority of Public Law No. 135, 77th Cong. See R.M. Barnett to Bethune, 31 August 1942, Aubrey Williams Papers, FDRL.   1121

107. Radio script on Kathryn Craven's Program, Station WNEW, New York City, 30 April 1943, Bethune Foundation.

Charlotte Hawkins Brown

Sandra N. Smith, *Chairman, Department of Curriculum and Teaching,* and Earle H. West, *Associate Dean and Professor, School of Education, Howard University*

1123

"Greatest Negro woman the race has produced."[1] "First lady of social graces."[2] "The twig bender of Sedalia."[3] "One of the foremost exponents of cultural education."[4] "Woman of the Year."[5] These things were said about Mrs. Charlotte Hawkins Brown. Who was she, and what did she accomplish that would elicit these superlatives? The purpose of this article is to sketch her life and work, and to assess her contributions.[6]

LIFE SKETCH

Charlotte Hawkins was born to Edmund and Caroline Hawkins, June 11, 1883, in Henderson, North Carolina. When she was six years old, her mother and step-father moved the family to Cambridge, Massachusetts, where she completed elementary and secondary school. Under the sponsorship of Alice Freeman Palmer, first woman president of Wellesley College and wife of a Harvard

---

[1] *Washington Sentinel,* December 9, 1933.

[2] Constance H. Marteena, *The Lengthening Shadow of a Woman* (New York: Exposition Press, 1977), p. 74.

[3] Cecie Jenkins, "The Twig Bender," typescript, Charlotte Hawkins Brown MSS., Schlesinger Library, Radcliffe College. (Hereafter designated as CHB MSS.)

[4] Book jacket, Charlotte Hawins Brown, *The Correct Thing* (Boston: Christopher Publishing House, 1941).

[5] *Greensboro Record,* February 21, 1955.

[6] There are many published and unpublished biographies of Brown, all intended for popular consumption and containing various errors. See: Charlotte Hawkins Brown, "Formal Training Explanation," and "Biography," typescripts in CHB MSS; Gwendolyn Cherry et al., *Portraits In Color* (N.Y.: Pageant Press, 1962), pp. 31–34; Sadie I. Daniel, *Women Builders* (Washington: Associated Publishers, 1931), pp. 133–163; Charles S. Johnson, *A Preface to Racial Understanding* (NY: Friendship Press, 1936), pp. 113–121; Constance Marteena, *Lengthening Shadow;* and the following reference books: *The Negro Almanac,* p. 758; *Dictionary of North Carolina Biography,* Vol. 1, pp. 242–243; *Afro-American Encyclopedia,* Vol. 2, pp. 408–409; *Who's Who of the Colored Race,* Vol. 1, p. 41; *Historical Negro Biographies,* pp. 167–168.

Journal of Negro Education, Vol. 51, No. 3 (1982)
Copyright © 1982, Howard University.

191

professor, Charlotte attended the state normal school at Salem. In the Fall, 1901, she accepted an appointment as a teacher of a small American Missionary Association (AMA) school in a rural area east of Greensboro, North Carolina. When the AMA withdrew its support, rather than accept a transfer, she decided to reopen the school and rely upon the help of Mrs. Palmer and her Boston friends. Mrs. Palmer died in 1902 and the school was renamed Palmer Memorial Institute (hereinafter PMI).

For the next forty years, Charlotte devoted her life to the building of PMI from a small elementary school serving children in the neighborhood to a high school and junior college enrolling boys and girls from many states and from the elite business and professional classes of black families. Without the support of organized philanthropy, she raised upwards of $1 million from wealthy friends in both the North and South to finance the development of PMI. This individual effort not only provided education for thousands of Black youths but also contributed to interracial cooperation and understanding in the South.

In 1911, Charlotte married Edward S. Brown, a graduate of Harvard who had rented rooms with her mother in Cambridge. The marriage ended after a year. A second marriage, in 1923, also failed, and Charlotte was known throughout her professional career as Mrs. Charlotte Hawkins Brown.

In addition to her work as educator, Mrs. Brown became active in interracial meetings, in women's club work, and in efforts for racial advancement. She was a skilled and powerful public speaker and was in such great demand that she delivered hundreds of addresses at colleges, interracial meetings, churches, and women's organizations. One address was reportedly heard by 25,000 persons in Madison Square Garden where she received a ten-minute standing ovation. Regularly during the summer, she lectured on interracial relations at Wellesley, Smith, Radcliffe, and Mount Holyoke colleges. Organizations in which she held office and membership included the Southern Interracial Committee, the Regional Council on Race Relations, National Council of Colored Women, the Urban League, the American Red Cross, the Y.W.C.A., and the South Atlantic Field Committee. She received honorary doctorate degrees from Howard, Lincoln, and Wilberforce.

Mrs. Brown retired as president of PMI in 1952, but remained as director of finance until 1955. She died at Greensboro, N.C., January 11, 1961. PMI continued under the leadership of Wilhelmina M. Crosson (1952–1966), Harold E. Bragg, (1966–1970), and Charles W. Bundrige (1970–71). PMI did not reopen after the 1970–71 academic year.

Mrs. Brown had known of Tuskegee and Booker T. Washington from childhood; his educational ideas were recognized and approved by her New England friends to whom she turned when the AMA discontinued its support. Thus it is not surprising that PMI in the early years emphasized industrial education for rural living. The charter, which was not drawn up until 1907, declared the purpose of the institution to be "the education of the colored race" in "improved methods of agriculture and industrial pursuits generally."[7] By 1904 enough money had been collected to construct a large permanent building to replace the blacksmith's shed which had housed the school earlier.

Although Mrs. Brown's later reminiscences plainly state that from the beginning she emphasized the development of culture and the social graces, it is difficult to validate this claim fully. An advertising pamphlet printed about 1916 described the school's unique work as "the development of farm life," and notes that it was the first school "to introduce industrial work in the rural schools of the county." Its vision of the future of its graduates embraced "domestic service, . . . farm life, . . . leadership in rural life, . . . community service . . . (and) useful Christian living." The pamphlet carried an endorsement by Mr. Washington, and also a Tuskegee trustee who said that Palmer was established on the same lines as Tuskegee and was "much stronger and more effective" than was Tuskegee at its beginning."[8] The use of this terminology may indeed have been dictated less by conviction than by Washington's advice "as to ways and means of obtaining help,"[9] but it is clear that the major theme was industrial education and the social graces were a low, minor key.

The subsequent careers of the earliest graduates confirm the reality of the industrial curriculum, which generally included the preparation of teachers. Two of the three graduates of 1905 became teachers; the third became a farmer. The seven graduates of 1907 went into the following occupations: housekeeper (1), rural school principal (2), carpenter (1), pastor (1), teacher (1) and physician (1). All five graduates of 1909 became rural teachers. Eleven graduates of 1911 became mechanics, farmers, housekeepers, teachers, and a

1125

[7]"Charter of Palmer Memorial Institute," CHB MSS, November 23, 1907, Box 3, Folder 67.
[8]*Palmer Memorial Institute*, Inc., CHB MSS, Box 4, Folder 90 (Internal evidence suggests a date of 1915 or 1916.)
[9]"Eulogy to Dr. Booker T. Washington," August 1920, typescript in CHB MSS, Box 1, Folder 13; CHB to Mrs. James C. Ernst, May 13, 1920, ALS in CHB MSS, Box 1, Folder 24.

stewardess. Four graduates of 1916 became teachers; the fifth worked as a domestic.[10]

In 1906, Helen Kimball of Brookline, Massachusetts, donated a parcel of land adjoining the school property to be used as the beginning of a farm. In 1909, Mary R. Grinnell, another Massachusetts friend, took the initiative in raising money for the "domestic science" building. In 1917, when the industrial building burned, Mrs. Brown wrote a benefactor for assistance, saying that the industrial equipment was "the heart of the school."[11] Thus, it is clear that during Palmer's earliest years, it was viewed by its founder and benefactors as designed to prepare black youth for rural living and for productive work. Its students were drawn from the immediate area, and returned to the same area, by and large, as teachers, farmers, and laborers. Nevertheless, Mrs. Brown hoped to make their homes "happy intelligent centers" where the beauty of a "picture, a good book, as well as a field of waving corn" could be appreciated.[12]

Prior to the loss of the industrial building in 1917, Mrs. Brown had depended entirely upon the financial contributions of her network of northern friends. Three years earlier, Galen L. Stone, a Boston broker and businessman, had been brought into the fold of contributors. His personal gifts, together with contributions he solicited and those of his son Robert (who also served on the Board of Trustees), became the single largest source of support of PMI. However, as fires, other emergencies, and the ever expanding plans of Mrs. Brown created continuous appeals for financial help, Stone quickly came to the conclusion reached earlier by other northern philanthropists (e.g., Peabody Fund, General Education Board) that northern philanthropy could not give permanent life to Southern institutions without Southern support. Accordingly, he warned Mrs. Brown that he was not inclined to continue to help PMI much longer except as "it will definitely come under the interest and supervision of the community in and about Greensboro."[13] In this respect, PMI was at a disadvantage since it was offering elementary and secondary level work at the very time when an extensive North-South collaboration was under way to effect support for public elementary and secondary schools. Mrs. Brown had other visions for her school than to let it become another public school. Nevertheless, she followed Stone's advice and cultivated local business-

1126

[10]"Report of Graduates of Palmer Institute," February 20, 1917, typescript in CHB MSS, Box 3, Folder 80.
[11]CHB to Galen L. Stone, January 12, 1918, ALS in CHB MSS, Box 1, Folder 31.
[12]CHB to Galen L. Stone, May 7, 1918, ALS in CHB MSS, Box 1, Folder 31.
[13]Galen L. Stone to CHB, April 10, 1918, ALS in CHB MSS, Box 1, Folder 31.

men, not only for contributions but for service on the Board of Trustees.[14] The result was that Stone could report to Wallace Buttrick, in writing to solicit aid from the General Education Board, that Mrs. Brown had secured the support of "some excellent white people of Greensboro."[15]

Stone not only contributed major amounts of money for buildings and the development of PMI, but guided its development in other ways as well. He pushed for more local support, as indicated above. He urged the adoption of a budget, the clearer communication of specific plans, and improved business methods. Acknowledging a letter requesting further donations, Stone wrote to Mrs. Brown complaining that she was "still pursuing the same rather irregular tactics. . . . I cannot tell from your letter what campaign you are planning to undertake." A few months later, he expressed vexation at her tendancy to "plan to spend money and continue to spend it before you had raised it, having counted on your ability to get it when the emergency might arise."[16] Indeed, there was no lack of emergencies created by fires, rising costs, and expanded facilities projected by Mrs. Brown, and she exhibited considerable ability in getting the funds to meet those emergencies. She responded to Stone's criticism by allowing his accountant to visit Sedalia and set her books in order. She also followed his advice to secure more local assistance by applying for and receiving a *per capita* payment for each county child attending PMI, a measure designed to continue until public schooling for black children should be available in the area.

Stone called Mrs. Brown's attention to the fact that PMI was too dependent upon her, and that the school should somehow be put on a more permanent basis. Consequently, in the early 1920s, negotiations were undertaken for the American Missionary Association to provide control and regular support for Palmer. The AMA specified certain financial conditions, and when those conditions were met by the raising of over $300,000 in a single year, Palmer became an AMA school. But Mrs. Brown was too forceful and independent a person to submerge herself and "her" institution under external auspices. The AMA connection was unsuccessful. In April, 1933, an administrative committee assigned the task of recommending what action to take in reference to PMI, voted to return PMI to its trustees saying that its creation "by a single individual" had led to "all sorts of special arrangements" which could not be justified. The school was returned to its independent status July 1, 1934, with

1127

[14]The leaflet in note 8 above listed 4 local and 34 northern trustees.
[15]Galen L. Stone to Wallace Buttrick, February 28, 1921, CHB MSS, Box 1, Folder 32.
[16]Galen L. Stone to CHB, November 6, 1920, ALS in CHB MSS, Box 1, Folder 32; Galen L. Stone

the understanding that Mrs. Brown would receive "the freedom in the management of the school which past history and the present situation seem to demand."[17]

As the decade of the thirties came to a close, several factors came together to push PMI toward a different emphasis. The public school movement, which had been stimulated by the Southern Education Board, had largely succeeded in bringing public elementary and high schools to most regions of the South. Thus Palmer faced the prospect of losing its local students who brought with them the state *per capita* payment. The sponsorship of the AMA was gone. Income tax laws and the depression seriously reduced the prospect of receiving large sums from wealthy benefactors; the foundations were helping public schools and colleges, not private secondary schools. Furthermore, an analysis of where the money was going at Palmer showed that as early as 1922 industrial training was the most expensive part of the curriculum. In 1935, the new administrative dean recommended that there be a change in the student labor program "to save expenses and get the work well done." Custodial work and farm work would be performed by full time employees, while the student work traditions would be honored by assigning "odd jobs" to them.[18]

The combination of financial constraints, the long time interests of Mrs. Brown, and the expressed desires of Galen Stone, contributed to the emergence of a new emphasis at PMI. In contrast to the earliest Northern supporters who favored industrial education because this training was thought best suited to the special "place" which the Negro would occupy in the social and economic order, Stone let it be known that his contributions to Palmer were not for the purpose of "educating and advancing Negroes" but in "making American citizens . . . in giving them the highest and best" education possible. He contended that there was to be no specially designed place for the Negro in American life, and therefore schools which enrolled black students should provide for development along all lines. Palmer students should not only sing Negro spirituals, but should develop a repertoire of the "best music."[19]

Mrs. Brown enunciated the goals for the "new" Palmer as requiring the elimination of the elementary school, and the addition of junior college. At both the secondary and college levels, more

1128

to CHB, May 9, 1921, ALS in CHB MSS, Box 1, Folder 32.

[17]"Action of the Administrative Committee of the American Missionary Association Concerning Palmer Memorial Institute," April 25, 1933, typescript in CHB MSS, Box 3, Folder 70.

[18]"Report of the Principal to the Board of Trustees," October 11, 1922, typescript in CHB MSS, Box 3, Folder 71; Nathaniel G. Sims, "Report to the President on the Organization of the Institute for the Academic Year 1934–35," typescript in CHB MSS, Box 3, Folder 73.

[19]CHB, "On The Passing of Mr. Galen L. Stone," typescript in CHB MSS, Box 4, Folder 107.

cultural emphasis was proposed. She reported that students were "more versed in books than habits of living," and that they had received little or no training "in correct habits, the manners required for public and private life" such as was available to whites at exclusive finishing schools. Thus, the vision articulated by Mrs. Brown was to provide this type of education "to a picked group of Negro youth, who in turn will give out this culture to other groups," and thus in time there would rise up "leaders whose very appearance will inspire youth to seek ideals of truth, beauty, and goodness." In this way, she thought, "the Negro race will find his open door to abundant life, through training for appreciation of all that is fine and beautiful."[20]

This change of direction required changes both in the composition of the student body and of the faculty. To meet these needs, the Sedalia Club of Cambridge launched a campaign to secure scholarship funds for 25 students above the second year of high school who were "talented in music, oratory, or painting." Faculty members were recruited from "the best New England and Eastern" colleges.[21]

1129

The first junior college class was graduated in 1934. At that time, total enrollment at PMI was approximately 250, nearly half of whom were "community" students. By 1937, the elementary school had been taken over by the public school, and total enrollment had dropped to 159, of whom only 6 were "community" students. But the addition of junior college students (55 in 1936) could not make up for the loss of local students, and the added expense of instruction on the college level made an impossible burden. Thus, the junior college came to an end in 1939.[22]

Mrs. Brown had known the meaning of financial exigency from the beginning of her work, and the 1939 fiscal crisis was nothing new. However, it was increasingly difficult to write letters or to make trips to the North to raise money. Consequently, Mrs. Brown reported to the trustees in 1939 that discussions had been conducted on the possible merger of PMI with North Carolina College for Negroes at Durham, and with Bennett College in Greensboro. No agreement was reached, however, and the alternative was to become more selective in admissions and limit enrollment to that "class of Negroes who will be able to pay sufficiently to meet the actual expenses beyond investments, wills, etc." As a concession to the

[20]"Pronouncement of the Ideals for the New Palmer," typescript in CHB MSS, Box 3, Folder 69; internal evidence suggests a date of 1930.

[21]J. C. Hyman, Publicity Director, "Palmer Memorial Institute Begins Fine Arts Courses," typescript in CHB MSS, Box 3, Folder 69, undated.

[22]A Brief Annual Report of the President of the Institution to the Board of Trustees for the Academic Year 1938–39; also 1940–41; typescripts in CHB MSS, Box 3, Folders 74 and 75.

school's traditional involvement with the local community, Mrs. Brown planned to raise scholarships for "8–10 fine boys and girls from the rural districts or from poorer families who have the brain and the desire to make good." During that particular year (1943), PMI enrolled a total of 178 students from 23 states, but only four were from the community. Apparently, the ideal, in addition to recruiting students who could pay their way, was to pick students "from as near the same social group as possible," that is, "from the very best families," who were willing to separate their children from the public schools in order to get this special training in a "cultural, Christian approach to life," and who would go on with advanced training to become leaders in community life wherever they might go.[23]

The increasing emphasis upon cultural education and upon enrolling an economically elite class did not mean the total loss of the emphasis upon the dignity of work. Throughout the decades of the 1940s and 1950s, each student was expected to give the school at least one hour of work per day, and the scholarship students gave more time. One student, recalling her experience at PMI in the mid-forties, reported that the "work ethic took priority in our development . . . Every student had duty work in one of the buildings, on the grounds or in the dining hall." This same student felt that formal academic study "did not occupy top priority," and that the emphasis on refinement, proper dress and decorum was sometimes "carried to the extreme."[24] This judgment may not be entirely accurate, however, for Palmer was fully accredited by the Southern Association of Colleges and Secondary Schools at a time when few black high schools enjoyed this recognition, and it sent almost all of its graduates to college. The results of a survey of graduates reported by Marteena[25] as well as our own survey indicate that an unusually high proportion of PMI graduates not only went to college but also completed advanced and professional degrees.

PMI was uniquely the fruit of one woman's labor. Mrs. Brown created it, and almost singlehandedly was responsible for soliciting contributions to sustain it for more than fifty years. Fiercely individualistic, Mrs. Brown appears to have regarded any other pattern of financial support as an acknowledgement of weakness, or as somehow weakening her hold on the institution. Through the school, she hoped to contribute to the amelioration of racial problems in

1130

---

[23]Annual Reports of the President, 1934–35; 1938–39, 1942–43; typescripts in CHB MSS, Box 3, Folders 73, 74, 76.

[24]Ann C. Hooper, "The Proper Thing to Say, To Do, and To Wear," in *The First Biennial Reunion of Palmer Memorial Institute*, August 3–5, 1979.

[25]Marteena, *The Lengthening Shadow of a Woman*.

two ways. First, the school itself was to be the product of interracial effort, demonstrating that blacks and whites could work together in mutual respect. Second, the school was to produce a type of black leader who would gain respect and acceptance among whites through the possession of universally accepted qualities of character and behavior. During her active life, over one thousand graduates went out from Palmer having been impressed with the idea of their own individual worth and with the idea that acceptance by other people depended upon their being "educationally efficient, religiously sincere, and culturally secure." There is no doubt that Mrs. Brown left a lengthening shadow of influence not only in terms of her impact on individual students, but in terms of what they accomplished because of what they gained from her.

Contributions as Race Leader

Although she perceived herself primarily as the builder of a school, Mrs. Brown also sought the role of race leader. In 1920, she wrote that her work and thoughts "for my people" were just as important as those of Booker T. Washington. She expressed the hope that "some incident like the Atlanta Exposition that gave Booker Washington to the world, may come to me some day." Having been thus discovered, she looked forward to being "sought . . . to interpret my people."[26]

During her early years in Cambridge, Mrs. Brown had experienced no racial discrimination, and indeed had acquired little racial sensitivity. Upon moving South to North Carolina in 1901, she moved into a world that required new behaviors. Following Washington's pattern, she chose to conform to southern cultural patterns while appealing to the human sympathy and Christian conscience of white society. In an open letter to the people of Guilford County, she reminded them that she had "respected the best traditions of the South" and had tried to do her duty as a "Christian young woman."[27] Evidence of conformity to custom is found in the seating arrangements at southern concerts by Palmer musical groups. On one such occasion, she indicated that the "entire middle aisle" would be reserved for "our white friends."[28] When arranging another concert, she asked the local sponsor to arrange ticket sales to Negroes "if you have a balcony or gallery."[29]

Mrs. Brown's first publication which addressed racial issues came in this early period of benign conformity. *Mammy*[30] was the

[26]CHB to Galen L. Stone, June 19, 1920, ALS in CHB MSS, Box 1, Folder 32.
[27]CHB to the people of Guilford County, December 8, 1920, ALS in CHB MSS, Box 1, Folder 28.
[28]CHB to Mr. Piper, April 1, 1920, ALS in CHB MSS, Box 1, Folder 28.
[29]CHB to Mrs. Bessie G. Hold, April 12, 1921, ALS in CHB MSS, Box 1, Folder 24.
[30]CHB, *Mammy: An Appeal to the Heart of the South* (Boston: Pilgrim Press, 1919); 18 pp.

story of a faithful aged couple, former slaves, who elected to live out their lives with their former owners. Years of dedicated service were rewarded with affectionate words but minimum subsistence and eventual disregard. Based upon actual persons, the story was intended to appeal to the hearts and Christian sentiments of southern whites to the end that they would support fair treatment for blacks. But even this mild approach to racial problems was critically received by her northern supporters, who were hurt that Charlotte would drag up things that properly belonged in the past.

There is evidence that Mrs. Brown's initial conservative racial strategy prior to the 1920s was not only modeled after Washington, but in fact demanded by some northern supporters as the price of continued financial support for Palmer. On more than one occasion, she wrote these friends asking, in effect, how much more humiliating treatment she must accept. The price of their money was to "tie my hands so I can't speak out when I am being crushed."[31] In order to satisfy these supporters and reduce southern hostility, she gave assurances that the purpose of Palmer was not to "infuse social equality into the veins of these children."[32]

Mrs. Brown's strong sense of personal worth and dignity meant that she could not long tolerate the personal affronts demanded by the conservative strategy. Gradually a more assertive approach evolved. One of the first irritants was the refusal by both northern and southern whites to address her by an appropriate title. To one correspondent who had offended her in this way, she wrote that "intelligent Negroes resent such discourtesies."[33] But even while enduring personal indignities, she refused to be limited in her inner thoughts. "I sit in a Jim Crow car," she wrote, "but my mind keeps company with the kings and queens I have known." External constraints must not be allowed to "segregate mind or soul."[34]

A traumatic incident in the Fall of 1920 precipitated a more aggressive racial stance for Mrs. Brown. She boarded a Pullman car in Greensboro on the way to a women's interracial meeting in Memphis. Upon emerging from her berth the next morning to take a seat in the coach, she was confronted by twelve "husky young white men" who forced her to move to the Negro coach. The humiliation was intensified by the fact that she was forcibly marched through three cars in which sat "southern white women passing for Christians" who were going to the same interracial meeting

1132

---

[31]CHB, undated final page of a letter, ALS in CHB MSS, Box 1, Folder 32.
[32]CHB to Mrs. Galen L. Stone, March 10, 1921, ALS in CHB MSS, Box 1, Folder 32.
[33]CHB to Mrs. W. E. Lowe, May 9, 1921, ALS in CHB MSS, Box 1, Folder 24.
[34]CHB, "Some Incidents in the Life and Career of Charlotte Hawkins Brown Growing Out of Racial Situations At the Request of Dr. Ralph Bunche," typescript in CHB MSS, Box 1, Folder 24.

"where they declared their purpose was to make the Negro woman unashamed and unafraid."[35] She sued the Pullman Company and obtained a settlement. However, her attorney suggested that she imitate the attitude of Mr. Washington and drop the matter. Mrs. Brown acknowledged that Washington was "truly a wise man for his day," but asserted that conditions were much different and "a few of us must be sacrificed . . . in order to get a step ahead." If this meant the loss of friends and financial support for her educational work, then she was "willing to become a martyr for Negro womanhood."[36]

Mrs. Brown chose to work primarily with the women of both races as the sphere of her racial leadership. By virtue of her background, especially her acceptance by upper-class white women in New England and New York, she felt that she had achieved a degree of self confidence that was lacking in southern black women.[37] Her leadership among women was expressed organizationally through such groups as the North Carolina Federation of Colored Women's Clubs, the National Council of Colored Women, the International Council for Women of the Darker Races, and many interracial meetings and speeches before white women's organizations. She felt that there were definite advantages to working with women. White women had recently been successful in the fight for voting rights, and without being threatened directly by economic competition, they could understand the humiliations suffered by black women and the aspirations of black women for their children and their families. Furthermore, since many racial injustices were being perpetrated allegedly to protect the honor of southern white women, it seemed especially appropriate to appeal to that same sense of honor in behalf of black women.

1133

Mrs. Brown's message to white women embodied several points. First, she expressed the importance of equal educational advantages for children, urging equality in such areas as length of school term, teacher salaries, and richness of curriculum. Rejecting any special Negro education, her appeal was always for the opportunity to develop along the same lines and to the same degree as anyone else. Inequalities, she argued, were usually justified in the minds of whites by thinking of the black servant class, the "Mary and John" who served and "were satisfied with old clothing, food, and other articles, without any definite realization of further responsibility to society."[38] Equality also meant integrated schools. Mixed

---

[35]CHB, "Some Incidents . . . ," typescript in CHB MSS, Box 1, Folder 24.
[36]CHB to F. P. Hobgood, Jr., October 19, 1921, ALS in CHB MSS, Box 1, Folder 30.
[37]CHB to Max Loeb, October 1933, ALS in CHB MSS, Box 1, Folder 26.
[38]CHB, "President Negro State Teachers Association . . . ," typescript in CHB MSS, Box 1, Folder 20, page 2.

schools, she argued, gave youths of both races the "opportunity to know each other," and would destroy "that un-American spirit of superiority of race" and replace it with "a common standard of superiority by character, intelligence and natural ability."[39]

A second theme in Mrs. Brown's leadership among women was the demand for "respectful recognition of womanhood." She reminded white women that they had sufficient regard for colored women to use them to nurse their children, and even to care for their children while they were vacationing in Europe. "At my mother's breasts," she said, "nursed three governors of North Carolina and two presidents of colleges." Yet the most ordinary human courtesies were denied these women.[40]

A third theme was the request for white women to help in reaching out to the Negro women who "labor day in and day out for the white people." While these working women were caring for other people's children, their own homes were being neglected and their children were living in unsanitary and unwholesome environments. The situation not only demanded education and cultural enlightenment, but fair wages and the elimination of distinctly "Negro jobs." "I cannot believe," she argued, "that God intended that any one race should be scullions for another race."[41] Implicit in this line of argument was the recognition of class differences among Negro women. Although Mrs. Brown spoke of herself as representing the working class of women, the maids and laundry women, she insisted that Negro women should not be judged by these women. There were, she noted, a large number of educated, cultured, refined black women of whom whites knew nothing, simply because the existing pattern of social relationships never brought the two together.

Finally, to allay the fears of white women, Mrs. Brown insisted that the "Negro woman wants everything—education, power, influence—in fact everything that the white woman wants but her white husband." Marriage was, she said, too complex a matter to have imposed on it the additional burden of racial difference.[42]

In addition to hundreds of addresses before white audiences and interracial women's groups, Mrs. Brown exerted significant leadership within the framework of black teachers, club women, and sorority members, that body of women who comprised the refined upper class of the race. There were several themes which

[39]CHB to Max Loeb, October 1933, ALS in CHB MSS, Box 1, Folder 26.

[40]CHB, "Changing Philosophies . . . ," typescript, CHB MSS, Box 4, Folder 107, p. 6.

[41]CHB, "The Importance of Overcoming Discrimination," typescript in CHB MSS, Box 4, Folder 107.

[42]*Buffalo Progressive Herald*, March 15, 1930; "The Importance . . . ," typescript in CHB MSS, Box 4, Folder 107.

she emphasized in these groups that were different from the themes directed toward white groups.

Mrs. Brown called upon black women to avoid imitating white women but to "hark back to those sturdy virtues that laid the foundation on which the finer things of the American people were founded." Rejecting the accusation that her emphasis upon culture was designed to make black women acceptable to white women by having them imitate whites, Mrs. Brown noted that social life among whites had deteriorated. Instead of following their example of riotous living, she called upon black women to teach children to be courteous, polite, kind, and to avoid night clubs, saloons, and the cocktail table.[43]

Deeply religious herself, Mrs. Brown called upon black women to make their homes "places of trust in God." Special attention should be given so that the minds of children were not "poisoned with hymns of hate and revenge."[44]

Finally, Mrs. Brown called for united support of such organizations as the Urban League and the NAACP which were working for fairness and justice. The earlier tolerant, patient strategy, she said, "kept us marking time with our hearts while our minds were being schooled in the methods . . . of striking a final blow for freedom." But the time for patience was running out and there must be "no two schools of thought" in the struggle for justice.[45]

Though these themes were consistently enunciated throughout Mrs. Brown's active career (1920--1950) as a race leader, certain developments can be noted. First, there was an increase in militancy and outrage, especially associated with World War II. In bitterly eloquent words, she called for no more delay in granting to all citizens the four freedoms for which blacks were being asked to sacrifice their lives. The time had come, she said, "to let the world know they prefer death to slavery or injustice."[46] In a New York address, she bluntly stated that the refusal to "open the doors of labor to black citizens was exhibiting "the very Hitlerism you are seeking to destroy." There would be no lasting peace, she prophesied, "so long as the white race seeks to deprive the darker people of the world of their God-given rights to live, to work, to have the education, the leisure, the culture that they covet for themselves."[47] Acknowledging that her advice bordered on sedi-

1135

[43]CHB, "The Role of the Negro Woman in the Fight for Freedom," typescript in CHB MSS, Box 1, Folder 14.
[44]Ibid.
[45]Ibid.
[46]Norfolk Journal and Guide, February 5, 1938.
[47]CHB, "The Importance . . . ," typescript in CHB MSS, Box 4, Folder 107.

tion, Mrs. Brown called for mass movements to challenge discrimination directly, and possibly to refuse service in the armed forces.[48]

Another development was the increased emphasis upon culture and refinement as a means of gaining acceptance by whites. In 1940, Mrs. Brown announced a "national crusade for good manners for my people," which would "usher in better days for us."[49] Since political appointment had eluded her, partially by choice, and the rise of effective civil rights organizations diminished the need for personal, charismatic leadership, the culture movement provided an area of unique emphasis that would give her individual recognition and leadership.

According to Mrs. Brown, her sense of beauty and refinement, deeply imbedded by her mother and grandmother and reinforced by her New England upbringing, had given her entree to the better class of southern white society who, against this backdrop, could understand better the personal indignity of racial prejudice. Two events projected her onto the national scene as the authoritative arbiter of good manners for blacks. First was her nationwide address, March 10, 1940, on the "Wings Over Jordan" radio program. Second was the publication in 1941 of the book, *The Correct Thing To Do, To Say, To Wear.*[50]

The radio address enunciated a clear class appeal "to that group of young Negroes from high schools and colleges whose education is above average." She asserted that social graces were not to be associated with either a servile status or with purely white customs, but were the universally "proper approach to life and its problems." In racial matters, the acquisition of social graces would "remove some of the commonest objections to our presence in large numbers." If black youths would practice "the little courtesies, the gentle voice, a knowledge of when to sit, when to stand, how to open and close a door," then the "wheels of progress" would be turned "with great velocity . . . toward equal opportunity and justice for all." The social graces were, she argued, "the key to the . . . heart of America, white and black."[51]

Mrs. Brown's book of etiquette, first published in 1941 and reprinted four times, set forth the detailed behaviors appropriate for both men and women in all kinds of settings including home,

[48]CHB, "Changing Philosophies . . . ," typescript in CHB MSS, Box 4, Folder 107.
[49]CHB to Arthur B. Spingarn, June 13, 1940, ALS in Spingarn MSS, Moorland-Springarn Research Center, Howard University.
[50]CHB, *The Correct Thing To Do, To Say, To Wear* (Boston: Christopher Publishing House, 1941); 142 pp.
[51]CHB, "The Negro and the Social Graces," radio address, March 10, 1940, Moorland-Springarn Research Center, Howard University; mimeographed form letter to listeners responding to the radio program, March 20, 1940, in Washington Conservatory of Music Collection, Moorland-Springarn Research Center, Howard University.

school, church, dances, concerts, and travel. Although the media viewed the book with some curiosity as the only book by a black author on social etiquette, Mrs. Brown contended that it was for "cultured people of all races."[52]

The emphasis on social graces led Mrs. Brown to become somewhat critical of the colleges, which, she said, were "too preoccupied with the more formalized aspects of education." To remedy this defect, she promoted the annual observation of "Good Manners and Culture Day" on black campuses and appeared regularly for seminars and lectures at schools such as Howard University and North Carolina College at Durham. Popular though she was as a speaker, if she ever wondered why she had not been discovered and projected into national race leadership as Booker T. Washington had been, she might have found the answer in sober reflection upon the significance and validity of her theme for the forties, "Acquire manners; the rest will come."[53]

SUMMARY AND EVALUATION

On whose terms and by what standards shall the work of such a person as Charlotte Hawkins Brown be evaluated? On one hand, the institution which she founded and built was unable to survive more than a decade after her death. On the other hand, over one thousand students were educated under her influence, and hundreds of thousands, both black and white, northern and southern, heard her speak for racial justice.

Beyond what she might have influenced other people to do, what did Mrs. Brown think was the significance of her own personal life? In one sense, it did not matter whether Palmer survived without her. She viewed her life as being a demonstration of what one black woman could do. As a representative of the black woman personified, her accomplishments would be a definitive refutation of racism and would demand for all black women the full respect which they deserved as human beings. One cannot doubt that Mrs. Brown almost singlehandedly accomplished much, far more than most other persons who enjoyed advantages she never had. In this sense, she vividly demonstrated the falsity of any theory of inherent inferiority on the basis of race. That the barriers of racial prejudice did not fall before this demonstration does not diminish the impact of her life but rather displays the entrenched strength of prejudice.

Undoubtedly, the continuing significance of Mrs. Brown lies not in an institution, or in organizations and clubs, but in the personal

---

[52]*Pittsburgh Courier*, April 20, 1940.
[53]Ibid. Also unidentified clipping, November 16, 1945, CHB Vertical File, Greensboro Public Library.

impact of one human being upon hundreds of other individual human beings. Whatever else Palmer was, it involved the close, direct influence of its founder upon young people in their formative years. The newspaper and magazine advertisements constantly emphasized this. In preparation for this study, we conducted a survey to which fifty PMI graduates, representing the period 1925–1969, responded. In response to a question about the effect of Mrs. Brown upon themselves, these alumni pointed to the "development of character" (respect for oneself, integrity, dependability, self discipline), the "motivation to be somebody," a sense of racial pride and responsibility, the importance of education and culture, and a commitment in whatever one does "to be true to yourself, do it well, share it with others." While they may have chafed under the rigid rules, and in retrospect perceived some of the social graces as having been superficial, these graduates agreed that the personal growth experienced at Palmer served them well.

Mrs. Brown's impact on interracial relationships is impossible to evaluate. Many testimonials could be cited ascribing great improvement in race relationships to her work, her speeches, and her influence upon individual persons. But the historical record is filled with assurances of wonderful race relationships in public print even while the groans of the oppressed were effectively stifled. Had the pattern of race relationships rested solely in the hearts of people, rather than being built into the social and political structures of the nation, Mrs. Brown's work might have been seen as making a far more lasting and pronounced difference.

Charlotte Hawkins Brown was a woman with pride in herself and her people. In her heart there burned a deep zeal for the great American principles of freedom and justice for all human beings, and she expressed this commitment with unusual oratorical eloquence. Her sense of personal independence, admirable though it was in some respects, nevertheless prevented her from forging the linkages that would have made her work more permanent. But she succeeded in showing for all the world to see "what one young black woman could do."

By ERLENE STETSON

Black Feminism in Indiana, 1893-1933

... Some day — the world is going to hear from both of us. Mary
McLeod Bethune to Madame S. J. Walker

Our woman's movement is woman's movement in that it is led
and directed for the good of women and men for the benefit of
all humanity, which is more than any one branch or section of it.
Address of Mrs. Josephone St. Pierre Ruffin National
Association of Colored Women Conference of 1896

1139

IT IS IMPORTANT THAT the experiences of American women be examined from
the point of assessing societal limitations on female experiences and expressions in each period of national history. What is less acknowledged is the need
for a basic reconstruction of the historical activities of American women that
takes into account the different kinds of female experiences and the social
contexts in which various women have lived. Ideally a study of feminism
should allow both to be done.

Feminism traditionally has been equated with suffrage by American historians. While a study of the movement for the vote is surely vital for an
understanding of the nineteenth century women's movement in the United
States, one limits the scope and significance of women's efforts by concentrating solely on the suffragists and the herculean antislavery efforts of black
women together with black men and white women. What is needed is an
expanded definition of feminism to include leisured women's (black and
white) pre-political activities before the Civil War (moral reform societies,
early temperance, education, women's fiction, abolition, and turn-outs by
laboring women in the factories of the North East), as well as more overtly
political activities of women after the Civil War which were largely responsible for the creation of the Sanitary Commission and which rallied the efforts
of thousands of American women behind nineteenth century organizations
such as the WCTU, NAWSA, General Fedration of Women's Clubs, WTUL,
Consumer's League, Socialist Party and the IWW.

Black feminism in Indiana is a largly untold story. It is a story that is closely
tied to women's club activities in Indiana.[1] Women's club activities are too
often dismissed as pleasant diversions in the province of the privileged or
educated. To the contrary, the history of black women's club activities in

---

[1] Women's club activities too often have been dismissed as the dilettantish diversion of leisured class women, or
as is the attitude toward black women, a tendency to label their movement as black bourgeois nationalism.
While the former is easily dismissed as a pernicious put-down, the latter reveals an ahistorical sense of the
power and force of a social movement for political good. Too often the apparent powerlessness of a group
obscures its real power; hence the popularity of the oft repeated 'the hand that rocks the cradle rules the
world' analogy.

Originally published in *Phylon*, Vol. XLIV, No. 4 (December 1983).

Indiana attests to the power and force of individuals and of a social movement for achieving good. Preeminently, it is a unique record of the contribution of black women in the area of racial progress ("uplift")[2] in particular and the making of Indiana into an enlightened and progressive state in general. Early concerns of black women along the lines of religion, education, fine arts, literature, industry, professions, home and child life, vocation, music, civics and interracial relations. The tangible evidences of their success were the establishment of day nurseries, kindergartens, working girls' homes, club houses, orphan homes, rescue missions and homes for delinquents, or the aged and infirm — all owned and staffed by black clubwomen.

Black women's visibility as clubwomen and their concerns for moral and physical "uplift" were given national attention as a result of an incident concerning the Chicago World's Fair in 1893.[3] Prior to 1893, black women had preferred to organize for the purpose of relief work. This was understandable given their status as recently freed slaves or as free women of color. Long before the Civil War made relief work a practical necessity, black women had formed organizations that directed attention to the needs of fugitives. The Female Benevolent Firm of Boston, Massachusetts was organized as early as 1848 to provide clothing and shoes to women and children who had been rescued by the Underground Railroad.

The Chicago World's Fair, advertised as a showcase through which the various nations might exhibit their industries and general achievements, was presided over by a Board of Lady Managers.[4] Mrs. Potter Palmer of Chicago, a clubwoman, was to oversee the United States' exhibits of accomplishment. Fearing that blacks would go unrepresented, Miss Hallie Quinn Brown, a teacher from Wilberforce University (Ohio), requested that she be allowed to sit on the board to oversee and represent the achievements of blacks. She was refused on the grounds that since she did not represent an organization she could not be a board manager. Undaunted, Miss Brown returned home and organized the Colored Women's League. Her hopes of serving on the board went unrealized, but a lesson had been learned nevertheless. So much so that by July, 1895, Miss Brown was more than ready to heed the call of Mrs. Josephine St. Pierre Ruffin of the Boston's Women's Era Club. Acting on a dissimilar but equally concerned impulse, Mrs. Ruffin issued a call to black women to come to Boston to help formulate a position paper in response to what she saw as a particularly vitriolic and slanderous anti-black female

1140

---

[2] The stock term that came to describe "rescue" work involving recently freed slaves (Southern racist propaganda would label them wretched freedmen) faced with freedom and all too quickly Jim Crowism. It is a word indelibly linked to the work of black clubwomen who dealt with the "plantation woman" and homeless children. Theirs was seen as a moral and social imperative.

[3] The information for this article is gleaned from: Elizabeth Lindsay Davis, ed., *Lifting As They Climb* (Chicago, 1933); William T. Alexander, *History of The Colored Race in America* (Palmetto Publishers, 1887); J. L. Nichols and William Crogmann (with essay by Mrs. Booker T. Washington on club history), eds., *The New Progress of a Race* J. L. Nichols, 1929; originally published in 1897 with H. F. Kletzing and Crogmann); numerous journals of the day (see attached bibliography); The National Association of Colored Women's Clubs (notes, minutes and memorabilia) headquartered in Washington, D.C., and the local Indiana Federation of NACW as gleaned from available reports at the Indiana Historical Society, Indianapolis. See bibliography for more sources; see Note 4.

[4] For a detailed account see Davis, op. cit. The authorized publication of the Board of Lady Managers is Mary Oldham Eagle Kavanaugh, ed., *The Congress of Women, World's Columbian Exposition* (Chicago, 1894); white women represented the women of the "colored" nations.

editorial appearing in a St. Louis newspaper. At Miss Brown's instigation, the women attending organized under one club calling themselves the National Federation of Afro-American women. Mrs. Booker T. Washington was elected president.[5]

The excitement of the July 29-31, 1895 meeting in Boston is sugested in the women's heady call for a repeat. This time no doubt influenced by both a sense of dramatics and a heartfelt need to continually reaffirm their sisterhood, they issued a call for a Congress of Colored Women for December of that same year. Their symbolism was geographically and historically fitting. They would meet in Atlanta, at the Atlanta Exposition. Mrs. Lillian Thomas Fox, Indianapolis clubwoman, attended and spoke at the meeting. Thus began a period of activism on behalf of black women in Indiana.[6] It Happened slowly, but happen it did. This was predictable, given the momentous epoch-making Atlanta meeting. Two things of great significance occurred. With New Yorker Victoria Earle Matthews presiding as chairperson of the executive committee of the Congress of Colored Women, the Federation signalled a widening of women's concerns outside their homes and local communities. While they reaffirmed their commitment to moral reform, the needy, rescue work, mother, child and home, they committed themselves to fight racist laws and practices (i.e., the separate car law). In their newfound confidence they promised themselves representation at the coming International Exposition in Paris (1900). These women shared their experiences of riding Jim Crow cars to attend the meeting and perhaps this more than anything brought them face to face with reality. They voiced their intent to create an Afro-American Women's paper. Perhaps now Miss Brown enjoyed her Parthian shot directed at the Chicago Board of Lady Managers that had called its affair "The Congress of Women" though Afro-American women were conspicuously absent. The Atlanta Congress of Colored Women was the first congress of black women in the United States and at that time possibly in the world. This little-known historical fact provides compelling evidence that the first grassroots all black mass women organized and led movement for social and political good happened among black women. Their efforts while directed at black women were not without wider implications for the masses of blacks as punctuated by their experiences with Jim Crow laws on their way to Atlanta. Never again would black women allow their work to remain isolated and privatized.

In this spirit did Miss Georgia A. Nance, Evansville, Indiana's president of the Young Ladies Trilby Club, attend the first annual (1896) meeting of the National Federation of Afro-American Women held in Washington, D.C. She paid two dollars as a delegate from Indiana.[7] Much happened on the order of

1141

---

[5] See Davis, op. cit., for historical account. Club reports contained a wealth of information, enough to provide a chronology for this essay.
[6] The various activities of the Indiana clubwomen is a matter of historical record as the Davis volume is interspersed with the names of Indiana delegates. From Evansville (southern Indiana) to South Bend (northern Indiana) the various buildings erected and supported solely by membership dues still remain to this day.
[7] See Davis, op. cit., for a recorded list of the various Indiana officers and delegates.

the Atlanta Congress. But the young Miss Nance must have been deeply impressed by the Federation's desire to represent all women. In recognition of the fact that the Federation was too closely identified with the club affiliations of Ruffin and Brown, the Federation decided to rename itself the National Association of Colored Women. This spirit of compromise and democratic principle provided the impetus for what happened in Indiana some eight years later.

Although Mrs. Josephine B. Bruce of Indianapolis served as First Vice-President of the second biennial meeting of the Association, held in Chicago, Illinois in 1899-1901, it was the already-mentioned Lillian Thomas Fox who made certain that Indiana women's voices were heard and that the concerns of black women in Indiana be given a prominence heretofore lacking. In the spirit of the Atlanta Congress, Fox issued a call to black women of Indiana. It is fair to say that Indiana's black women's activist history had begun when forty-two delegates arrived at Bethel A.M.E. Church in Indianapolis on April 27, 1904. They united under one federation — the Indiana Association of Colored Women's Club. With Mrs. Fox presiding, Mrs. Herrold was elected president. Their first annual meeting, held in Marion, Indiana on April 26-27, 1905, with Mrs. Herrold presiding and reelected, revealed their concerns to be both modest and laudable. Their aims were: (1) to show the world what black women had accomplished under the most adverse circumstances; (2) to dedicate their lives to serving the less fortunate ("lifting as they climb"), and (3) to give strength to each other through their mutual cooperation. Subsequent presidents included, in 1907 Mrs. Minnie Scott of Anderson, Indiana; in 1914 Mrs. Gertrude B. Hill of Indianapolis; and in 1921 one of the most popular, both at home and abroad, Mrs. Sallie Wyatt Stewart of Evansville, Indiana. Mrs. Stewart was followed by Carrie Crump of Indianapolis and Mrs. Bessie C. Jones of West Baden.[8]

The growth of the Indiana federation was nothing short of phenomenal. By 1933, it represented some fifty-six clubs and a membership of two thousand. Its budget easily exceeded twenty thousand dollars. The women in the federation represented various professions. They were teachers and hairdressers mostly. But they were also various and sundry business representatives, bookkeepers, ministers, barbers, modistes, juvenile court officers, steam launderers, grocers, stenographers, real estate agents, insurance agents, attorneys and various self-employed who called themselves cake specialists, agriculturists, and manufacturers of hair preparations. They represented some forty-nine cities in Indiana. Literally, they came from all over Indiana. No city was too small. Billionairess Madame C. J. Walker of Indianapolis would participate at both the local and national levels. Frequently, she gave tours of her mansion. She talked about strategies and problems of the black businesswoman. The interstate and intrastate supportive network between women compares with anything known today. The businesswoman Madame C. J. Walker and Mary McLeod Bethune were women united in a common cause. This alone was significant.

1142

---

[8] See Davis, op. cit..

The significance and relevance of the Indiana Association of Colored Women's Clubs are to be seen in the visibility that it gave to heretofore existent scattered and unaffiliated clubs. This resulted in network building that exposed women not only to a larger community of Indiana women, but it also provided a common forum for the systematic study of the conditions under which women lived. It gave an importance to the club work of black women that had been unknown, and brought to public attention neglected areas of women's concerns. The federation, unlike any one club, had the benefit of the combined strength of women united as one. To this end it could far more credibly reflect and validate black women's responses to sociopolitical realities, enabling them to incorporate necessary features of self-help, self-pride, and self-respect in keeping with previous activities of moral and social reform. The latter would be especially important given the recent experience of black women under slavery and beginning efforts to institutionalize racism.[9]

1143

Perhaps more importantly than all of these, the Indiana Association signified the recognition on behalf of black women in Indiana that the changing reality of late nineteenth and early twentieth century society created a welcome imperative for a united effort of women to meet the changing needs of a rapidly increasing industrialized nation. Given the fact that in ever-increasing numbers black women were getting college eductions (careers outside the marriage confines) and entering industries, the federation's timing was a bit delayed if anything. Working side by side with men in factories and industries, women were doing what had once been called "men's work." Their emergence from the home to the larger world (of work and of travel) and their shifts in roles were reflected in the programmatic concerns of the Indiana federation. A look at their publication reveals a distinct shift from "mother's meetings" and the "plantation woman" to home-making classes, research, statistics, suffrage, anti-lynching committees, domestic work and women in industry. It is fair to say that the anti-lynching committees were the most active in the whole of Indiana, and had to be.

The accomplishments of the Indiana Association of Colored Women's Clubs belied its modest aims as is easily seen in the various homes, rescue missions, schools, nurseries and kindergartens that the Association owned and operated. By 1933, they owned over nineteen thousand dollars' worth of property. A cursory look at their success is a challenge to any social service today. If there are accolades to be given, the role of the church cannot be overlooked. The churches, in the very beginning, provided meeting places for these women. What the clubs single-handedly achieved themselves was the intellectual stimulation they provided black women. Specifically, black women

---

[9] This becomes all the more understandable as one understands the history of Indiana as regards race relations. At best, Indiana was a bundle of contradictions: a haven for the mulatto progeny of slavemasters, an area as homophobic as dixie as regards the presence of blacks; its restrictive codes were among the severest anywhere (Klan activity to this day is quite strong), and a humanistic pocket where the Society of Friends and antislavery persons joined in mutual comraderie with blacks. Hoosier law ('lynch law') made it necessary for black clubwomen in Indiana to forego the tea to tackle the faggot.

presented position papers on such topics as WCTU, "The Status of the Afro-American Woman Before and After the War," and topics related to women in industry, labor laws, compulsory education laws among others. The noted clubwoman, Mrs. Mary Church Terrell, is nationally known for her speech-making powers that were cultivated in such milieu. Temperance seemed to have been a specific concern inasmuch as these club women noted a direct relation between a broken home, alcoholic husband-father and wife and child abuse. Clearly, early feminism was directly concerned with the preservation of the family and provides a provocative lesson, that charity ought to be at home, that a woman's humanity has to be guaranteed at home before it can begin elsewhere.

1144   Although black women in Indiana were active participants and aptly represented in the National Association of Colored Women from its inception, this fact was never more aptly demonstrated than in the late twenties and early thirties. It was through The Indiana Association's past President Mrs. Sallie Wyatt Stewart of Evansville that Indiana reached its zenith of representation in the national organization. Mrs. Stewart went as an Indiana delegate to the National Association meeting in Denver, Colorado in 1918. After that meeting she served continuously in office in the National Association, for four years as Chairperson of the Social Science Department, for two years as chairperson of the executive board, for four years as vice president at large and for five years (1928-1933) as president, and thereafter as an honorary one.

Mrs. Stewart's contribution to the National Association of Colored Women was reflective of her business acumen as a real estate agent and teacher in the Evansville Public Schools. She organized the National along lines of fiscal soundness, creating a board of control that had charge of all finances related to the National. Mrs. Stewart insisted on record-keeping and business methods in the interest of accountability and sound organization. Her plan for reorganization[10] (which was eventually adopted) called for the abolishment of a proliferative number of departments (at the time there were twenty-seven) to concentrate on two departments: (1) Mother, Home and Child, and (2) Black Women in Industry. Mrs. Stewart's singular success was in having systematically reorganized the National Association of Colored Women in plans of action (program priority over fund-raising) and in methods of working.

The accomplishments of Mrs. Stewart alone and what she did for Evansville in the area of high school curriculum and social services for blacks is as yet unwritten history. The relevance of this study is not what any one woman did but rather the documenting of the power and the presence of a group of women who found each other even as they were finding themselves.[11] Today's

---

[10] See "Indiana Chapter," in *Davis*, op. cit.. Various archival holdings (Bennett College, North Carolina; Spingarn Moorland at Howard University; The Schomburg Collection; the James Weldon Johnson Collection at Yale University contain a wealth of information on specific women members. See Note 3, and bibliographical reference on periodicals.

[11] The women's club movement was not without the problems endemic to women's movement in the late nineteenth century. The myth of white Anglo-Saxon Protestant superiority manifested itself among these women who on occasion were very much complexion conscious. The rivalry between Mary Church Terrell and Mary McCleod Bethune was not without a color-complexion bias. Furthermore, club women saw "the plantation woman" as a distinctly inferior breed. The social science journals of the day proliferated with articles on the connection between inferior genes, a "bad" environment, and the criminal (read black, read poor) classes. It is the felt and real accomplishments of this group that prompt this essay.

generations of black men and women might do well to note that affirmative action was begun with early black feminism. The Women in Industry department agitated for wholesome work conditions, shorter working hours, better wages, insurance coverage and unemployment compensation. Their attempts at professionalizing the workplace included systematic studies and surveys; they inventoried employers and called mass meetings when necessary. In a word, the history of black feminism in Indiana is a record of acting out of sheer faith that the good in humanity will triumph.

1145

Carrie Still Shepperson:
The Hollows of Her Footsteps

By JUDITH ANNE STILL (Mrs. Judy Anne Headlee)*

26892 Preciados Drive, Mission Viejo, California 92691

"Hath not a Jew ahs," drawled a slender, walnut-skinned Negro boy, holding a large volume of Shakespeare out in front of him.

"Not ahs, . . . *eyes*," interrupted the teacher firmly. "And do stand straighter, young man."

"Yes'm, Mrs. Shepperson," answered the boy, then squared his shoulders purposefully.

Neither the teen-age Shylock nor any of his classmates sitting on the sidelines cared to defy the directions of their teacher, Mrs. Shepperson. Her word was law.

---

*The author is the daughter of William Grant Still and business manager for William Grant Still Music, and a free-lance writer. She is the widow of geologist and mini-submarine expert, Larry Allyn Headlee, and the mother of four children. She has been an instructor of college English and a personal correspondent for the actress Ann-Margaret. This article has been previously published in *Forum* magazine, University of Houston, Texas, XV (Spring 1977), 60-65.

At the present time, William Grant Still Music is engaged in the process of donating to the University of Arkansas the private papers and memorabilia of the noted Little Rock composer, William Grant Still. Still was the first Negro to conduct a major symphony orchestra in the United States, when in 1936 he directed the Los Angeles Philharmonic Orchestra in his own compositions in the Hollywood Bowl. He was the first black man to conduct a major symphony orchestra in the Deep South, when in 1955 he directed the New Orleans Philharmonic Symphony Orchestra at Southern University. He was the first of his race to conduct a white radio orchestra in New York City. He was the first to have an opera produced by a major company in the United States, when in 1949 *Troubled Island* was performed at the City Center of Music and Drama in New York City. He wrote 150 compositions in all, including operas, ballets, chamber works, symphonies, and arrangements of folk themes, especially Negro spirituals. In 1971 he was awarded an honorary doctoral degree by the University of Arkansas.

Originally published in *The Arkansas Historical Quarterly*, Vol. XLII, No. 1 (Spring 1983).

The time? The first decade of the twentieth century in Little Rock, Arkansas. The milieu? Brick and frame schools near small businesses, theaters, blacksmith shops, and cane fields. Sun-bonneted ladies, water-melons selling for five cents each, and the bodies of the Negro and white bandits displayed, bullet ridden, in the funeral parlor window.

Of the two colored English teachers who were teaching at the all-Negro M. W. Gibbs High School, Mrs. Shepperson was the more strict and more beloved. It was not only that she helped the students to put on Shakespearean plays so that they could earn money for a library; it was not only that she taught them to sing and to do fine needlework and to use perfect grammar; it was also that she believed in the abilities of her students to handle all of these difficult tasks. She always looked at them circumspectly, as if she knew how much more they could do if they only worked long enough and hard enough.

Her name, before she married Charles Shepperson, was Carrie Lena Fambro Still. Though she was an Afro-American, her features were not essentially Negroid. She had mulatto skin and penetrating dark eyes beneath low-slung eyebrows. She had coal black, Spanish hair, worn parted in the middle, long in back, and fluffed around an aristocratic forehead. Her lower lip was set, as if it were riveted to the middle of her jaw.

Those who remember her, oddly enough, have difficulty describing her. They say that she was attractive, that she was of medium height, straight of stature, and that her voice was cultured. Beyond that, they will say only that, when she walked into a room, everyone snapped to attention. Like Melville's Ahab, she was magnetic and predominant.

She exercised discipline fully and without favoritism. Her only son was in her class at school, and in order not to appear that she indulged him above the other students, she was often more severe with him than with the others. Once when he was reading Chaucer aloud to the class, he laughed coarsely at the word "dung." Without warning, his mother's ruler came down on his wrists. Then, when he pouted, she snapped, "Pull in that lip, young man."

The boy had met his match in his mother, in spite of his precocious and stubborn nature. He seldom got away with dipping pigtails in ink-wells, or throwing crayons at poor Professor Gillam — and only once did he play hookey to watch the trains pass through town. In fact, some-

1148

times he was even punished for the pranks of his friend, Leander Mc-Dowell. Leander was fond of putting tacks and water on chairs of both teachers and students.

Speaking of Mrs. Shepperson in later years, her son has said, laughing, "She had an educated whipping strap. If I crawled under the bed to escape, the strap curled under ahead of me."

But the discipline kept the mischievous child in tow, and he became valedictorian of his class and, afterwards, one of the most important composers in America. In fact, much has been written about Carrie Fambro's son, William Grant Still, the dean of Negro composers — the man whose opera was promoted by Eleanor Roosevelt and Mayor Fiorello LaGuardia, and the first man of color to conduct a major symphony orchestra in the Deep South. Little, however, is really known of his mother.

1149

Recently an educational filmstrip was made about Still for the elementary schools, picturing Carrie Still as a simple homebody, clad in an apron cooking wonderful meals in the kitchen while young Still and Mr. Shepperson listened to the latest pre-1910 classical recordings. But the image was false. Carrie was no Hattie McDaniel. Her attempts to cook always resulted in disaster — like the time that she seasoned a roast with bluing. She was fortunate that she had her mother, Anne Fambro, to prepare meals for the family.[1]

Of course, her lack of culinary talent did not concern her overmuch. She had too many things to interest her outside of the kitchen. Most significantly, she did not give over any of the cares of child upbringing to the grandmother. When little William was impish, and the grandmother tried to tell the daughter that it was his "Injun blood" showing, Carrie just frowned at her and dealt with him in her own stalwart fashion.

She was firm with her son because she saw that he was a handsome, sensitive lad with great genius. She knew that he was vulnerable to those who would prey upon his sensitivity and his genius, and that, without habituation to difficulties, he would soon lose heart. As William Still himself put it later on,

---

[1] Anne Fambro took her last name from the slaveowners in whose house she lived in Atlanta, Georgia.

In shaping my attitudes, my mother had a most important role to play. She was constantly "molding my character," trying to keep me from "following the path of least resistance," impressing on me the fact that I *must* amount to something in the world. . . . She gave me chores to do: cutting the kindling and the wood, bringing it and the coal indoors; starting the fires every morning; sweeping the house. When in high school I wanted long trousers like the other boys, I had to go to work to pay for them. My mother could easily have given them to me, but it was part of her discipline to let me earn them.[2]

1150

In addition to the stress on physical output, Carrie worked on vocabulary building, pronunciation, and grammar. She said that good English could help her son to reach people who were worth reaching and who would not listen otherwise. She made sure that he, and his fellow students, always said "get," not "git," and "she and I," not "her and me." For all of his life Still could tell why, grammatically, one cannot say, "It is me," instead of "It is I." And he could tell how such knowledge opened doors for him in the field of serious music.

Knowledge and talent had opened doors for Carrie too. She was born on June 15, 1872, in Milner, Georgia, the daughter of a light-skinned plantation owner from Florida, and Anne Fambro, a light coffee-colored Negro-Choctaw house servant. Her Spanish father was fond of his charming, sagacious daughter, and saw that she was well-dressed and educated in the arts of embroidery, painting, music, and language.

From the first she showed signs of fierce pride. If some hapless child in her Georgia neighborhood made derogatory remarks about her "half-breed" origins, she was more than likely to beat him soundly. Then, after the conflict, she would tell her mother without shame, "I *won't* take anything from anybody."

And she never did.

Deciding that she wanted to teach, she went to Atlanta University. Then, with degree in hand, a trim and handsome teacher of English, she took a position in Alabama. It was not too long afterwards that she

---

[2] Robert B. Haas, ed., *William Grant Still and the Fusion of Cultures in American Music* (Los Angeles, 1972), 76.

Carrie Still Shepperson

1151

William Grant Still, Sr.

Judith Anne Still Headlee

William Grant Still

met William Grant Still, Sr., who was also a teacher.

Racially, Still was a Negro-Scotch-Irish-Indian, with a fine Harry Belafonte face and a smartly-trimmed mustache, good hair, and a broadleafed mouth. Most important, he was a man of spirit. In his early twenties he had protested the fact that Negro teachers were paid less than whites, and was burned out of a one-room schoolhouse. On the same occasion, a friend of his was shot. The incident did not deter him, however, from his interest in teaching.

When he and Carrie met, they were immediately drawn to each other by the similarity in their natures — their mutual sense of the justice of things and their common ability to combat hostility. Still, however, had to dissolve a relationship with another woman in order to woo and wed Carrie. The other woman, who was of a servant mentality, was jealous and bitter, and vowed revenge. In spite of her threats, Carrie became Mrs. Still on June 26, 1894, and the mother to the son, William, on May 11, 1895. But the marriage was not destined to survive. Mysteriously, the elder Still died suddenly when his son was only a few months old. Rumor had it that the rejected lover had taken her revenge with poison.

1153

So Carrie was a bride, a mother, and a widow almost within a year. Deeply within herself she grieved. But outwardly, she set her lip and promised her baby that he would never suffer materially for the loss of a parent. She considered going to live near her father — he had sent word from his Florida plantation that he wanted her to come. He promised her a home and an orange grove.

Carrie wanted to go, but she had her son to consider. Little William was not as fair as his mother and father. He was readily identifiable as a colored person. If he and his mother lived in Florida, they would have to put up with the Florida "Jim Crow" laws, which were possibly more stringent than racial restrictions in other areas of the South.

Carrie would not give up her dignity in order to have an easy life; once again her pride and high temper won out. She said of her son, "He's not a stereotyped Negro, or Indian, or Scotch-Irishman. He's an American, in the finest sense of the word. He must never let anyone take away his humanity with a label."

Ultimately, she went to Little Rock, Arkansas, to try to earn a living. She and her son moved in with their Aunt Laura at 912 West 14th Street, two miles from the main part of town.[3] Little Rock was a rural city then; it had a "downtown" area, but it also had many open lots dotted with grazing cattle, as well as cane fields on the outskirts of the houses.

Carrie, through her teaching, was able to purchase the house in which they were living — a fine, two-story gray frame house, with shingles and a broad front porch, standing in a middle-class interracial neighborhood. Oddly enough, interracial neighborhoods were not unusual in the South in the early part of the century. Only in recent years has the idea become current that blacks in the South have always lived to themselves in poverty and ignorance and bitterness.

1154

The truth was that Carrie and her son, and her mother who came to live with them, were not ignorant, poor, or hated. They co-existed peacefully with their neighbors, and among their neighbors were people of all races. In fact, down the street lived a German boy named Billheimer who was later to become president of Silverwoods. Also nearby was the house of a white boy named Allan, who, like Leander McDowell, was always to be a devoted friend of William Still.

And yet there was more to it than co-existence. The good life that they came to enjoy was also the result of Carrie's many community services and exemplary talents. In the hot summers she went into the back-woods of Arkansas to thatched one-room school houses of places like Olmstead, a small community northwest of Jacksonville, to teach. There, where barefoot boys and scorpions both tried to make places for themselves in a world of naivetè and raw courage, she taught the people to say "fire" instead of "far," and "sit" instead of "set."

When the summers were over, Carrie returned to bring culture to Little Rock. She spearheaded the formation of a Lotus Club, or literary group, whose members read the classics and the latest "best sellers," and discussed the books at meetings. Carrie's fondness for her Lotus Club work even led her to write a book herself, which has since been lost. The manuscript, done in her beautiful scroll-like penmanship, concerned the prejudices against Negroes and women in her day.

Besides being an author, she was also a musician. An accomplished pianist, she formed and directed a group of spiritual singers. Sometimes

---

[3] This was Laura Oliver Hyatt.

she filled the neighborhood with music when she led her family in song out on the front porch on warm evenings. Sometimes she wrote little songs for the children to sing at school and in church.

At other times she taught fine embroidery to young girls, and won prizes for her beautiful needlework at the fair. Her own wardrobe was enriched with the high-fashion garments that she created, some in silk and taffeta, and most with the leg-of-mutton sleeves and high collars of the day. She did not care too much for bustles, and her favorite dress was a blue-lavender with delicate flowers on it.

In her spare time she painted china. Today only one piece of her hand-painted china remains — a beautiful double-handled sugar bowl. Its shades of misty green and blue-gray materialize mystically out of a white, gold-trimmed background, and evolve into a string of orchids around the middle of the bowl.

1155

Because Carrie was talented, thorough, and well-proportioned, she soon had many suitors. And yet she was a lady to be treated with respect. Once when a saucy streetcar conductor took the liberty of calling her by her first name, she confronted him angrily and would not let the car continue until she had received his apology.

Eventually, of course, she found a good man. She married a well-fixed postal employee named Charles B. Shepperson on November 27, 1904. Charles Shepperson was a man who loved the arts and appreciated classical music. He was destined to introduce his stepson to the best in serious classical recordings and in Arkansas theatrical productions.

Once married, Carrie Shepperson's financial status was enough enhanced that she was able to pursue the goal dearest to her heart: the financing of a library for the colored people in Little Rock.

Carrie felt that the most important thing for people to have in a growing culture — besides freedom — was education. But in those days, though Negro and white usually lived together amicably, the slave era was still near enough in memory that no white person thought it necessary to make books available to the nonwhite population. Negroes could buy books, but not borrow them.

So Carrie ordered and paid for theater costumes, through a mail order catalogue, and in a fall semester started her students rehearsing plays to enact before the citizens of Little Rock. Her son William played

Little Hiawatha in one of the first dramatic productions. He remembered his disappointment when his Indian dance did not draw the penny-tossing applause that another boy received when he sang "Back to Baltimore."

Later his mother helped the high school students to produce the *Merchant of Venice* and *A Midsummer Night's Dream,* leading them staunchly through the intricacies of Shakespeare's vocabulary. Tickets sold well for all of these productions, and soon the anxiously-awaited library was set up within the confines of Capitol Hill School.

The students and the other townspeople were satisfied with the library, with the Shakespeare, and with the unflagging cultural pride of Carrie Shepperson. Further, they were fond of the English teacher for her other qualities. She could laugh on occasion. She laughed when little Will sneaked some homemade sherbet in the kitchen and tried, bug-eyed, to conceal a mouthful of the icy stuff when she came in. She laughed with Charles Shepperson too. Once when she was playing a very tedious piano piece called the "Burning of Rome," Shepperson hauled in a large pail of water and set it by the piano.

"What's that for?" she asked, surprised.

"To put the fire out," was the answer.

She smiled about that the rest of the day.

She might have smiled also had she heard some of the comments that are made today about the people of her time. "Negroes seventy-five years ago were ignorant, and were not allowed to develop their talents." "White men built America." She would probably tell anyone who made such statements that the nation-builders were not all white, and that they were not all men. And then she would demand that the misguided apologize for their ignorance.

Indeed, it was Carrie who had tried to teach her son about nation-building. Although she insisted that he be a top scholar, and nurtured his love for music by sending him to violin lessons regularly, she hoped that he would use his intellect to become a doctor of medicine rather than a musician. Negro musicians in her time were commonly thought to be an immoral lot, and she hoped for better things for him.

Young Still, wanting above all to please her, went to Wilberforce

University to study medicine for four years. And yet the lure of the musical world was too strong. He made it clear to her that he had to realize his desires, and she understood. She told him always to follow the inner sense of dignity that great men keep within themselves, and, when in need of real help, to turn to the Ninety-first Psalm for strength.

For He will deliver thee from the snare of the fowler, . . .
And under his wings shalt thou take refuge:
His truth is a shield and a buckler. . . .

So he tucked the Psalm and his mother's faith in among the keepsakes of his soul, and went off to Boston and to New York to begin a musical career with W. C. Handy, Paul Whiteman, Artie Shaw, and Edgar Varese.

While Still was in the East, he received word that his mother had cancer and was not expected to live. He returned to Little Rock just in time to be with her at the last. He found her hair whitened and her eyes weakened by the illness. Although she was in a great deal of pain, she expressed maternal anxiety over her son's vulnerability to greedy, deceptive people. She cautioned him to take care of his material and spiritual inheritance. Then she died.

She left him a solid square block of twelve houses in the center of Little Rock,[4] some emerald jewelry, a pinkish-ivory cameo brooch, a watch pin, her painted china, and the book she had written. As it turned out, her worries about her son's credulous nature were prophetic. He subsequently lost all of these things that she had willed to him to a dishonest aunt, a capricious first wife, and an avaricious property manager. He was much too busy with his music to care for his possessions properly. Only one thing remained that had been hers: the uncompromising moral strength and integrity to overcome the prejudices and jealousies that would confront him in his lifetime.

---

[4] This block of houses was said to be on Ninth Street between Cross and Ringo streets in Little Rock. Melba McDowell, who lived in Little Rock, told Verna Arvey (Mrs. William Grant Still, and the author's mother) that Carrie Shepperson owned all twelve houses at her death. However, when questioned recently, Josie Gilkey, a classmate of William Grant Still who now lives in Los Angeles, California, insisted that some of the property was disposed of prior to Carrie's death, leaving the son just a row of houses.

Carrie Lena Fambro died on May 18, 1927,[5] at the same time that Lindbergh made his historic flight across the Atlantic. And, like Lindbergh's, the force of her influence has extended over the years. William Grant Still, returning to Mississippi in 1974 for the successful presentation of his opera, *Bayou Legend,* thought of his mother once again in "the quiet gentleness of respect and grateful love."

We too can know fine people by the mystic aura that their incredible spirits spread over the decades. We can know Carrie Shepperson — we can look at her orchid-wreathed, sea-green china and feel her sense of purpose and dedication — and yet we may fall like sand into the hollows of her footsteps. For there was something in the quiet majesty of her mind, and in the splendid rigidity of her soul that somehow went into the making of the nation.

1158

---

[5] Carrie Shepperson was buried in a perpetual care grave in the Fraternal Cemetery in Little Rock. She was laid to rest next to her husband, C. B. Shepperson, who had died years earlier of drowning.

Discontented Black Feminists: Prelude and Postscript to the Passage of the Nineteenth Amendment

ROSALYN TERBORG-PENN

A significant number of black women and black women's organizations not only supported woman suffrage on the eve of the passage of the Nineteenth Amendment but attempted to exercise their rights to vote immediately after the amendment's passage in 1920. Unfortunately for them, black women confronted racial discrimination in their efforts to support the amendment and to win the vote. Consequently, discontented black feminists anticipated the disillusionment that their white counterparts encountered after 1920. An examination of the problems black women faced on the eve of the passage of the woman suffrage amendment and the hostility black women voters endured after the amendment passed serves as a preview of their political status from 1920 to 1945.

1159

The way in which black women leaders dealt with these problems reveals the unique nature of feminism among Afro-American women. Black feminists could not overlook the reality of racism and class conflict as determining factors in the lives of women of their race. Hence, black feminists of the post-World War I era exhibited characteristics similar to those of black feminists of the woman suffrage era and of the late nineteenth-century black women's club movement. During each era, these feminists could not afford to dismiss class or race in favor of sex as the major cause of oppression among black women.

Prelude to Passage of the Nineteenth Amendment

On the eve of the passage of the Nineteenth Amendment, black women leaders could be counted among other groups of women who had worked diligently for woman suffrage. At least ninety black women leaders endorsed woman suffrage, with two-thirds of these women giving support during the decade immediately before passage of the amendment. Afro-American women organized suffrage clubs, participated in rallies and demonstrations, spoke on behalf of the amendment, and wrote essays in support of the cause. These things they had done since the inception of the nineteenth-century woman's rights movement. However, the largest woman suffrage effort among black women's groups occurred during the second decade of the twentieth century. Organizations such as the National Federation of Afro-American Women, the National Association of Colored

Originally published in *Decades of Discontent: The Woman's Movement, 1920-1940*, Lois Scharf and Joan M. Jensen, eds. (Westport: Greenwood Press, 1983).

Women (NACW), the Northeastern Federation of Colored Women's Clubs, the Alpha Kappa Alpha Sorority, and the Delta Sigma Theta Sorority actively supported woman suffrage. These organizations were national or regional in scope and represented thousands of Afro-American women. Some of the women were from the working class, but most of them were of middle-class status. Across the nation, at least twenty black women suffrage organizations or groups that strongly endorsed woman suffrage existed during the period.[1]

Three examples provide an indication of the diversity in types of woman suffrage activities among black women's organizations. In 1915 the Poughkeepsie, New York, chapter of the Household of Ruth, a working-class, black women's group, endorsed woman suffrage by sending a resolution to the New York branch of the National Woman's Party (NWP) in support of the pending state referendum on woman suffrage. With the need for an intelligent female electorate in mind, black women of Texas organized voter leagues in 1917, the year Texas women won the right to vote. Among these was the Negro Women Voters' League of Galveston. Furthermore, in 1919, the Northeastern Federation of Colored Women's Clubs, representing thousands of women from Montreal to Baltimore, petitioned the National American Woman Suffrage Association (NAWSA) for membership.[2]

The enthusiastic responses of black women to woman suffrage may seem astonishing when one realizes that woman suffrage was a predominantly middle-class movement among native born white women and that the black middle class was very small during the early twentieth century. Furthermore, the heyday of the woman suffrage movement embraced an era that historian Rayford Logan called "the nadir" in Afro-American history, characterized by racial segregation, defamation of the character of black women, and lynching of black Americans, both men and women. It is a wonder that Afro-American women dared to dream a white man's dream — the right to enfranchisement — especially at a time when white women attempted to exclude them from that dream.[3]

The existence of a double standard for black and white women among white woman suffragists was apparent to black women on the eve of Nineteenth Amendment passage. Apprehensions from discontented black leaders about the inclusion of black women as voters, especially in the South, were evident throughout the second decade of the twentieth century. During the early years of the decade, black suffragists such as Adella Hunt Logan, a club leader and suffragist from Tuskegee, Alabama; Mary B. Talbert, president of the National Association of Colored Women; and Josephine St. Pierre Ruffin, a suffragist since the 1880s from Boston and the editor of the *Woman's Era*, a black women's newspaper, complained about the double standard in the woman suffrage movement and insisted that white suffragists set aside their prejudices to allow black women, burdened by both sexism and racism, to gain political equality.[4]

1160

Unfortunately, with little influence among white women, the black suffragists were powerless and their words went unheeded. By 1916 Carrie Catt, president of the NAWSA, concluded that the South had to be conciliated if woman suffrage was to become a reality. Thus, in order to avoid antagonizing southern white women who resented participating in the association with black women, she urged southern white delegates not to attend the NAWSA convention in Chicago that year because the Chicago delegation would be mostly black.[5]

The trend to discriminate against black women as voters continued, and in 1917 the *Crisis*, the official organ of the National Association for the Advancement of Colored People (NAACP), noted that blacks feared white female voters because of their antiblack woman suffrage and antiblack male sentiments. Afro-American fears went beyond misgivings about white women. In 1918 the editors of the *Houston Observer* responded to black disillusionment when they called upon the men and women of the race to register to vote in spite of the poll tax, which was designed especially to exclude black voters.[6]

Skepticism about equality of woman suffrage among blacks continued. Mrs. A. W. Blackwell, an African Methodist Episcopal church leader in Atlanta, estimated that about 3 million black women were of voting age. She warned, however, that a "grandmother clause" would be introduced after passage of a suffrage amendment to prevent black women, 90 percent of whom lived in the South, from voting.[7]

Disillusionment among black suffragists became so apparent that several national suffrage leaders attempted to appease them with reassurances about their commitment to black woman suffrage. In 1917 Carrie Catt and Anna Shaw wooed black female support through the pages of the *Crisis*. In the District of Columbia, the same year, Congresswoman Jeanette Rankin of Montana addressed an enthusiastic group of Alpha Kappa Alpha Sorority women at Howard University. There she assured the group that she wanted all women to be given the ballot regardless of race.[8]

However, in 1917 while the New York state woman suffrage referendum was pending in the legislature, black suffragists in the state complained of discrimination against their organizations by white suffragists during the statewide woman suffrage convention at Saratoga. White leaders assured black women that they were welcomed in the movement. Although the majority of the black delegates were conciliated, a vocal minority remained disillusioned.[9]

By 1919, the year before the Nineteenth Amendment was adopted by Congress, antiblack woman suffrage sentiments continued to plague the movement. Shortly before the amendment was adopted, several incidents occurred to further disillusion black feminists. Mary Church Terrell, a Washington, D.C., educator and national leader among black club women, reported that white suffragists in Florida discriminated against black

1161

women in their attempts to recruit support for the campaign. In addition, the NAACP, whose policy officially endorsed woman suffrage, clashed with Alice Paul, president of the NWP because she allegedly said "that all this talk of Negro women voting in South Carolina was nonsense."[10] Later, Walter White, the NAACP's assistant to the executive secretary, complained to Mary Church Terrell about Alice Paul and agreed with Terrell that white suffrage leaders would be willing to accept the suffrage amendment even if it did not enfranchise black women.[11]

Within a week after receiving Walter White's letter, Mary Church Terrell received a letter from Ida Husted Harper, a leader in the suffrage movement and the editor of the last two volumes of the *History of Woman Suffrage*, asking Terrell to use her influence to persuade the Northeastern Federation of Colored Women's Clubs to withdraw their application seeking cooperative membership in the NAWSA. Echoing sentiments expressed earlier by NAWSA president Carrie Catt, Harper explained that accepting the membership of a black organization was inexpedient for NAWSA at a time when white suffragists sought the cooperation of white southern women. Harper noted that the major obstacle to the amendment in the South was fear among whites of the black woman's vote. She therefore asked federation president Elizabeth Carter to resubmit the membership application after the passage of the Nineteenth Amendment.[12]

At its Jubilee Convention in Saint Louis in March 1919, the NAWSA officially catered to the fears of their southern white members. In response to a proposal by Kentucky suffragist Laura Clay that sections of the so-called Susan B. Anthony amendment that would permit the enfranchisement of black women be changed, the convention delegates agreed that the amendment should be worded so as to allow the South to determine its own position on the black female vote.[13]

During the last months before the passage of the Susan B. Anthony amendment, black suffragists had been rebuffed by both the conservative wing of the suffrage movement, the NAWSA, and by the more radical wing, the NWP. Why then did Afro-American women continue to push for woman suffrage? Since the 1880s, most black women who supported woman suffrage did so because they believed that political equality among the races would raise the status of blacks, both male and female. Increasing the black electorate, they felt, would not only uplift the women of the race, but help the children and the men as well. The majority of the black suffragists were not radical feminists. They were reformers, or what William H. Chafe calls social feminists, who believed that the system could be amended to work for them. Like their white counterparts, these black suffragists assumed that the enfranchised held the key to ameliorating social ills. But unlike white social feminists, many black suffragists called for social and political measures that were specifically tied to race issues. Among these issues were antimiscegenation legislation, jim crow

1162

legislation, and "lynch law." Prominent black feminists combined the fight against sexism with the fight against racism by continuously calling the public's attention to these issues. Ida B. Wells-Barnett, Angelina Weld Grimke, and Mary Church Terrell spoke out against lynching. Josephine St. Pierre Ruffin and Lottie Wilson Jackson, as well as Terrell and Wells-Barnett took steps to challenge jim crow facilities in public accommodations, and antimiscegenation legislation was impugned by Terrell, Grimke, and Wells-Barnett.[14]

Blacks understood the potential political influence, if not political power, that they could harness with woman suffrage, especially in the South. White supremacists realized it too. Although there were several reasons for southern opposition to the Nineteenth Amendment, the one common to all states was fear of black female suffrage. This fear had been stimulated by the way in which Afro-American women responded to suffrage in states that had achieved woman suffrage before the passage of the federal amendment. In northern states with large black populations, such as Illinois and New York, the black female electorate was significant. Chicago elected its first black alderman, Oscar De Priest, in 1915, the year after women won the right to vote. In 1917, the year the woman suffrage referendum passed the New York state legislature, New York City elected its first black state assemblyperson, Edward A. Johnson. In both cities the black female vote was decisive in the election. In the South, Texas Afro-American women mobilized in 1918 to effectively educate the women of their race in order to combat white opposition to their voting.[15]

By 1920 white southern apprehensions of a viable black female electorate were not illusionary. "Colored women voter's leagues" were growing throughout the South, where the task of the leagues was to give black women seeking to qualify to vote instructions for countering white opposition. Leagues could be found in Alabama, Georgia, Tennessee, and Texas. These groups were feared also by white supremacists because the women sought to qualify black men as voters as well.[16]

Whites widely believed that black women wanted the ballot more than white women in the South. Black women were expected to register and to vote in larger numbers than white women. If this happened, the ballot would soon be returned to black men. Black suffrage, it was believed, would also result in the return of the two-party system in the South, because blacks would consistently vote Republican. These apprehensions were realized in Florida after the passage of the Nineteenth Amendment. Black women in Jacksonville registered in greater numbers than white women. In reaction, the Woman Suffrage League of Jacksonville was reorganized into the Duval County League of Democratic Women Voters. The members were dedicated to maintain white supremacy and pledged to register white women voters.[17]

In Texas, where women could vote before the passage of the Nineteenth

1163

Amendment, black women, nevertheless, were discriminated against. In 1918 six black women had been refused the right to register at Forth Worth on the ground that the primaries were open to white Democrats only. Efforts to disfranchise black women in Houston failed, however, when the women took legal action against the registrars who attempted to apply the Texas woman suffrage law to white women only. A similar attempt to disqualify Afro-American women in Waxahachie, Texas, failed also.[18]

1164

Subterfuge and trickery such as the kind used in Texas was being used throughout the South by 1920. In North Carolina, the predictions of Mrs. A. W. Blackwell came true when the state legislature introduced a bill known as the "grandmother clause" for women voters. The bill attempted to protect illiterate white women from disfranchisement, but the legislators had not taken into account that "grandfather clauses" had been nullified by the Supreme Court. Nonetheless, black leaders called to the women of the race to stand up and fight. This they did.[19]

In 1920 black women registered in large numbers throughout the South, especially in Georgia and Louisiana, despite major obstacles placed against them by the white supremacists. In defense, Afro-American women often turned to the NAACP for assistance. Field Secretary William Pickens was sent to investigate the numerous charges and recorded several incidents which he either witnessed personally or about which he received reports. In Columbia, South Carolina, during the first day of registration black women apparently took the registrars by surprise. No plan to disqualify them had been put into effect. Many black women reported to the office and had to wait for hours while the white women were registered first. Some women waited up to twelve hours to register. The next day, a $300 tax requirement was made mandatory for black women. If they passed that test, the women were required to read from and to interpret the state or the federal constitutions. No such tests were required of white women. In addition, white lawyers were on hand to quiz and harass black women. Although the *Columbia State*, a local newspaper, reported disinterest in registering among black women, Pickens testified to the contrary. By the end of the registration period, twenty Columbia black women had signed an affidavit against the registrars who had disqualified them. In the surrounding Richland County, Afro-American women were disqualified when they attempted to register to vote. As a result, several of them made plans to appeal the ruling.[20]

Similar reports came from Richmond, Virginia, where registrars attempted to deny or successfully denied black women the right to register. A black woman of Newburn, North Carolina, signed an affidavit testifying to the difficulty she had in attempting to register. First she was asked to read and to write the entire state constitution. After successfully reading the document, she was informed that no matter what else she did, the registrar would disqualify her because she was black. Many cases like this one were handled by the NAACP, and after the registration periods ended in the South, its board of directors presented the evidence to Congress. NAACP officials and others testified at a congressional hearing in support of the proposed enactment of the Tinkham Bill to reduce representation in Congress from states where there was restriction of woman suffrage. White supremacy prevailed, however, as southern congressmen successfully claimed that blacks were not disfranchised, just disinterested in voting. Hence, despite the massive evidence produced by the NAACP, the Tinkham Bill failed to pass.[21]

The inability of the NAACP to protect the rights of black women voters led the women to seek help from national woman suffrage leaders. However, these attempts failed also. The NWP leadership felt that since black women were discriminated against in the same ways as black men, their problems were not woman's rights issues, but race issues. Therefore, the woman's party felt no obligation to defend the rights of black women.[22]

1165

That they would be abandoned by white female suffragists in 1920 came as no surprise to most black women leaders. The preceding decade of woman suffrage politics had reminded them of the assertions of black woman suffrage supporters of the past. Frederick Douglass declared in 1868 that black women were victimized mainly because they were blacks, not because they were women. Frances Ellen Watkins Harper answered in 1869 that for white women the priorities in the struggle for human rights were sex, not race. By 1920 the situation had changed very little, and many black suffragists had been thoroughly disillusioned by the machinations of the white feminists they had encountered.[23]

Postscript – Black Feminists, 1920-1945

Afro-American Women continued to be involved in local and national politics during the post-World War I years. However, few organized feminist activities were apparent among the disillusioned black feminists of the period. Afro-American women leaders and their organizations began to focus on issues that continued to plague both the men and the women of the race, rather than upon issues that concerned white feminists. The economic plight of black women kept most of them in poverty and among the lowest of the working classes. Middle-class black women were still relatively few in number. They were more concerned about uplifting the downtrodden of the race or in representing people of color throughout the world than in issues that were limited to middle-class feminists. Hence, during the 1920s there was little concern among black women over the Equal Rights Amendment debate between the more conservative League of Women Voters (LWV) and the more radical NWP. Although the economic roles of many white American women were expanding, the status of black women remained basically static between the wars. As a result, black feminists identified more with the plight of third world people who found themselves in similar oppressed situations. Former black suffragists were more likely to participate in the Women's International League for Peace and Freedom (WILPF) or the International Council of Women of the Darker Races than in the LWV or the NWP.

In 1920 Howard University professor Benjamin Brawley examined the economic status of black women. He found that there were over 1 million black females in the United States work force in 1910. Fifty-two percent of them worked as farmers or farm laborers, and 28 percent worked as cooks or washerwomen. In essence, 80 percent of black women workers were doing arduous, menial work. Brawley speculated that conditions had not changed much by 1920.[24] In 1922 black social worker Elizabeth Ross Haynes found that 2 million black women in the nation worked in three types of occupations: domestic and personal service, agriculture, and manufacturing and mechanical industries. Of the 2 million, 50 percent were found in domestic service. Only 20,000 were found in semiskilled jobs in manufacturing and mechanical industries. Haynes's findings in 1922 were in keeping with Brawley's speculations.[25] Unfortunately, by 1945 the position of black women in the work force had not changed significantly. Black women ranked lowest on the economic scale among men and women, black and white.

Geographically, during the period, the black population was shifting from the rural South to the urban North and West. Nearly 90 percent of the adult black female population lived in the South in 1920. By 1930 less than 80 percent of that population did. In 1940 the percentage had dropped to nearly 75 percent.[26] Even with this drop, however, three-fourths of the adult black women of the nation remained in the South, where they were virtually disfranchised. The black women who found their way north and west lacked the political influence necessary to change the status of black women because of their economic powerlessness. What temporary gains black women made in World War I industry quickly faded away during the postwar years.

In 1935 the average weekly wage for a black domestic worker was $3.00 and washerwomen received a mere 75¢ a week. Working conditions, as well as wages, were substandard, and black women were exploited by white women as well as by white men. In observing the working conditions of New York City domestic workers, Louise Mitchell found that standards had not changed much by 1940. Some women worked for as little as $2.00 a week and as long as 80 hours a week. Mitchell noted Women's Bureau findings that indicated that women took domestic work only as a last resort. She concluded that black women were the most oppressed of the working classes.[27]

As the United States entered World War II, black women found more opportunities in industry. However, jobs available to black women were

1166

the ones for which white workers were not available. War industry jobs were often found in urban centers outside of the South. Consequently, the majority remained outside of the mainstream of feminist consciousness because feminist interests were not their interests, and those black feminists of the woman suffrage era found little comfort from white feminists. Several of the black feminists of the woman suffrage era remained in leadership positions during the 1920s and the 1930s, while others faded from the scene. In addition, new faces became associated with black female leadership. Among these were Amy Jacques Garvey and Mary McLeod Bethune. Although all of these women either identified themselves or have been identified as feminists, their major concerns between the world wars were racial issues, with the status of black women as a major priority.

1167

A look at the 1920s reveals that most of the black women's organizations that were prominent during the woman suffrage era remained so. Nonetheless, new groups were organized as well. Elizabeth Carter remained president of the Northeastern Federation of Colored Women's Clubs, which celebrated its twenty-fifth anniversary in 1921. The leadership of the NACW was in transition during the 1920s. Mary B. Talbert retired as president and was succeeded by a former suffragist, Hallie Q. Brown, in 1922. In the middle of the decade Mary McLeod Bethune assumed the presidency. In 1922 several NACW leaders organized the International Council of Women of the Darker Races. Margaret Murray Washington, the wife of the late Booker T. Washington and the first president of the National Federation of Afro-American Women, was elected president.[28]

In addition to these established black women's organizations, there was the women's arm of Marcus Garvey's United Negro Improvement Association (UNIA). At its peak, in 1925, the UNIA had an estimated membership of 2 million and can be considered the first mass movement among working-class black people in the nation. Amy Jacques Garvey, Marcus Garvey's wife, was the articulate leader of the women's division and the editor of the women's department of the UNIA official newspaper, *Negro World*. A feminist in the international sense, Amy Jacques Garvey's feminist views embraced the class struggle as well as the problems of Third World women. A black nationalist, Garvey encouraged women of color throughout the world to organize for the benefit of themselves as well as their own people. Although she gave credit to the old-line black women's clubs, Garvey felt their approach to the problems of Third World women was limited. A Jamaican by birth, she called for revolutionary strategies that did not merely reflect the reform ideas of white middle-class women. Instead Garvey called upon the masses of black women in the United States to acknowledge that they were the "burden bearers of their race" and to take the lead in fighting for black independence from white oppression. Amy Jacques Garvey combined the UNIA belief in the power of the black urban working class with the feminist belief that women could think and do for themselves. The revolutionary implications of her ideas are reflected in the theme of the women's pages of *Negro World*—"Our Women and What They Think." Garvey called for black women's dedication to social justice and to national liberation, abroad as well as at home.[29]

Garvey was a radical who happened to be a feminist as well. Her views were ahead of her time; thus, she would have fit in well with the mid-twentieth century radical feminists. However, the demise of the UNIA and the deportation of Marcus Garvey in 1927 shattered much of Amy Jacques Garvey's influence in the United States and she returned to Jamaica. In the meantime, the majority of black feminists of the 1920s either joined the white social feminists, such as Jane Addams and the WILPF, or bypassed the feminists altogether to deal with race issues within black organizations.

1168

The leadership of the WILPF was old-line and can be characterized as former progressives, woman suffragists, and social feminists. Jane Addams presided over the organization before U.S. entry into World War I and brought black women such as Mary Church Terrell, Mary B. Talbert, Charlotte Atwood, Mary F. Waring, and Addie W. Hunton into the fold. Terrell had been a member of the executive committee since 1915. As a league representative, she was elected a delegate to the International Congress of Women held in Paris in 1919. Upon her arrival, Terrell was impressed with the conference delegates but noticed that there were none from non-western countries and that she was the only delegate of color in the group. As a result, she felt obliged to represent the women of all the nonwhite countries in the world, and this she attempted to do. At the conference meeting in Zurich, Switzerland, Terrell agreed to represent the American delegation and did so by speaking in German before the largely German-speaking audience. In addition, she submitted her own personal resolution to the conference, despite attempts by American committee members to change her wording. "We believe no human being should be deprived of an education, prevented from earning a living, debarred from any legitimate pursuit in which he wishes to engage or be subjected to humiliations of various kinds on account of race, color or creed." Terrell's position and thinking were in keeping with the growing awareness among black women leaders in the United States that Third World people needed to fight oppression together.

Although Mary Church Terrell remained an active social feminist, her public as well as her private views reflected the disillusionment of black feminists of the woman suffrage era. In 1921 she was asked by members of the WILPF executive committee to sign a petition requesting the removal of black troops from occupied German territory, where they were alleged to be violating German women. Terrell refused to sign the petition because she felt the motives behind it were racist. In a long letter to Jane Addams, the executive committee chairman, Terrell explained why she would not sign the petition. She noted that Carrie Catt had investigated the charges against the black troops and found them to be unfounded. The troops, from French colonies in Africa, were victims, Terrell contended, of American propaganda against black people. Making a dramatic choice between the feminist organization position and her own loyalty to her race, Terrell offered to resign from the executive committee. Addams wrote her back, agreeing with Terrell's position and asking her not to resign.[31] In this case, when given the choice between the politics of feminism and race pride, Terrell felt that her energies were needed most to combat racism, and she chose to take a nationalist position in the controversy.

Several other attempts were made at interracial cooperation among women's groups during the early 1920s, but most of these efforts were white-dominated and short-lived. An exception was the Cooperative Women's League of Baltimore, founded in 1913 by Sarah C. Fernandis. This group maintained relations with white women's civic leagues in connection with local health and sanitation, home economics, art, and education projects. In 1925 the league initiated its twelfth annual program.[32] This organization was quite conventional, a far cry from feminist — black or white. However, the activities were, like most black women's group activities of the times, geared to strengthen local black communities.

Other black-white cooperative ventures on a grander scale included the Commission on Inter-Racial Cooperation of the Women's Council of the Methodist Episcopal Church South. In October 1920 the commission held a conference on race relations. Only four black women were invited and they were selected because of their husbands' prominence, rather than for their feminist views. The conference pledged a responsibility to uplift the status of black women in the South, calling for a reform of the conditions under which black domestics worked in white homes. The delegates passed resolutions supporting improved sanitation and housing for blacks, fair treatment of blacks in public accommodations, the prevention of lynching, and justice in the courts. Significantly, no mention of protecting black women's suffrage was made. Several months later, the National Federation of Colored Women's Clubs met at Tuskegee, Alabama, and issued a statement that seemed to remind the Methodist Episcopal women of their pledge and called for increased cooperation and understanding from southern white women. Interestingly, the black women included suffrage in their resolution.[33]

Nothing came of this attempt at interracial cooperation, for neither the social nor the economic status of black women improved in the South during the 1920s. The trend toward interracial cooperation continued nevertheless, and in 1922 the YWCA appointed a joint committee of black and white women to study race problems. Once, again, only four black women were invited to participate. Principles were declared, but little came of the gathering.[34]

In the meantime, most black women's organizations had turned from

1169

attempts to establish coalitions with white women's groups to concentrate upon pressing race problems. Lynching was one of the major American problems, and black women organized to fight it. On the national front, black women's groups used political strategies and concentrated their efforts toward passage of the Dyer Anti-Lynching Bill. In 1922 the Northeastern Federation of Colored Women's Clubs appointed a delegation to call on Senator Lodge of Massachusetts to urge passage of the Dyer bill. In addition, the Alpha Kappa Alpha Sorority held its national convention in Indianapolis and sent a telegram to President Warren Harding urging the support of his administration in the passage of the bill. Also that year, the NACW met in Richmond and appointed an antilynching delegation to make contact with key states needed for the passage of the Dyer bill in Congress. In addition, the delegation was authorized to meet with President Harding. Among the black women in the delegation were veteran antilynching crusader Ida B. Wells-Barnett, NACW president Hallie Q. Brown, and Rhode Island suffragist Mary B. Jackson.[35]

1170

Perhaps the most renowned antilynching crusader of the 1920s was Spingarn Medal winner Mary B. Talbert. In 1922 she organized an executive committee of 15 black women, who supervised over 700 state workers across the nation in what Talbert called the Anti-Lynching Crusade. Her aim was to "unite a million women to stop lynching," by arousing the consciences of both black and white women. One of Talbert's strategies was to provide statistics that showed that victims of lynching were not what propagandists called sex-hungry black men who preyed upon innocent white women. The crusaders revealed that eighty-three women had been lynched in the United States since Ida B. Wells-Barnett had compiled the first comprehensive annual report in 1892. The Anti-Lynching Crusade was truly an example of woman power, for the crusaders believed that they could not wait for the men of America to stop the problem. It was perhaps the most influential link in the drive for interracial cooperation among women's groups. As a result of its efforts, the 1922 National Council of Women, representing 13 million American women, resolved to "endorse the Anti-Lynching Crusade recently launched by colored women of this country."[36]

Although the Dyer bill was defeated, it was revised by the NAACP and introduced again in the House of Representatives by Congressman Leonidas C. Dyer of Missouri and in the Senate by William B. McKinley of Illinois in 1926. That year the bill failed again, as did similar bills in 1935, 1940, and 1942. However, it was the effort of blacks and white women organized against lynching that pressed for legislation throughout the period. Without a doubt, it was the leadership of black women, many of whom had been active in the late nineteenth-century women's club movement and in the woman suffrage movement, who motivated white women in 1930 to organize the Association of Southern Women for the Prevention of

Lynching. Although a federal antilynching bill never passed the Congress, by the end of the 1940s public opinion had been sufficiently convinced by the efforts of various women's groups that lynching was barbarous and criminal. Recorded incidents of lynching ceased by 1950.

Even though interracial cooperation in the antilynching campaign was a positive factor among black and white women, discrimination against black women by white women continued to plague feminists. In 1925, for example, the Quinquennial of the International Council of Women met at the Washington Auditorium in the District of Columbia. The council sought the cooperation of NACW president Mary McLeod Bethune and arrangements were made to have a mass choir of black women perform. The night of the concert, black guests were placed in a segregated section of the auditorium. Mary Church Terrell reported that when the singers learned of what was happening, they refused to perform. Foreign women delegates were in the audience, as well as white women from throughout the nation. Many of them were angry because the concert had to be cancelled. Terrell felt that this was one of the most unfortunate incidents of discrimination against black women in the club movement. However, she agreed with the decision of her black sisters not to sing.[37]

1171

National recognition of black women did not really come until 1936, when Mary McLeod Bethune was appointed director of the Division of Negro Affairs, National Youth Administration, under the Franklin D. Roosevelt administration. The founder of Bethune-Cookman Institute in Daytona, Florida, Bethune had been a leader in the black women's club movement since the early 1920s. NACW president from 1924 to 1928, she founded the National Council of Negro Women (NCNW) in 1935. What feminist consciousness Bethune acquired was thrust upon her in the mid-1930s because for the first time, a black woman had the ear of the president of the United States and the cooperation of the first lady, who was concerned not only about women's issues, but about black issues. In 1936 Bethune took advantage of her new status and presented the concerns of the NCNW to Eleanor Roosevelt. As a result, sixty-five black women leaders attended a meeting with Eleanor Roosevelt to argue the case for their greater representation and appointments to federal bureaus. They called for appointments of professional black women to the Children's Bureau, the Women's Bureau, and each department of the Bureau of Education that dealt with the welfare of women and children. The NCNW also wanted the appointment of black women to administrative positions in the Federal Housing Administration and Social Security Board. In addition, they called for enlarging the black staff of the Bureau of Public Health and for President Roosevelt to suggest to the American Red Cross that they hire a black administrator.[38]

The NCNW requests reflect two trends among middle-class women in the mid-1930s. First, they were calling for positions that black women had never held, nor would achieve until a generation later; consequently, their ideas were revolutionary ones in terms of federal policies. Second, they were calling for policies to benefit not only their sex, but their race; hence, the NCNW reflected the position established by black feminists a generation before.

Mary McLeod Bethune's leadership was acknowledged by black women's groups throughout the nation, and she accepted the responsibility by referring to herself as the representative of "Negro womanhood." In 1937 she visited the Flanner House, a black settlement house in Indianapolis whose black woman superintendent, Clio Blackburn, said the institution's aim was to help black people help themselves. If no other person represented this standard to black women at this time, Mary McLeod Bethune did. The following year she met with the Alpha Kappa Alpha Sorority in Boston to assist them in a benefit for the Mississippi Health Project, a project to help black people in that region which was sponsored by the national sorority.[39]

1172

Middle-class black women clearly reflected their dedication to uplifting the race at a time when most Afro-Americans were thwarted not only by race prejudice but also by economic depression. Although activities that involved race uplift were not feminist in orientation, many black feminists took an active role in them. In an interview with Mary McLeod Bethune in 1939, Lillian B. Huff of the *New Jersey Herald News* asked her about the role of black women leaders and how Bethune related to her leadership position. Bethune, who had come from humble origins, felt that black women had room in their lives to be wives and mothers as well as to have careers. But most importantly, she thought, black women should think of their duty to the race.[40]

Bethune's feelings were not unique to black women, for most black feminists and leaders had been wives and mothers who worked yet found time not only to struggle for the good of their sex, but for their race. Until the 1970s, however, this threefold commitment — to family and to career and to one or more social movements — was not common among white women. The key to the uniqueness among black feminists of this period appears to be their link with the past. The generation of the woman suffrage era had learned from their late nineteenth-century foremothers in the black women's club movement, just as the generation of the post World War I era had learned and accepted the experiences of the preceding generation. Theirs was a sense of continuity, a sense of group consciousness that transcended class. Racial uplift, fighting segregation and mob violence, contending with poverty, as well as demanding rights for black women were longstanding issues of concern to black feminists.

The meeting of the National Conference on Problems of the Negro and Youth at Washington, D.C., in 1939 was a good example of this phenomenon among black women. Bethune called the meeting and invited a range of black leaders from Mary Church Terrell and feminist Nannie Burroughs, who were both in their seventies, to Juanita Jackson Mitchell, the conference youth coordinator. The young Mitchell had been a leader among black civil rights activists in the City-Wide Young People's Forum in Baltimore a few years before. Bethune noted the success of the meeting of young and old, all of whom had a common interest in civil rights for Afro-Americans.[41]

By 1940 Mary Church Terrell had written her autobiography. At the age of seventy-seven, she was one of the few living links with three generations of black feminists. In her introduction, Terrell established her own interpretation of her life story, which in many ways reflected the lives of other black feminists. "This is the story of a colored woman living in a white world. It cannot possibly be like a story written by a white woman. A white woman has only one handicap to overcome — that of sex. I have two — both sex and race. I belong to the only group in this country which has two such huge obstacles to surmount. Colored men have only one — that of race"[42]

1173

Terrell's reference to her status as an Afro-American woman applied throughout United States history to most black women, regardless of class. In view of this, it is not surprising that black women struggled, often in vain, to keep the right to vote from 1920 to 1940. A brief reference to this struggle, a story in itself, reveals that they fought to keep the little influence they had although black feminists anticipated that many of them would lose. Nonetheless, black female enthusiasm was great immediately following passage of the Nineteenth Amendment. In Baltimore alone, the black electorate increased from 16,800 to over 37,400 in 1921, indicating that the number of black women voters surpassed the number of black men registered to vote. By 1922, however, attempts to thwart the influence of black women voters were spreading across the South. As a result, the NACW recommended that all of its clubs lobby for the enforcement of the Nineteenth Amendment.[43]

By 1924 feminist Nannie Burroughs had assessed the status of black women of voting age and their relationship to white feminists. Burroughs noted that white women continued to overlook or to undervalue the worth of black women as a political force in the nation. She warned white female politicians to tap the potential black female electorate before white men exploited it.[44] With the exception of Ruth Hanna McCormick, who recruited Mary Church Terrell to head her 1929 Illinois campaign for the United States Senate, warnings such as Burroughs's did not seem to influence white female leaders. For example, disillusioned members of the Republican Colored Women State Committee of Wilmington, Delaware, protested unsuccessfully when they lost their representation on the state Republican committee. A merger of the Women's Advisory Committee, a white group, with the State Central Committee had caused the elimination of black women representatives. The decline in black women's participation in Republican party politics was evident by 1928, when only 8 out of 104 black delegates to the Republican National Convention were women. The same year, the NACW program did not even bother to include suffrage among its priorities for women of the race.[45]

Although President Roosevelt made good his promise to Mary McLeod Bethune, so that by 1945 four black women had received outstanding federal appointments, the political viability of black women in the early 1940s was bleak. The list of black elected officials from 1940 to 1946 included no women.[46] Agents of white supremacy continued to subvert what vestiges of political influence blacks held. For example, in 1942 Congressman Martin Dies, chairman of the congressional committee investigating un-American activities, attempted to link several national black leaders to the Communist party. Among the group was Mary McLeod Bethune, who remained the only black woman prominent in national politics.[47]

1174

Hence, over twenty years after the passage of the Nineteenth Amendment racial discrimination festered in most areas of American life, even among feminists and women in political life. Prejudice did not distinguish between middle-class and working-class black women, nor between feminists and nonfeminists who were black. Although black women continued to use what political rights they maintained, the small number of those politically viable made little impact upon public policies.

Notes

1. See Rosalyn Terborg-Penn, "Nineteenth Century Black Women and Woman Suffrage," *Potomac Review* 7 (Spring-Summer 1977): 13-24; and Rosalyn M. Terborg-Penn, "Afro-Americans in the Struggle for Woman Suffrage" (Ph.D. dissertation, Howard University, 1977), pp. 180-85.

2. *Indianapolis Freeman*, 28 August 1915; Monroe N. Work, ed., *The Negro Year Book, 1918-1919* (Tuskegee Institute, Ala.: The Negro Year Book Publishing Co., 1919), pp. 57-59 (hereafter cited as *Negro Year Book*, by year); Rosalyn Terborg-Penn, "Discrimination Against Afro-American Women in the Woman's Movement, 1830-1920," *The Afro-American Woman: Struggles and Images*, edited by Sharon Harley and Rosalyn Terborg-Penn (Port Washington, N.Y.: Kennikat Press, 1978), p. 26.

3. See Rayford W. Logan, *The Negro in the United States* (Princeton, N.J.: Van Nostrand, 1957); and Terborg-Penn, "Discrimination Against Afro-American Women," pp. 17-27.

4. Terborg-Penn, "Afro-Americans in the Struggle for Woman Suffrage," chapter 4.

5. David Morgan, *Suffragists and Democrats: The Politics of Woman Suffrage in America* (East Lansing, Mich.: Michigan State University Press, 1972), pp. 106-07.

6. *Crisis* 15 (November 1917): 18; *Negro Year Book, 1918-1919*, p. 60.

7. Mrs. A. W. Blackwell, *The Responsibility and Opportunity of the Twentieth Century Woman* (n.p., n.d.), pp. 1-5. This pamphlet is housed in the Trevor Arnett Library, Atlanta University.

8. *The Crisis* 15 (November 1917): 19-20; *New York Age*, 10 May 1917.

9. *New York Age*, September 20, 1917.

10. Walter White to Mary Church Terrell, 14 March 1919, Mary Church Terrell Papers, Box no. 3, Library of Congress, Washington, D.C. (hereafter cited as MCT Papers); Charles Flint Kellogg, *NAACP: A History of the National Association for the Advancement of Colored People, 1909-1920* (Baltimore: Johns Hopkins Press, 1967), p. 208.

11. Walter White to Mary Church Terrell, 14 March 1919, MCT Papers, Box no. 3.

12. Ida Husted Harper to Mary Church Terrell, 18 March 1919, and Ida Harper to Elizabeth Carter, 18 March 1919, MCT Papers, Box no. 3.

13. Aileen Kraditor, *The Ideas of the Woman Suffrage Movement, 1890-1920* (Garden City, N.Y.: Anchor Books, Doubleday and Co., 1971), pp. 168-69; *Crisis* 17 (June 1919): 103; Ida Husted Harper, ed., *The History of Woman Suffrage, 1900-1920* (New York: J. J. Little and Ives Co., 1922), pp. 580-81.

14. Terborg-Penn, "Afro-Americans in the Struggle for Woman Suffrage," chapters 4 and 5.

15. *Ibid.*, pp. 207, 217-18, 225.

16. *Crisis* 19 (November 1920): 23-25; *Negro Year Book, 1921*, p. 40.

17. Kenneth R. Johnson, "White Racial Attitudes as a Factor in the Arguments Against the Nineteenth Amendment," *Phylon* 31 (Spring 1970): 31-32, 35-37.

18. Terborg-Penn, "Afro-Americans in the Struggle for Woman Suffrage," pp. 301-02.

19. *Ibid.*, pp. 303-04.

20. William Pickens, "The Woman Voter Hits the Color Line," *Nation* 3 (October 6, 1920): 372-73.

21. *Ibid.*, p. 373; NAACP, *Eleventh Annual Report of the NAACP for the Year 1920* (New York: NAACP, 1921), pp. 15, 25-30.

22. William L. O'Neill, *Everybody Was Brave* (Chicago: Quadrangle Press, 1969), p. 275.

23. Terborg-Penn, "Afro-Americans in the Struggle for Woman Suffrage," p. 311.

24. Benjamin Brawley, *Women of Achievement: Written for the Fireside Schools* (Nashville, Tenn.: Woman's American Baptist Home Mission Society, 1919), pp. 14-17.

25. Elizabeth Ross Haynes, "Two Million Negro Women at Work," *Southern Workman* 15 (February 1922): 64-66.

26. United States Department of Commerce, Bureau of Census, *Population Trends in the United States, 1900-1960* (Washington, D.C.: U.S. Government Printing Office, 1964), pp. 231, 234.

27. Gerda Lerner, ed., *Black Women in White America: A Documentary History* (New York: Random House, Pantheon Books, 1972), pp. 226-27; Louise Mitchell, "Slave Markets Typify Exploitation of Domestics," *Daily Worker*, 5 May 1940.

28. *Negro Year Book, 1922-24*, p. 37.

29. *The Negro World*, 24 October 1925, 5 March 1927. See Mark D. Matthews, "'Our Women and What They Think,' Amy Jacques Garvey and *The Negro World*," *Black Scholar* 10 (May-June 1979): 2-13.

30. Mary Church Terrell, *A Colored Woman in a White World* (Washington, D.C.: Randsdell, Inc., 1940), pp. 330-33.

1175

31. *Ibid.*, pp. 360-64.

32. *Crisis* 30 (June 1925): 81.

33. *Negro Year Book, 1921-22*, pp. 6-9.

34. *Negro Year Book, 1922-24*, pp. 18-19.

35. *Ibid.*, pp. 37-38; *Crisis* 23 (March 1922): 218; *Crisis* 24 (October 1922): 260.

36. *Crisis* 24 (November 1922): 8.

37. Terrell, *A Colored Woman in a White World*, pp. 370-71.

38. Mary McLeod Bethune, Vertical File, Howard University, Washington, D.C., Clippings Folder, 1930, *Black Dispatch*, 16 April 1936 (hereafter cited as Bethune Vertical File and the source).

39. Bethune Vertical File, *Indianapolis Recorder*, 14 December 1937, *Boston Guardian*, 18 October 1938.

40. Bethune Vertical File, *New Jersey Herald News*, 14 October 1939.

41. Bethune Vertical File, *Black Dispatch*, 28 January 1939.

42. Terrell, *A Colored Woman in a White World*, first page of the introduction.

43. *Crisis* 23 (December 1921): 83; *Negro Year Book, 1922-24*, p. 37.

44. *Negro Year Book, 1922-24*, p. 70.

45. Terrell, *A Colored Woman in a White World*, pp. 355-56; *Negro Year Book, 1922-24*, p. 70; *Negro Year Book, 1931-32*, pp. 13, 92-93. Blacks did not vote the Democratic party on a large scale until the second Franklin D. Roosevelt administration.

46. *Negro Year Book, 1947*, pp. 286-87, 289-91.

47. Bethune Vertical File, *Black Dispatch*, 10 October 1942.

Links, Incorporated: Friendship and Service

EULA S. TRIGG

1177

Links, Incorporated was founded in 1946 at Philadelphia by two friends who gathered together a group of women to organize a new type of club, the aim of which would be three-fold, social, charitable, and intercultural in scope. It was the dream of the founders, Margaret Hawkins and Sarah Scott, that this club would direct the talents of women toward a more unified support of those causes which reflected the basic needs of their fellow human beings, with emphasis on the black minority to which they belonged. It would also provide varied opportunities for the members to identify themselves as black women who had a purposefulness and a goal beyond the social aspects of their lives.

That dream became a reality on November 9, 1946, for on that day in the city of "Brotherly Love", a candle was lit, a link in the chain of friendship and service was forged that was to have far reaching results. Very significantly, one of the charter members of Philadelphia, Lillian Walls suggested the name "Links" as symbolical of enduring and binding friendship.

As the club expanded its horizons enthusiasm ran so high that women in neighboring cities were invited to add other "links" to the chain. Incorporated in 1951 in Trenton, New Jersey, this organization has developed into 144 chapters in thirty-three states and the District of Columbia, with approximately 3500 women.

Originally published in *The Negro History Bulletin*, Vol. 39, No. 5 (May 1976), pp. 584-589.

1

Aside from the many and varied services and programs, there have been substantial contributions from Links, Incorporated to the following organizations:

$37,000 to the National Association for the Advancement of Colored People
$100,000 to the N.A.A.C.P. Legal Defense and Educational Fund
$100,000 to the Urban League
$250,000 to the United Negro College Fund and other programs for higher education including Sickle Cell Disease Research.

1178

Each chapter is committed to the support of these National projects and to the implementation of the program areas; Services to Youth, Freedom and the Arts, and National and International Trends and Services.

It was within the framework of the ideals subscribed to by the founders of the Philadelphia Chapter that Washington, D.C. became the third chapter in the chain of Links. Organized by Bernice Thomas and Ruth Young, it was installed in April, 1948, with six members, Vashti Cook, Katie Harris, Anne C. Reid, Eula Trigg, Ruth Young and Bernice Thomas, the first president.

From its inception, the chapter has sponsored projects geared primarily toward improving and enriching the lives of children and youth. Activities have included aid to children in institutions, the Industrial Home School Annex, Junior Village, Children's Hospital, Children's Department of Freemen's Hospital and the Meriwether Home.

Implementing the three-fold objectives of Links, Incorporated, the emphasis shifted from material contributions to cultural programs. In 1954, realizing that segregation was depriving the black child of the opportunity to see and enjoy "live theatre" the chapter presented three plays, from the noted Clare Tree Major's New York Children's Theatre and a Louisa Mustin's Puppet Show in the Lisner Auditorium. This was the first desegregated Children's Theatre in Washington.

Again in 1964, the Washington premier of the Seymour Barb comic opera based on the story of "Little Red Riding Hood" was presented at Cramton Auditorium, Howard University. Still interested in Junior Village, some of the youngsters housed there were given free transportation and tickets to these plays.

Washington, D.C. Chapter, Links, Incorporated

1179

Left to right: Lessie Yancey, President of the Chapter; Elizabeth D. Koontz, Director, Women's Bureau, U.S. Dept. of Labor, and Eula S. Trigg.

3

As part of the program for providing educational opportunities for the academically talented youth, two girls received a yearly scholarship to attend the college of their choice.

The chapter's assistance to children was not confined to the United States but extended to Niger, Africa, where one of its members, the late Vashti Cook, wife of then Ambassador Mercer Cook, resided.

Throughout the years outstanding black artists, both national and local, have been presented in concerts, plays, and art exhibits. More recently the members have worked with a church group of young adults seriously involved in social community problems.

1180

This year marked the initiation by the Washington Links of an annual Black History Awards Program for senior students in one of the high schools of the city each year. This year it was Dunbar High School where seniors were invited to participate in an Essay Contest on some phase of Black History. A total of three hundred dollars was contributed to the three winners by the chapter. The Association for the Study of Afro-American Life and History (ASALH) co-sponsored the project and awarded appropriate books to the three winners and Negro History Bulletins to all contestants. All of the entering students also received certificates from the Links.

A panel of three judges, coordinated by Dr. Michael Winston, Director of the Howard University Moorland-Spingarn Research Center, read and evaluated the student papers. The two other judges were Ms. Jacqueline Trescott, Washington Post staff writer, and Mrs. Isadore Miles, retired teacher of the city schools and Howard University.

The Awards Program was held 26 February at the Dunbar High School auditorium. The winners were (1) Doreen Quick, (2) Sharlene Howard, and (3) Karl Dean. Max Robinson, CBS News anchorman was the main speaker, with remarks by Ms. Trescott, Mrs. Phyllis Beckwith, Dunbar principal, and Ms. Ruth Parham, Social Science teacher who supervised the student writers. The entire Black History project was highly successful and inspirational and the Washington Links look forward to duplicating it each year, featuring a different high school's seniors.

As a part of the 200th anniversary of our nation, a Black Heritage Bicentennial Tour and Luncheon was held on 15 May. The program included visits to monuments and museums dedicated to black leaders and commentary by knowledgeable persons throughout the tour. The project was capably planned and managed by Christine Davis, chairwoman, Lessie Yancey, co-chair, and committee on National Trends.

The latest project, which is now in process, to be finalized in the fall of 1975, is the establishment of a Revolving Student Loan Fund at Howard University. This will enable the chapter to help numerous students each year who might otherwise be forced to drop out of college.

As the Washington, D.C. Chapter with its present membership of 36, looks forward to the future, it expects to grow and expand its dimensions in order to meet the challenges and concerns of this rapidly changing and evolving world. It salutes the founders and the dedicated women who have made significant contributions to the chain of Links, Incorporated.

1181

BRIEF PROFILES OF CHAPTER MEMBERS

Journalism

Thelma D. Perry, President of the Washington, D.C. Chapter of Links, Inc., resigned from college teaching several years ago to become Executive Editor of the *Negro History Bulletin*. Prior to college work she practiced law in the District of Columbia and remains a member of the District Bar. Her articles have been published widely in scholarly journals. Thelma's 384 page book, "History of the American Teachers' Association" was published in 1975 by NEA. Among her biographical listings are Dictionary of International Biography, Directory of American Scholars, International Authors and Writers Who's Who, and Who's Who Among Black Americans.

Dentistry

Dr. Jeanne Craig Sinkford became the first woman to head a major medical institution when she was appointed Dean of the College of Dentistry at Howard University on July 1, 1975. She has received many awards for her pioneering efforts as a female in dentistry and community activities. The Capital Press Club included her in its 31st Anniversary Salute to Black Pioneers. Alpha Kappa Alpha Sorority cited her for Exceptional Professional Achievement at the North Atlantic Regional Conference. Jeanne was recently admitted to the prestigious Institute of Medicine of the National Academy of Sciences. She is also Chairperson of the Appeals Board of the Commission on Accreditation of the American Dental Association.

Community Endeavor

Dolly Assevero as a member of the Caribbean American Intercultural Organization, was responsible for planning and sponsoring exchanges in cultural and recreational activities between the United States and the Caribbean area. She is a member of the Advisory Board of the D.C. Youth Symphony and docent of the Corcoran Gallery of Art. Chairwoman of our International Trends Committee, Dolly brings interesting foreign lecturers to chapter meetings.

1182

Helen Cannady is a member of the Executive Board of the Planned Parenthood Association of America. Deeply involved in homemaking and youth activities, she's also recording secretary of the chapter.

Laura Carson, a former principal in the D.C. Public Schools, served on the D.C. Board of Mental Health for eight years. She was chairwoman of a community "Blow Your Top Shop" Committee where adults with problems had the opportunity to talk and receive counseling. As chapter financial secretary Laura works closely with treasurer Eula Trigg.

Adelaide Clark has been appointed President of the D.C. Bicentennial Commission in charge of receiving and entertaining state delegations to Washington. She is also a member of the Board of the Women's State Bank of Maryland. On April 28th, she received an award from the Junior Citizens Corps, Inc. for outstanding service.

Mamie Crawford, since resigning from the faculty of Howard University, has been actively involved with the social and civic programs of St. Stephen and the Incarnation Church. Through the years she has worked with the Scouts and other projects for youngsters.

Helen Harris is a member of the Parents' Council of the Washington Association of Independent Schools whose aim is to improve academic and social programs through seminars and workshops in which the students are involved. She is on the membership committee of the Medical Chirugical Association. Helen is also a chairwoman of our chapter's 1976 annual Day-at-the-Races Project.

Anne Teabeau, descendant of Frederick Douglass, has been an active volunteer in the Museum of African Art. She is now a member of the Board of Trustees.

Lessie Yancey was appointed reading specialist at the Beauvoir National Cathedral Elementary School where she taught for several summers. Through an organization known as W.O.W. she interviews teenagers for summer jobs. One of her major interests is providing services geared to the needs of senior citizens.

Education and Administration

Henrietta Avant, chapter vice-president, is a former assistant professor of education and supervisor of student-teacher programs at the Blanford Laboratory School, Petersburg, Virginia. A former principal in the public schools of Washington, D.C., she is now actively engaged in volunteer services. She is a member of the Library Guild of St. Albans National Cathedral and a cashier in the gift shop at Howard University Hospital, among other voluntary activities.

Dr. Theresa Brown was chairwoman and Professor of English at D.C. Teacher's College and has written many scholarly articles in the field of English literature. She is listed in Who's Who of American Women and Who's Who in American Education. She is a member of the faculty of Howard University.

Anne Burwell was Director of the Washington Community School of Music for two years. She is now Professor of Piano at Howard University. Anne chaired our Christmas giving project for indigent people. She is involved with symphony and other cultural programs.

Bernice Davis is counselor for highly motivated children preparing for life careers at the Walt Whitman High School in Maryland.

Doris Francis, a former volunteer at the Crispus Attucks Day Care Center in Boston, is now a teacher of young children (3-5 years) at the Webb-Trinidad Day Care Center in Washington, D.C.

Jeanne Lofton, with a Master's Degree in Slavic languages and literature, was invited by the Voice of America to tape programs in Russian on secondary education in America. As a result of the tapings she was invited by U.S.I.A. to go to Russia as a consultant on secondary education with the Graphic Arts Tours. Jeanne chairs our chapter's L.C.L.C. (Links Committee on Local Concerns).

1183

7

Irene McDuffie, as counselor in the D.C. Public Schools, was successful in obtaining scholarships for culturally deprived children with academic ability.

Mercedes Palmer, former Director of the Laboratory School at Texas Southern University, is dedicated to and involved in early childhood education. She is consultant for a National Childhood Day Care Association. She co-chairs with Adelaide Clark a committee that promotes cultural enrichment for city day-care children.

Jean Reed, a homemaker, was formerly Director of the International Student Center at Fisk University, Nashville, Tenn.

1184

Dr. Anne C. Reid, as Professor of drama at Howard University directed and produced "The Wild Duck" by Ibsen, which toured the Scandinavian peninsula and Germany. It was used as a model for setting up the United States International Cultural Exchange program. On November 18, 1975, she received the Pioneer Award from Audelco for outstanding work in the theatre. She is now Professor of Theatre Arts, University of Maryland, Baltimore County.

Dr. Evaretta Rutherford, chairperson of curriculum and teaching in the School of Education, Howard University, was appointed Curriculum Consultant for Educators to Africa for the summer study program in West and East Africa conducted by Howard University and the African-American Institute. She was recommended to the U.S. State Department to serve as Senior Fulbright Professor at the University of Botswana, Lesotho, Swaziland, South Africa 1972-1973.

Beatrix Scott, a former teacher in the secondary schools of Washington, D.C. was also a member of the Board of Examiners. Her services to the community include: President of the Iona Whipper Home for Unwed Mothers, Residential Chairwoman of the U.G.F. Drive, and National President of the Alpha Kappa Alpha Sorority. More recently she was appointed Public member of the Foreign Service Promotion Board of the State Department.

Vernon Sinkford, a former teacher of English in the Public Schools of Washington, D.C., was chairwoman of the Publicity Committee for the Washington, D.C. Chapter of Links. She has held other important club and civic offices.

Bernice Thomas, a former teacher in the D.C. Public Schools, assisted in the training of student teachers. While a member of the National Executive

Council of Links, Inc., she chaired the Handbook Committee which compiled and distributed copies to 42 chapters—1951-1953.

Government and Politics

Isobel Clark was formerly Assistant Director of the National Urban League and Director of Social Welfare for the United States in the Virgin Islands. At present she is Consultant in Education, Human Resources, and Urban Affairs for colleges, management consultants, and the Federal Government. She directs publicity for the chapter.

Christine Davis served twenty-three years as Chief of Staff of the Committee on Government Operations in the U.S. House of Representatives and was administrative assistant to two members of the United States Congress. She resigned to become Director of the Washington Bureau of Tuesday Publications, Inc.

1185

Marjorie Lawson, an attorney and immediate past chapter President, was appointed Judge of the Juvenile Court by President Kennedy making her the first black woman appointed to the bench in Washington, D.C. President Johnson appointed her United States representative to the Commission for Social Development in the United Nations. More recently she has been appointed to the Tax Revision Committee to make recommendations for Tax Structure for the District of Columbia.

Eunice Matthews is the Mayor of Highland Beach, Inc. one of two self-governing municipalities in Anne Arundle County of Maryland. As President of the National Women's Auxiliary to the National Medical Association, she introduced a five point program which is still in use. She has received awards from the National Medical Association and the Alpha Kappa Alpha Sorority for outstanding service.

Annette Richter is Personnel Security Specialist, Office of Security Agency for Internal Development, Department of State. She is the tireless, capable, corresponding secretary of the chapter.

Alice Spraggins is Vice President of the D.C. Democratic Women's Organization and an active member of the National Democratic Women's Organization. She works with the Parents' organization at Gallaudet College—The Kendall Demonstration School for the Deaf, and other such groups.

Allie Weeden, a licensed attorney, was co-organizer and first President of "Federally Employed Women", an organization concerned with equal opportunity for women employed by the Federal Government. In 1971, she received the National Public Service Award from the General Services Administration of the United States Government. Allie spearheaded the March, 1976 chapter project of contributing more than two dozen books to the library of the National Office of Links, Inc.

Medical Social Services

1186   *Martha Ann McMahon*, as Acting Director of Social Services at Howard University Hospital, is responsible for the supervision and administration of services of patients and in-service programs for members of her staff.

Religion and Human Relations

Minnie Freeman, the first woman to chair the Trustee Board of Plymouth Congregational Church, has been appointed Assistant Moderator. She is a writer-editor of the United States Information Agency, and authors other articles. Minnie is chairwoman of our chapter's projected trip to Las Vegas.

Eula S. Trigg was the first black woman elected President of the Sodality Union (C.L.C.) Archdiocese of Washington composed of approximately 15,000 women. She also chaired the Foster Home Recruitment Committee of the D.C. Welfare Department. She is a member of the Board of Trustees at St. Ann's Infant and Maternity Home. She chairs the D.C. chapter's overall Planning Committee.

A Complex Bond: Southern Black Domestic Workers and Their White Employers 1187

SUSAN TUCKER

Alice Walker, in *Meridian*, shows a young black protagonist summing up her knowledge of white women in order to decipher what her lover could possibly see in someone as undesirable as a white girl. She has had very few first-hand dealings with white women and draws instead upon the memories of her grandmother, a former domestic, and her mother, who has occasionally worked for whites:

> For she realized what she *had* been taught was that nobody wanted white girls except their empty-headed, effeminate counterparts—white boys . . . As far back as she could remember it seemed something *understood*: that while white men would climb on black women old enough to be their mothers— "for the experience"—white women were considered sexless, contemptible and ridiculous by all . . . They were clear, dead water.
>
> Her mother, though not a maid, had often worked for white families near Christmastime in order to earn extra money, and she told her family—in hushed, carefully controlled language . . . about the lusty young sons . . .
>
> But what had her mother said about white women? She could actually remember very little, but her impression had been that they were frivolous,

Originally published in *Frontiers: a journal of women studies*, Volume IX, Number 3 (1987), pp. 6-13.

helpless creatures, lazy and without ingenuity. Occasionally one would rise to the level of bitchery, and this one would be carefully set aside when the collective "others" were discussed. Her grandmother—an erect former maid who was now a midwife—held strong opinions, which she expressed in this way: 1. She had never known a white woman she liked after the age of twelve. 2. White women were useless except as baby machines which would continue to produce little white people who would grow up and oppress her. 3. Without servants all of them would live in pigsties.[1]

1188

This paper explores such remembrances, and the corresponding remembrances by white women of black women. For all but the last two decades, southern women, white and black, have primarily been known to one another as Meridian knew of white women—through a domestic worker. She, more than any other person in the segregated south, witnessed the very personal lives of both blacks and whites. She thus became the key person through whom each race claimed to know the other. This paper, then, asks, How do black female domestic workers and their white employers remember one another? And what do these memories tell us about past race relations among southern women?

Data for this research was gathered between 1979 and 1985. Extensive, open-ended interviews were conducted with 100 black and white women: domestic workers, children of domestic workers, employers, and children of employers, all born between 1880 and 1960 in an area that runs from Baton Rouge, Louisiana, to Pensacola, Florida. Because I grew up in this area—the Gulf South—and because much of my personal and professional commitment to change in the South stems from witnessing the life of a black domestic worker, I wanted to know if memories of and about domestic workers had affected the views of others. I specifically asked questions designed to record the interviewees' lifelong memories of each other. I wanted to look closely at how two groups of southern women viewed themselves and each other in terms of race and sex. I conducted all the interviews with white women and a little over half the interviews with black women; the remaining interviews with black women were conducted by Mary Yelling, a black interviewer. Interviewees were selected through the help of social service agencies, churches, college alumnae associations, relatives, friends, and friends of friends.[2]

To study the relationships of black and white southern women involves dissecting a complicated entanglement of race relations and economics. In particular, to study black female domestics and their white female employers involves examining the meaning of frequent contact between two groups of

2

women separated by race and class and yet connected by long years of knowing one another. For within the entanglement of race relations, economics, and power struggles based upon race and economics there grew a complex bond of mutual dependence and mutual distrust, and sometimes, a guarded but nevertheless remembered affection.

Within this complex bond many southern women came to know each other. For example, during the 1950s and 1960s, when I was growing up, half of all working black women in my hometown of Mobile, Alabama, were domestic workers.[3] Until 1968, I had never spoken to a black female who was not either a domestic herself or the daughter, niece, or granddaughter of a domestic.

Until this time, for me as well as many other southern white and black women, the white home was our only meeting place. This was certainly true for upper- and upper-middle-class whites and for the many families of black domestics. But this was also true for middle-class blacks who, like Meridian's mother, made extra money by serving at parties, taking in wash, or other tasks; and for lower-middle-class and working-class whites, who took their clothes to washerwomen and often had a "day worker" come in once a week to clean their homes.

1189

Even less well-off white families could afford domestics, because black women had little other choice of employment. As late as 1945, it required only half as large a family income to employ a servant in the South as it did in other parts of the country;[4] the South was known as the white housewives' utopia.

For southern women, this "utopia," resting as it did on the labor of black women, had other meanings as well. Most important, perhaps, was the symbolic one, for the "utopia" was rooted in the Old South and in the person of the ever-giving, nurturing, and loyal "Mammy." The South retained little of the plantation life so romanticized in film and novels, but it did retain power over blacks and a relatively elite lifestyle, in that it could employ black women for low wages. The domestic, then, was often used to illustrate how the Old South worked at its best.

For example, in one of my first interviews, a white woman stood angrily by her mantelpiece and began telling me how she did not care to do the interview, how no one would ever understand past ties between whites and blacks. Pointing up to a family portrait, she said:

See that little girl up there? That was Grandmother. And she had a slave named Annie. Well, Annie came with Grandmother and they lived here. Her mother had died when she was a little girl and she was an only child and she was devoted to Annie.

And when the war was over, the Civil War, Annie was right there in the house with them. And, of course, they had everything stripped from them. They didn't have anything. They were poor.

All right, Annie went out and got herself a job and brought her pay home to help buy the groceries, to feed the children in the family for Grandmother. And Annie is buried in our cemetery lot right now. She was part of the family. She stayed with the family all the rest of her life. And she went out when everything was gone to get work, and brought money home to help Grandmother. Now that's true! And how do you explain it?

1190

How does one explain it, except to see these as two individual women, black and white, whose legend of mutual help persists until today? The problem is, of course, to document also the legends told by black domestics and the children of black domestics, in order to hear more than just one side of each legend.

Still, I did find Annie's marker in the cemetery. "Annie Johnson," it reads simply, "1840-1920." There is no indication on the gravestone, as there is on others in this same cemetery, of her status as mammy, nurse, or companion. There is no indication that she was, as the legend passed down through the white family has it, anything other than a part of the family.

In Katherine Anne Porter's story, "The Old Order," the white child Sophia Jane assigns her beloved servant and companion a birthdate and marks it in the family Bible:

> . . . inserting it just below her own. "Nannie Gay," she wrote in stiff, careful letters, "(black)," and though there was some uproar when this was discovered, the ink was long since sunk deeply into the paper, and besides no one was really upset enough to have it scratched out. There it remained, one of their pleasantest points of reference.[5]

I prefer Sophia Jane's demarcation of Nannie, *within* the family, but (black). I prefer it because it more accurately reflects how most, if not all, domestics became a part of the white family: first, in slavery, "inserted" there by whites; and later, "inserted" there by economic conditions that left them little other choice.

My interviewee's remembrance, however, is a significant one, and one that I was to hear in various forms in other interviews. Her argument, joining white employer and black domestic in the care and protection of one another, was a favorite example used to illustrate the harmonious ways of the Old South, particularly as remembered by older white women. Such stories were often carried further by white women, and to a lesser extent by black women, to illustrate how white employers and black domestics shared a common distaste for and distrust of men. Such stories discussed husbands who were alcoholics or otherwise neglectful of responsibilities. Two white women told me that it was only with black domestics that they felt free to relate their grievances. Black domestics spoke of revelations of infidelity, drug addiction, financial losses, and incest. With black women, such "secrets" were "safe"—according to the racial etiquette that ensured that what went on in the white home would never be mentioned by a black to another white. But they were also "safe" because until recently white women have not acknowledged that such problems existed at all levels of society. White women seem to have felt that black women—who lived in a society said to be violent—would understand and comfort. In response, white women felt they helped black women in their struggles with abusive men. One white woman described a call at night from a black domestic leaving her husband: "Mother was more than glad to help. She saw this woman as her 'sister' in a common struggle that centered around religion, but also on attitudes toward men, in general."

Black women may have felt a similar security in telling their marital problems to someone outside their own community. Their descriptions of such conversations, however, had a less secretive tone. Instead, they spoke humorously of men—white and black—as "half-people," "boys," "playing at life." Speaking of her own husband and the husband of her employer, one black woman reflected:

> Was he worse than my husband? . . . If you put each one of 'em in a sack, I think they would fall out together. There's a very few good men. It's a very few.

Black women revealed less in these confidential exchanges because as they correctly saw, shared gender did not erase the fact that most white women did not wish to change a system in which their own standard of living rested upon the cheap labor of all blacks, male and female. As one white woman said in describing her life:

> I'll tell you the truth . . . my husband died in 1960 and I have done just as well having Dorothea come every day and Julius come once every two weeks.

I have no illusions about white men, either, you see. One colored woman every day and one colored man working every now and then to do the heavy work makes for more than a replacement for a husband! Of course, I did love him. But he was a child. Like the Negroes in a way. I think most Southern women will admit that . . . if you can get them alone. Certainly ones with young children and old ones like me. What good are men to us?

For white women like this one, employing a black domestic allowed a lifestyle very different from that of her contemporaries in other parts of the country. How did such a lifestyle affect the white women to whom I spoke? Of the forty-eight white women I interviewed, two of the women born before 1940 entered politics and one became a doctor; two born after 1940 became lawyers; many were active in volunteer work. Upper-middle-class for the most part, not one of them expressed an interest in the women's movement. Though by no means a random sample of southern white women, the women interviewed seemed typical in their lack of interest in feminism—educated white women of the South are perhaps more conservative in their views on feminism because any study of feminism would address the full equality of all people, thereby challenging attitudes towards race and class as well. And on a less philosophical but nevertheless important level, in the South educated white women, who in other areas of the country first made up the ranks of the National Organization for Women and other feminist groups, are perhaps less inclined to support change because the traditional roles of women, as mothers or other caretakers within the family, have been easier, more rewarding ones—roles that have not blocked the road outside the domestic sphere, that have not been tinged with exhaustion and underutilization of intellect. The traditional roles of many white southern women, more often than not, have been made easier at the expense of black women.

For example, many white women told me how pleasant young motherhood had been with the help of black women—first a baby nurse who came and stayed for the three weeks following the birth of a child, and later other black nursemaids. Again and again younger white women, mothers today who do not have this help, told me that they remembered their mothers' lives as being very different from their own because of black women:

The thing I always remember was how close Rachel was to my mother. I mean, I think about it today and almost yearn for that sort of relationship. I can remember Rachel fixing breakfast for Mama and it would just be a

1192

6

poached egg and toast and coffee on a tray, but just the way it looked, I remember. And I remember how she'd take it into Mama's room and sit it on the dressing table.

Today, I feel so . . . tired. I have these two children and I'm pregnant and I'd love someone to bring me breakfast. And Rachel came everyday—well six days a week and did that. I can never remember her going on vacation or anything. She'd go with us on vacation . . . and she came at seven in the morning and left at 6:30 after she'd fed us and had us all cleaned up.

The help of a black domestic also meant the emotional support of a woman who was already symbolically cast as mother in southern culture. A recurrent sentence in the interviews with white women was, "She was closer to me than my own mother." This was probably accurate; in homes that employed full-time help, black women domestics were the more active caregivers. They were the ones who were there in day-to-day emergencies. They were often the ones who told girl children about menstruation, about sex, about relationships with men because they were often with these children at crucial times in their lives. One black woman told me of a young white woman in labor who refused to go into the delivery room without her. It was the maid who cut the newborn's umbilical cord. This was in the 1950s, long before "significant others" were allowed to be present at birthing.

1193

White women in the South generally view black women as stronger, more instinctive mothers than whites.[6] They entrust their children to black domestics, believing them to be more "natural" mothers. Indeed, the most visible role of the black domestic within white southern literature has been that of a mother surrogate. Even in late twentieth-century works, she is most often the mothering character and she is often shown in contrast to an ineffectual white mother.[7]

Black domestics are also seen as emotionally and physically stronger than white women, even though in fact black women have poorer health and a lower life expectancy than do white women. Black people, several women told me, "age slower than white people." And black women in particular, another white woman told me, "stay strong until they die." In describing the care of her dying mother by an older black woman, one white woman said: "Black women are stronger. They can do this more easily than I could."

Such a belief in the strength of the black domestic is built upon the mythical quality southern white women ascribe to black domestics. To white women employers, black domestics seemed to have almost magical qualities. They were called healers, therapists, listeners: "They sensed things. If you weren't feeling well, they could just pick up a rag or something and touch you and it felt better."

Such idealization, and the fact that the stories were often ones handed down through generations of mothers and daughters, suggest that the strength of the black domestic had an important function in the minds of southern white women. Primarily, of course, it "explained" how such a person could labor and continue to give under harsh societal and economic conditions. White women often clearly saw the injustice under which black women lived. But by proclaiming the strength of black women, white women could ignore these injustices. Specifically, they could ignore their own part in the continued exploitation of black women in the workplace. And they could also ignore some of their own guilt for not speaking out against other forms of exploitation, such as the sexual exploitation of black women by white men.

But the strength ascribed to these black domestics in repeated statements by white women seems also to have helped the white women in their own struggles. Particularly, the image of the strong black mother seems to have encouraged white girl children. It may be that this image provided a much-needed vision of woman's strength in a male-dominated society.

How did black domestics view this role assignment? And how, in general, did they view their complex bond with white women employers? Black women, too, saw themselves as the more "instinctive mothers"—both to their own children and to the children of whites. They did not wish to be cast as "mammy" and they did not perceive their child-rearing as romantically as whites did, but they saw themselves as warmer and more balanced in their approach to children. They felt white women "didn't know how to love children; white women didn't stay around to know how." And they saw their care of white children as a "decent" or "Christian" response. White women, they felt, did not have the same standards as they—of decency or Christianity: "She couldn't have raised that child. She was too busy with looking out for herself," said one. At the same time, black domestics who did not wish to work with children resented being always cast as experts: "They all think we blacks just love children." Black domestics were also very clear that their care for white children was not the same as their care for their own children. "I loved them," said one black domestic, "like you'd love anyone you knew as a baby—but I wouldn't go help her now, say, like I'd go to my own daughter."

1194

The black domestics I spoke with worked because they had to, because they had children to support alone, or because their husbands' earnings could not support the family. In every interview with black women, there were poignant stories of returning to work shortly after childbirth; of leaving their own children with relatives, neighbors, older children; of seeking jobs near home. As symbolic and surrogate mothers to whites, many of them felt intensely the irony and sadness of their lives—that to support their own children, they had to mother other women's children. They also felt immensely the luxury white women had (and often refused) of being able to choose to care for their own children: "You'd be there just taking good care of their children and yours were probably just somewhere running wild." One woman described the drowning of her own son while she was at work, minding white children.

1195

And yet, black women also expressed a very strong pride that they did provide for their families. Many of the older black women interviewed had migrated from rural areas to southern cities between 1900 and 1950. To agricultural workers in a section of the country that was no longer economically profitable, domestic work in the cities did offer a better standard of living. Today, it is hard to imagine, as one black woman told me, how she worked in the city for $10 a week in 1941 and felt this to be a fortune compared to the $3 a week she could make as a domestic in the country. She left her three-year-old daughter with her family (who were sharecroppers paid not in cash, but from the commmissary's stock of food) in order to have actual cash, "to buy a little bit of canned meat, rice, and material. All these meant a lot."

Another rural-born black woman told of an aunt who worked for a wealthy urban family and who, before her death, found jobs with various branches of the white family for six nieces. The aunt's goal was to bring her family out of the poverty of the country. It appears from a reading of scholarly works on domestic workers, and on the history of black women's work, that black women, more than any other ethnic group except the Irish, migrated alone—without men—to better their lives.[8] In the network of aunts, nieces, cousins, mothers, daughters, and finally whole families lay much of the real strength black domestics did have.

From such networks, black women learned to look upon both their jobs and themselves with a great deal of humor and dignity. With laughter, they often spoke of the uniformity with which whites of all social classes seemed to need blacks "to take care of them." They saw clearly their role as signifiers of status within the white community. As one black woman told me, "See, these white people, soon as they got able, they used to get a colored person to wash for them." That is how, she explained, she came to be employed at ten years old in 1904, baby-sitting and washing for a woman who worked in a cotton mill.

Another black woman, born in 1938, told me of her experience with poor whites in this way:

> Now I did get a job sort of as a maid for a poor family once. I mean they were so poor till their house was just so dirty. And they had rabbits in the back yard. And the girls used to roll their hair with paper from the bread. . . . And (the mother) had tons of kids. You know, she worked in a dime store downtown herself! And I think her older daughters were working in the theater. They had the kinds of jobs we couldn't get . . . And it was a struggle for them to pay me that little $20 a week. . . . And their house was a lot worse than ours. . . . They were poor but they thought they could afford a maid!

1196

This black woman, like many others, maintained her identity outside her work—within her home and her church. As another black woman told me, "My aunt said, 'Never marry yourself to a job, because heh, domestic work, you can find anytime.' " Another recalled, as her reason for "not loving those white folks like they say they love you," a story her mother had told her:

> I always had a feeling that people, they like you as long as you're able to do their work. My mother told me that. I told you she worked for a very rich family. And she was up in their house one day helping out with the old grandmother. And this old black man who had worked for them since he was a boy, he passed up there in the house with them. So my mother said, "Oh, I know they're gonna miss him."
> And the old lady said, laughing, "I don't know, Margaret, you can always get another darky, just as good or better."

In order to preserve this valued independence, three black domestics explained, they avoided borrowing much from whites, even if this meant going without much-needed money. This refusal was considered by older black domestics to be an almost revolutionary concept, for not to borrow from whites "meant you might just be hurting your family for your principles." Although work in cities did mean being paid in cash, black domestics, like their rural counterparts, were still linked to white families in ways that were but one step from the plantation system. Wages were pitifully low and not governed by federal minimum wage laws until the 1970s. Instead, black women's subsistence-level wages were supplemented by cast-off clothing, furniture, food, and loans. Older black women accepted such "gifts" because they had no other choice:

> Of course, at first, I didn't get enough money. . . . At that particular time, it was a certain salary they paid you and that's what they paid unless they gave you extra for being nice.
> I got a lot of extra. For doing and being nice and kind to those kids. And they always treated all my kids just like they treated me. Like Old Miz Nevitte, when the kids graduated or something, she'd give me a check.

From 1900 to the present, however, black women have increasingly felt an uneasiness about such "gifts." "I told them I didn't tote,"[9] said one, discussing the "old days" after slavery, when whites did not pay except by giving food in "the service pan." Black women correctly associated these gifts with a system designed to keep them in the service of whites, without the monetary means to achieve a higher standard of living. A domestic who worked in the 1950s described the effect of such offers:

1197

> 'Want some watermelon?' she'd say. 'Take your mother a slice of watermelon.'
> That made me detest domestic work. And the more I would work for people and see the books they had, the furnishings, everything in their houses, all nice, I just couldn't understand why we couldn't have this. Why we couldn't get paid more, instead of being just offered a slice of watermelon or whatever?

If they worked for a wealthy enough family, like the aunt who brought her nieces to the city, domestics did often make a slightly better wage, and they tended to remain with the same employer for longer periods of time.[10] They also seemed more inclined to use loans from whites to buy land, homes, automobiles, and educations for their children. Five black women spoke of such loans. They often spoke quite gratefully of these whites, telling me stories of gifts of "good things, not just what they didn't want"; they spoke of gifts that could actually be categorized as gifts between equals, not just the cast-offs offered almost as an apology for low wages.

And yet, even these domestics were painfully aware that their bond with whites rested upon the paternalistic system that served to keep blacks subordinate. The following story pinpoints their knowledge of their unfair position. It is from an interview with a black woman born in 1930, who at the time she describes was working for a white family for $20 a week. Her father became ill, and the hospital in the town refused to operate on him without being paid first.

> I called Miz Jones . . . told her I couldn't come to work 'cause my Daddy was very sick and I had to try and see if I could help my mother to get some money.
> She said, 'How much money?'
> I said, 'A hundred and forty dollars is what Mama needs before the doctors would touch him.'
> Now, you understand I'm only making $20 a week so by the time I'd get a hundred and forty dollars is a long time. But at any rate, she said, 'I'll talk to my husband, Mr. Jones.'
> So she told him, 'Leila's father is sick and has to have an operation and they won't touch him unless somebody else says the money will be paid.'
> See, she knew the system.
> So, Mr. Jones called the hospital and told them to operate on the man and start right away and don't make no more much ado about it.
> I never will forget that . . .
> I was so thankful. But I still knew it wasn't right. The whole system was wrong. Because, of course, Mr. Jones never did have to pay a cent. The fact was that the doctors wouldn't touch my Daddy until somebody white said they'd pay the money.

1198

Black women like this one saw clearly the unfair discrepancies between their own lives and those of the white families for whom they labored. The same white women who idealized domestics were often seen by those domestics as frivolous, dependent, and silly. Idleness encouraged craziness in white women, one black woman told me, explaining alcoholism and depression in her employer. Although the money they earned was very little, black women did recognize that having money of their own gave them an independence white women lacked. Two black women told me humorous stories of white women who had "allowances" from their husbands. Another described the emptiness in the life of her employer, who "shopped for a living."

Black women, also, in most cases, knew that the white women for whom they labored saw them as independent, strong people, worthy of admiration and emulation. Their awareness that they were seen as healers, as professional caretakers, did in many cases enable them to feel a sense of reciprocity and tenderness towards white women employers. One black woman described the death of a white child and her constant support of the white mother during the following months. Between these two women, as between other black and white women who shared important points in each other's lives, a true bond of affection did develop and endure.

But such bonds failed not only to rectify social and economic injustices, but even to end the persistent silence between white and black women about these injustices. The same white employers who saw black women as strong and persevering, who wondered "how they did it," did not even, for example, talk to black domestics about societal troubles.

In recitals of everyday meetings between black domestics and white employers there are many small examples of how this silence prevented change. For example, a white woman who had expressed affection towards her black domestic also explained that, when the domestic's husband was among the first to be laid off in a job, the employer was afraid to mention race as a factor in his dismissal. She also told me how she paid the woman during pregnancy leave but made her promise not to speak of this to anyone in the white family—and particularly not to other domestics,[11] lest they also ask for paid pregnancy leave. She did not want her friends to know. Surely, an open stand on the part of this white woman could have ended the silence, at least in her immediate environment. This could have been a beginning, even if a small one. 1199

Instead, southern white women like this one were early taught that it was "impolite" to discuss race and they seem to have fallen back on this as a standard response in their confusion and guilt over social injustices. I was told over and over that race was not mentioned between black domestics and white employers because "you didn't want to hurt their feelings." Recalling how her young daughter had asked, in the presence of a domestic, why Willie Bell could not sit in the little booths at the drugstore, a white woman said, "I just froze. We didn't think it right to bring up unpleasant things. We thought it would hurt their feelings." When I asked if this black domestic's feelings were not hurt by the daily reminders of segregation, she replied, "I suppose now that they were. But then we didn't think of it. We thought it was a rule."

Another white woman described the silence this way:

Once when Beatrice went home sick, Mother went over to her room to clean it up. There was like a writing paper box and on the top, as you opened the lid, there was a picture of Mother's best friend. It was probably something that Mother had thrown away . . . and underneath that were all these things that Beatrice had cut out of the newspaper about racial matters. We never knew why that was or why. But I know that she really loved Mother. And I know Mother really loved her.

This white interviewee was typical of others in that she brought up the silence and the affection in close proximity. Thus, although the code of silence governed all southerners, white women's choice of words—words such as *feelings*, *politeness*, *love*—suggests that they formed their own peculiarly female justifications for the written and unwritten laws of segregation. And although their particular justification took into account their connections to black women, the end result of their silence was that they, too, participated in the entire system designed to keep blacks at a subsistence level.

1200

The silence of white women was reinforced by the silence of black women. As has been noted by many black writers, silence as a form of mask-wearing was central to the survival of black people both in slavery and later. Most of the black domestics interviewed mentioned that any discussion of race with white women might get them labeled "uppity" and could mean a loss of vital income. Not only were their wages crucial to their families' survival, but these black domestics seemed also to be go-betweens in finding legal, medical, and other forms of help for neighbors and friends, as well as their own families. Charles S. Johnson, a black sociologist who studied the rural South during the first half of the twentieth century, found that "for those [blacks] still living in the country there is, it would appear, one unfailing rule of life. If they would get along with least difficulty, they should get for themselves a protecting white family."[12] Perhaps because many of the older black women interviewees had migrated from the country to the cities, I found this means of coping still prevalent.

To prepare black children for adulthood in a white-dominated world, black children, then, like white children, were early instructed in the code of silence. Robert Coles, studying black southern children in the 1960s and 1970s, found that black parents thought it necessary that children "grow up scared of whites."[13] As one black woman told me—"You just flat didn't mention anything. You acted—even in the 1960s—like you was pleased [with] *every*thing. *Pleased*." Said another, "When the Roosevelts were speaking for black people you just went along like you'd never even heard of them."

Such reticence has left a legacy of silence between white and black southern women that is only now fading. Like Meridian, the women we interviewed seem to be still guessing about one another, still extrapolating

14

from the earlier, segregated versions of black or white women they have known or known of. Said one younger white woman, "Sure, I know black women at work to say hello to, to talk with about the weather. But, as far as really knowing them, knowing their home life or even their thoughts, there is a certain restraint, a wall between us. I'm afraid of saying the wrong thing." And said a black woman, "Every white woman reminds me a little bit, underneath—even those I know at work, know well—of the woman my mother worked for. I don't get too close to them. I'm careful what I say." Said another black woman, "They don't put out that back door now,[14] they'll even call you 'Mrs.' if you tell them, but underneath, you scratch them and it's still, you're black and they're white and you got to work up courage to speak up."

1201

The need to end such a legacy of silence is great. As black and white southern women begin to meet one another on more common grounds, we must look honestly at the ways in which our mothers and grandmothers have been known to one another. Particularly, we can then begin to look at the vocabulary we have used, as women, to explain, and even to justify our complicity in the hierarchy of laws and customs that exploit women. In so doing, we can begin to sort out the ways that class, race, and gender have figured in the history of southern women.

And in so doing, we can begin to work for change in areas, such as domestic work, that have been hidden from the public eye. Black domestic workers are, after all, still the lowest paid of all workers. Despite various legislative measures enacted in the 1970s, some do not receive minimum wage. Many will not receive Social Security benefits because they cannot afford now to have money withheld from their paychecks. Almost never do they have any insurance paid by their employers. Their working conditions are determined, still, by a complicated entanglement of race relations and economics. An end to the legacy of silence could signal the beginning of measures to correct such conditions.

It is important, therefore, that we do not lose sight of either the present conditions or the past history of domestic workers.[15] And if we can begin to urge that domestic workers be justly compensated for their work—work that is, more than any other, what has been labeled "women's work"—will we not, then, also begin to fight for a more just compensation of all work?

NOTES

1. Alice Walker, *Meridian* (New York: Harcourt, Brace, Jovanovich, 1976), pp. 103-105.

2. Because the numbers of white household workers and nonwhite employers of household workers were statistically low in this area of the South, I chose to interview only black domestics who labored primarily for whites, white employers of black domestics, and the children of these two groups.

3. See U.S. Bureau of the Census, *Decennial Census* for the years 1950 and 1960 for cities in Alabama. See also the census for Louisiana, Mississippi, South Carolina, Georgia, and Florida.

4. C. Arnold Anderson and Mary Jean Bowman, "The Vanishing Servant and the Contemporary Status of the American South," *American Journal of Sociology*, 54 (November 1953), 215-30, especially p. 223.

5. Katherine Anne Porter, "The Old Order," in *The Leaning Tower and Other Stories* (New York: Harcourt, Brace and Company, 1934), pp. 37-38.

6. The idea of the black woman as the strong, instinctive mother to the white family for whom she worked is discussed by Lillian Smith, *The Killers of the Dream* (New York: Norton, 1961); by Catherine Juanita Starke, *Black Portraiture in American Fiction: Stock Characters, Archetypes and Individuals* (New York: Bantam Books, 1971), pp. 125-35; and by Richard King, *A Southern Renaissance: The Cultural Awakening of the American South, 1930-1955* (New York: Oxford University Press, 1980), pp. 172-93. Although King and Smith both discuss the view of black woman as seductress, I found no evidence that white women viewed black women in this way. White interviewees, instead, seemed to sometimes categorize black women "as having different morals," and in this way, they seemed to rationalize the rape of black women by white men. In interviewing over 100 black and white women, I did not find any instance where black women were described as being sexually more ardent. Rather, white women—if they spoke at all of the sexuality of black women—saw these black women as "more accepting of their bodies," "looser, but not in a bad way," "just different." The view of black woman as seductress seems to be a stereotype used primarily by southern men to excuse rape: a stereotype popularized by women only in romantic novels.

7. In the nineteenth century, the black domestic was represented by such characters as Nanny in *The Recollections of a Southern Matron* (1836) by Caroline Howard Gilman, Mammy in *Uncle Tom's Cabin* (1851) by Harriet Beecher Stowe, Aunt Phillis in *Aunt Phillis' Cabin* (1852) by Mary H. Eastman, Mammy in *Diddie, Dumps, and Tot* (1883) by Louise Clark Pyrennelle, Mom Bi in "Mom Bi: Her Friends and Her Enemies" (1884) by Joel Chandler Harris, and Mammy Krenda in *Red Rock* (1898) by Thomas Nelson Page. All these works show the black domestics as a devoted mother surrogate to white children.

Twentieth-century works such as Julia Peterkin's *Green Thursday* (1924), William Faulkner's *The Sound and the Fury* (1929), Margaret Mitchell's *Gone with the Wind* (1936), Lillian Smith's *Strange Fruit* (1944), Ann Petry's *The*

1202

Street (1946), Carson McCullers' *The Member of the Wedding* (1958), Harper Lee's *To Kill a Mockingbird* (1960), Shirley Ann Grau's *The Keepers of the House* (1964), Lisa Alther's *Original Sins* (1981), Toni Morrison's *Tar Baby* (1981), and Roy Hoffman's *Almost Family* (1982)—to name a few—continue in the tradition of idealizing black domestics, presenting household workers who mother white families.

8. This is suggested in David Katzman's *Seven Days a Week: Women and Domestic Service in Industrializing America* (New York: Oxford University Press, 1978), which looks at the period 1870 to 1920, and Daniel Sutherland's *Americans and their Servants: Domestic Service in the United States from 1800 to 1920* (Baton Rouge: Louisiana State University Press, 1981). Elizabeth Pleck's "The Two-Parent Household: Black Family Structure in Late Nineteenth-Century Boston," in *The American Family in Social-Historical Perspective*, ed. Michael Gordon (New York: St. Martin's Press, 1973), pp. 152-77, also touches upon the migration of single black women. Further study of census and other records is needed to fully assess how often black women migrated alone, with the intent of living with an aunt or older sister once they arrived.   1203

9. "Toting" was the practice of accepting food from the employer's kitchen as "supplement" to paid wages, or less frequently in place of paid wages. "Toting" was also referred to as "taking home the service pan." To tote means to add up to—in this case to add up to the total payment earned for work.

10. Twelve of the fifty-two black women interviewed had worked for the same family for twenty years or more. Four of the younger black women interviewed had mothers who had worked for the same family for long periods of time. These women, of course, are not a sample representative of all domestic workers. Further studies are needed to determine the average length of employment with one family.

11. "Waiting on" was the term used to describe pregnancy leave. The employer chose whether to leave the position available for the worker, that is to "wait" on her. This leave seems generally to have been, and to be still, unpaid. Black women often recalled sending someone else—a sister, daughter, or other relative—in their place to work "to keep the job going" for two or three months.

12. As quoted by Eugene Genovese in *Roll, Jordan, Roll: The World The Slaves Made* (New York: Pantheon Books, 1974), p. 118.

13. Robert Coles, *Children of Crisis: A Study of Courage and Fear* (Boston: Little, Brown and Company, 1964), p. 66.

14. To "put out that back door" means to open the back door of a car, showing the person about to enter that he or she must ride in the back seat, must not be seated in the front seat by the (white) driver.

15. Recent sociological studies include Robert Hamburger's *A Stranger in the House* (New York: Macmillan, 1978), a book of oral histories of northern domestic workers; a chapter in Bettina Aptheker's book, *Woman's Legacy: Essays on Race, Sex, Class in American History* (Amherst: University of Massachusetts Press, 1982), a study of domestic work within a Marxist framework; Elizabeth Clark-Lewis' "This Work Had A' End: The Transition From Live-in to Day

Work," (*Southern Women: The Intersection of Race, Class and Gender*, Working Paper 2; Memphis: Center for Research on Women, Memphis State University, 1985), a comparison of live-in versus live-out work among domestic workers in the Washington, D.C. area from 1900 to 1920; Judith Rollins' book *Between Women: Domestics and Their Employers* (Philadelphia: Temple University Press, 1985), a study of the relationship of domestic workers to their employers in the Boston area in the 1980s; Linda Martin and Kerry Segrave's *The Servant Problem: Domestic Workers in North America* (Jefferson, N.C.: McFarland, 1985), a look at the status of domestic workers from 1940 to the present; and scattered publications of the Department of Labor and the National Committee on Household Employment. Historical studies include Katzman's *Seven Days a Week* and Sutherland's *Americans and Their Servants*. Literary criticism includes only one book-length work, Trudier Harris' *From Mammies to Militants: Domestics in Black American Literature* (Philadelphia: Temple University Press, 1982).

1204

Susan Tucker is a Fellow at the Newcomb College Center for Research on Women, Tulane University. Trained as a librarian, she has worked since 1978 in the gathering and compiling of bibliographic material on the relationship of southern domestic workers and their employers. In 1980 she began recording oral memories of and about these two groups of women in the Gulf South. Some of the interviews conducted on this project will be published in 1988 by Louisiana State University Press. This article grew out of early efforts to analyze and write about these recorded memories after six years spent transcribing and editing amidst mothering and other domestic and professional jobs. For their willingness to discuss ideas and for their help in the editing of this paper, she is sincerely grateful to Beth Willinger, Newcomb College; Barbara Ewell, Loyola University; and the editors at *Frontiers*.

SYLVIA WOODS

You Have to Fight for Freedom

I WAS BORN March 15, 1909. My father was a roofer. In those days they put slates on the roofs and he was a slater. It was a very skilled job. You had to nail the slate. They used to make a fancy diamond with different colors. Every time the white guys got ready to do this they sent him for the bucket of beer so that he wouldn't learn it. But when they got ready to send him for the beer, he would find something wrong. He didn't know where his hammer was or he had to get something before he went, and in the meantime he would be watching. He learned it and he could do it beautifully. He'd say, "I'm the best. I stole it from those bastards but I'm the best." He became so good he didn't have to work with contractors any more. He could go out on his own.

And he was a union man. There was a dual union—one for whites and one for blacks. He said we should have one big union but a white and a black is better than none. He was making big money—eight dollars a day. I used to brag that "My father makes eight dollars a day." But he taught me that "You got to belong to the union, even if it's a black union. If I wasn't in the union I wouldn't make eight dollars a day."

New Orleans is a trade union town. My father had seen the longshoremen organize and they made a lot of money. Unions were not new to this city. And I mean they had unions! When they came out on strike, there were no scabs. You know why there were no scabs? Because you carried your gun. The pickets had guns and they would blow your brains out.

Originally published in *Rank and File: Personal Histories by Working-Class Organizers*, Alice and Staughton Lynd, eds. (Boston: Beacon Press, 1973).

My father got into the Garvey movement when the Garvey movement was being born. I was about maybe nine or ten at the beginning of the Garvey movement. We couldn't wait for Sundays to come because we went to the big meeting in Longshoremen's Hall. The band would be playing and we would march. Everybody had a title and everybody had a uniform. My husband used to say that any organization that puts a black in a uniform, that's all he needs. It makes him something special. If you have a uniform it gives you a little more dignity. The other thing was freedom. You want to leave this oppression and go back to the mother country and have some freedom. This was the beginning of my realizing that you have to fight for freedom.

1206

I'll never forget, there was a little woman there and she used to speak every Sunday. When that woman got up to talk, my father would just sit thrilled and then he'd look at me: "Are you listening?" I'd say, "I'm listening." "I want you to hear every word she says because I want you to be able to speak like that woman. We have to have speakers in order to get free." And then when we got home he would say, "Now what did she say?" I could say it just like her, with her same voice, all of her movements and everything. This would please him no end.

He was a gentle man. He believed in women doing things. He never slapped my mother. If the housework didn't get done, he didn't see it. There were more important things to do.

He was a very kind man. He never raised his voice. He never wanted my mother to give us a licking and my mother was hard on us. She really would give it to us, but he would say "No" if he was home.

I had a grandmother who was very religious and my mother was kind of because that was her upbringing. After she married my father she sort of got away from it. But my grandmother made us go to church and she would frighten us: "You're going to die and go to Hell 'cause you're telling a lie and when I get through beating you, you're not going to tell any more lies." I was actually afraid I might go to Hell. My father would say, "That's a lot of crap. This is what the white folks tell you so that you will be scared. They go to church and come right out of church and lynch a nigger before

you can say scat. Now, are they scared that they're going to Hell?"
My grandmother used to get so angry with him. "Tom, you are
going to send those children's souls to Hell." He said, "The white
folks send them to hell every day. They were sent to hell when
they were born right here on earth, Ma." She would pray and we'd
all have to go and pray and he'd say, "Don't believe all that. Go
and kneel down but don't be saying all that crap."

My grandmother was born in slavery. It's a funny thing, we never
thought to talk to her about it. She never talked to us except to
say, "Scrub the kitchen," or do something or don't do something,
or "Come with me."

If she hadn't had a stroke I wouldn't have been married until I
was maybe forty because she took me everywhere. When I was
twelve years old she was still picking me up from school. "You
got to watch girls. You can't be too careful with girls."

When I was maybe ten years old, I changed schools. On the way
to school, I had to go through a park that was for white people
only. We could walk through the park but we couldn't stop at all,
just pass through it. There were swings in this park and, oh, I so
much wanted sometimes to just stop and swing a little while, but
we couldn't because we were black. I would walk through this park
to my school where there weren't any swings.

Every morning all the kids would line up according to classrooms
and we would have prayers and sing the Star Spangled Banner and
then we'd march to our respective groups after this business.

I decided I wasn't going to sing the Star Spangled Banner. I just
stood there every morning and I didn't sing it. One morning, one
of the teachers noticed that I wasn't doing it. So she very quietly
called me over and asked me why didn't I sing the Star Spangled
Banner. I said I just didn't feel like singing it. So she said, "Well
then you have to go in to the principal and explain that to him.
All of the children in the school take part and you've got to do
it too."

OK, I went in to the principal and he asked me why I wasn't
singing the Star Spangled Banner. He threatened me with a lot of
[stuff like] I'd have to bring my mother. I said, "I don't care. I'll
tell her to come but she won't come because she has to go to work."

1207

I said my grandmother would come, not my mother. "Alright, then you'll have to bring your grandmother." I said, "She don't care if I don't sing the Star Spangled Banner." (I didn't know whether she would care or she wouldn't care.) He said, "You won't be able to come to school here." And I said, "So, OK, I won't come."

He says, "Why don't you want to sing it?" Finally I told him. "Because it says 'The land of the free and the home of the brave' and this is not the land of the free. I don't know who's brave but I'm not going to sing it any more." Then he said, "Why you've been singing it all the time haven't you? How come you want to stop now?" And I told him about coming through the park and if I could not swing in those swings in the park, and I couldn't sit in the park, and I could only walk in Shakespeare Park, then it couldn't be the land of the free. "Who's free?" He didn't say anything.

Then he said, "Well, you could pledge allegiance to your flag." I said, "It's not my flag. The flag is with freedom. If the land is free and the flag is mine, then how come I can't do like the white kids?" And then I told him that the next white kid I see, I'm beating him up. "I'm telling you right now, he's just going to get all beat up. I don't care." He says, "But you can't do that. You could go to Jones Home." So I said, "Well, I'll go to Jones Home. I don't care. But he'll get beat up. I know that!"

Anyway, he told me that I didn't have to sing the song and I didn't have to pledge allegiance but I had to stand in the back of the line. So who cares about standing in the back of the line? Sometimes the white administrators would come to the school and look the niggers over. (We called it that. "Well, there's the white folks looking the niggers over.") And he didn't want them to see me. But I didn't mind getting in the back of the line as long as I didn't have to sing that song. But I was so hurt and disillusioned, I would not have sung it no matter what. I'm sure that this man must have sympathized with me although he gave no indication that he did. He had said he was going to make me bring my parents but he never mentioned it again. I never sang it again from the time I was ten years old. I still don't pledge allegiance to the flag and I don't sing the Star Spangled Banner.

1208

My mother had two children, my brother John and me, and then we had a brother Joseph. I'm eleven years older than him. She had to work and I had to take care of the two boys. Every morning when she got ready to go to work Joseph would cry, "Mama, please stay home!" She had to go off and leave him and I know how her heart must have been broken. In the evenings I would take him to meet her. We walked two blocks to the streetcar. The first street-car would come along and she wouldn't get off. He'd say, "Where is Mama?" I'd say, "She will be on the next one." So the next one would come and she wouldn't get off and he would cry, "When is she coming?" She left him crying; she found him crying. You know she felt sorry for me her little girl, her first born, taking this burden.

1209

She went to work in "the white folks' yard," as the blacks would say. She did the washing—and then there wasn't any washing machine—she did it by hand. This man used to have fifteen white shirts a week. She took care of the child, the house, the washing, the ironing, everything but the cooking. I think she made two dollars a day.

My mother was very strict with me. The school used to have dances for the youngsters on Saturday. I could go if John went with me (that's my older brother). He would say, "Don't dance with him. I saw him carrying on in the corner. You dance with him and I'll be telling Mama." And then, "Come on. Let's go." "But John, just one more . . ." "Let's go! I'm ready to go." I'd say, "I'll bring in your wood for a week." "OK, bring in my wood for a week. You can dance another dance." Then I'd have to do all of his chores for a week in order to dance another dance.

They were really strict and tight, so I wouldn't get spoiled, so I wouldn't have a baby. (They didn't know that I wasn't going to have any babies.) Then my grandmother had this stroke and I had to take care of her. And I had to mind Joseph. I didn't mind minding him—we were happy.

Finally, I got tired of it. Then Henry came along and he was talking about we would get married and then we would go to Chicago. I had never been on a train in my life. I would have married just to get on that train and come to Chicago.

He lived two blocks away from us. We grew up together. But my mother didn't know his parents. The first time he came he asked my mother if he could come to see me and she said, "Have your mother come up here Sunday and we'll discuss it." I was fifteen. The next winter I got married. When he got serious my mother was sorry she had let him come. We got married and my mother just hated it. My father didn't want me to get married either. My father was a skilled laborer making eight dollars a day and here is this man who didn't even have a trade. Henry was working as a porter in a dress shop. "How do you intend to take care of her?" my father asked him. "She can't cook. She is lazy. You will not find anybody as lazy as that girl! I'm telling you what you are getting. She doesn't want to do a thing in the house and her mother has to get after her to wash the dishes. She slops them up. She don't dry them. You take down a plate to eat and water drops in your face. She is the laziest thing you have ever seen." Henry said, "Yes, sir. That's all right. We'll get married."

Henry came to Chicago. He got a job and he sent me a one-way ticket. I was so happy. It took him three months to send it to me because the train fare was $35. Thirty-five dollars was a lot of money. When I got the ticket I told my mother, "I got my ticket, Ma. I can go to Chicago!" She looked at it and it was a one-way ticket. She said, "Put that thing in that dresser over there and leave it there. When your father gets enough money, he'll buy you a two-way ticket and then you'll be able to go. You're not going away from here with a one-way ticket." I cried and cried. She said, "You take your round-trip ticket and if they say your eye is black you can tell them the devil with them and you'll come home." So I had to wait. It took almost a month before she got that ticket.

The minute I got off the train and I told Henry that I had the two-way ticket, he couldn't wait until the next morning to go down town and sell the other half of it so that he would have some money, because he had lost the job in the meantime. It was in the heart of the Depression. He's a little guy and in those days they just didn't hire little guys.

So I had to go to work. I had never had a job in my life. I came from a family that didn't allow the girls to work because they didn't know who you were going to work with and you couldn't mix and mingle with anybody and everybody. All you could do is go to school.

I got this job in a laundry. The first morning I went there, this guy asked me, "Did you ever work in a laundry before?" I said, "No." He said, "Well there's no point in your coming here because we only hire people who know how to work in a laundry." I said "OK" and I left. The next morning I went back because I didn't know any place else to go. "Weren't you here yesterday?" "Yes." He said, "Well, I told you that we don't hire people who don't know how to work in a laundry." I said, "Well, maybe you'll need somebody one day. I'll come back tomorrow." So the next day I came back. When I walked in the door he said, "Come with me." He took me upstairs and he said to the foreman, "Teach her how to shake out."

1211

You had to shake these clothes out and put them on long poles. You know how things look when they come out of a wringer. You had to shake them out so that they could run them through the mangle. Two girls put the things through the mangle. One girl did the sheets and the other did the small things like towels and pillow slips. I worked really hard. I kept those poles full. The women would say, "You mean you never worked before?" I'd say, "I never had a job before."

When I went back the next day, my arms were aching. I just couldn't lift them up. The women were angry with me. They said, "You just don't want to work." There was this one big fat woman and she said, "That kid's tired. You know it's the first time she's ever worked. What in the hell do you expect of her? If anybody else says anything to her, they're going to have to reckon with me." She was pulling those great big bags and tying them up and pitching them just like they were nothing. Nobody wanted to reckon with her. I limbered up in the afternoon and I did a little better.

So then I wanted to start shaking sheets because there is an art to shaking sheets. You pick these sheets up and—wham—if you did it right they popped. You made the sheet pop and then you threw it over that pole. This fascinated me. "Come on over here. You can shake out the sheets." I was going so fast. There were four poles and if we kept those poles full, then I could monkey around.

I'd go over and watch the women feed the sheets into the mangle. One day I said to this white gal (only white feeders—black shakers and black folders, the hardest jobs—white table girls), I said, "Will you let me see if I can run this?" She said, "Sure." By the next week I knew how to feed.

So the next week I wanted to fold. I hurried up and filled the poles and they showed me how to fold. I wasn't there three weeks before I knew how to do everything.

I was working for ten dollars a week and I asked this white woman on the mangle, "How much do you make?" She said, "Fifteen dollars." I said, "You mean you're making fifteen and he's only paying me ten?" She said, "Yes, but I'm a feeder." I said, "Well that girl over there"—and she was a Negro woman—"she only makes ten and she was feeding. I'm going to ask him for a raise." She said, "Kiddo, don't do it because you'll be fired if you do." "He doesn't have to fire me. I'm going to quit. I'm not working for ten dollars a week."

The next morning I said to the owner, "Hey Charlie." "What do you want?" He never stopped walking. You had to walk behind him to talk to him so I walked right behind him. I said, "I'm not working for ten dollars any more." "What do you mean you're not working for ten dollars any more? I hired you, you didn't know how to do a goddamned thing, I did you a favor." I said, "I know how to feed and fold and stack." He said, "It's impossible. You've only been here three weeks. I don't believe it."

He came up and he watched me work. I stood at that mangle and fed those sheets in. He said, "Speed it up!" I put it up to its highest notch and ran it. He said, "All right, I want to see you fold." I snatched those sheets out of that mangle, me and this other girl. . . . He didn't say a word. He turned around and he walked out.

Everybody said, "He's going to fire you. He's going to get you." I said, "I don't give a damn if he fires me. I don't have to work here. I know how to feed and fold. I can go to King's Laundry down at the next block."

The next week he raised me to eighteen dollars. That was the top for the table girls. He said, "Now don't you tell anybody." The minute I got that check I went right back up and said, "Hey everybody, I got a raise!" "Aw, you're crazy." I said, "Look at my check! Eighteen dollars." So they called him up and they asked, "How come she's getting eighteen dollars" instead of saying, "Give me eighteen dollars too!" He looked at me and said, "God damn you, I made a mistake when I hired you. I told you not to tell anybody."

Then they organized a night shift. There was so much work that they just couldn't get it all out. So they put all the black workers on nights. I used to work from five o'clock in the evening until three o'clock in the morning, every night. I was getting $18—top salary.

No whites. All blacks but the blacks were stealing them blind. They were wrapping sheets around them and wearing them home and taking everything. They said, "Well, hell, we are just getting the rest of our pay." The foreman would go downstairs and everybody would stop. They wouldn't do a thing.

One night a white woman was hired. "Who is this white woman?" Everybody was looking around. She was hired to watch us to see that we didn't do any stealing. The boss came up and said that this woman was going to be the forelady. I said, "I don't know what the rest of you think but I'll be goddamned if she's going to be forelady over me. We've been working nights for over a year. We've the most seniority. We're all black women here and if he has to have a forelady I don't know why he couldn't have one of us. She's got to go." So everybody got mad. They closed the mangles down.

And then the boss comes up. He walks right up to me and says, "What's going on here?" I said, "We're not working." He said, "Why not?" I said, "We're not going to have a white forelady over all black women. Until you get her out of here, we're not going to work. If you are going to have a forelady you have to get one of us. Either one of us or nobody." So he goes out and calls the cops.

1213

The cops came in and said we had to get out if we weren't going to do any work. We really messed the place up. We mixed the bundles up until the cops didn't know what to do. They told them that I was the ringleader and they put me in the patrol wagon but the white policeman just took me home.

We went up to my house and held a meeting. It was all new to me and I didn't know how far to take it. We didn't fight any more. We just left. But they didn't put a white forelady over us!

My husband got fired that night—he was working there—and they fired my brother. I just went down the next block to another laundry and got a better job. I was making $20 a week as a table girl and all around girl.

1214

From there I went to a laundry in Oak Park that paid 32 cents an hour, and that was a lot of money! This laundry was owned by a family and they would give us a turkey every year for Christmas and two weeks vacation with pay. This was unheard of. Other laundries were paying 18 and 20 cents an hour, their top rate was 25 cents an hour, but Brooks in Oak Park paid 32 cents.

When the union came to organize, I went to all the meetings and I was the spokesman for our laundry, for Brooks. The union said that they had negotiated with the laundry owners for 26 cents an hour. And I said, "You have got to be kidding! We are already making 32. You have to negotiate for 35."

I got mad and quit the union because the best they could get was 26 cents. I just pulled out the whole Brooks laundry. We walked out of the goddamned union.

The guy came running after me, "You can't do this. You have to come back." "I'm not coming back because you had no business to negotiate the contract. You should have brought it to us first." They had signed the contract and it was a closed shop and eventually everyone had to join the union. So I quit the laundry.

I was still in the laundry when the war came. My friend Martina and I decided we were going to go to work in a war plant, Martina and I both, so that we could earn some more money. And we were sick and tired of working in a laundry.

We went over to Wilson Jones. That's a place that made notebooks and papers. There I learned to run a punch press. Then

I heard about Bendix Aviation that made carburetors for airplanes. It was right around the corner from where I lived. They used to wear blue uniforms, pants and a blouse, and I loved it. The black gals would put on a white shirt under the blue and they'd bring the collar of it out. They'd wear white socks and they'd get blue sneakers. You really had an outfit. You had the cap. "I've got to get a job in there!"

So I went to Bendix looking for a job. I used to go about three times a day. I would go in the morning and they would tell me I was too fat. Then I'd go home and put on a hat and I'd go back in the afternoon and they'd say, "Well, we're not hiring right now." I would sit there and hear them begging white girls to take jobs, so I picked a fight with them. I said, "What do you mean you're not hiring? You were begging that woman. You told her you had a job at nights on the punch press, and nobody can operate a punch press better than I." He said, "We don't have punch presses here." I said, "Whatever you have, I can do it." But I didn't get hired. They had their quota.

Finally they wanted to give me a job. What is the job doing? Cleaning up the bathroom. I wasn't taking no washroom job! "I want to work on a *machine*." Martina took the job, which was good because otherwise I never would have gotten in there.

One day she called me up at home. "Hurry up and come on over here. There's a man here says he'll hire you." We always thought that this guy had some connection with the Communist Party. He hired everything black that came in. Martina went to him and she said, "I have a friend who wants to work in the factory and she's been coming and coming and they never will hire her." He said, "Tell her to come. I'll hire her." So he hired me. When I walked in the door of the plant I said, "I'm going to make you sorry for every day that I walked around to this shop hoping to get hired!"

I worked on the carburetors. I was on an assembly line that had two sides and a belt ran down the center and I was burring—taking all of the burrs off the carburetor. Right across from me was a young Polish woman named Eva. She was going to show me how to do it. We did about ten of them. Then I said, "You don't have to

1215

help me any more.'' She said, ''Do you think that you can keep
up with the line?'' ''I can keep up with the line.'' So I did. Eva
and I became real good friends because when she got stuck I would
reach over and help her.

One night she said, ''There's a union meeting tonight. Will you
go with me to the union meeting?'' And I said, ''Ahh, I'm tired.''
She said, ''Aw, come on and go.'' She said, ''I want to buy you
a drink anyway,'' because I had helped her. I said, ''OK, you can
buy me a drink but I don't want to go to a union meeting.''

So we went to this tavern and then we started talking union. I
got kind of high, you know, and ''OK, we'll go to the union meeting.''

1216

This was United Automobile Workers. I was the only black there.
All the stewards were coming in and saying how they couldn't
organize the workers: ''I can't get anybody to join''; ''So-and-So
said the union is no good . . .''

I said, ''You know why you can't get anybody to join? Because
you don't have anything to sell them. You aren't selling them union.
You're letting them sell you non-union from what I hear you saying
here. You'll never get the workers to join the union if you let them
tell you the union isn't any good. I wouldn't join a union that's
no good either.'' A steward must sell the union, telling the workers
how much strength they have when they are organized.

I looked at this guy who was the organizer and his face was just
lighting up. ''Union! What do you mean? I'll bet you if I was the
steward I could sign them up.'' The next day I was elected steward
of my department. Two nights later everybody in that department
was signed up.

I only joined the union for what it could do for black people.
I didn't care anything about whites. I didn't care if they lined them
all up and shot them down—I wished they would! I had no knowledge of the unity of white and black. I had no knowledge that you
can't go any place alone. The only thing that I was interested in
was what happened to black people.

Of about three thousand, twenty-five per cent were blacks. Ninety
per cent were women. I was making ninety cents an hour—great
big money! I never thought I would live to make that much money.

When the union thought they were ready they notified the Labor Relations Board and an election was held in the shop. The union won. Then we were going to have an election of officers for the union. I was nominated for financial secretary. I didn't know how to account or keep books and I didn't want to be bothered but I accepted the nomination.

Then Mamie Harris came to me and tried to convince me that I shouldn't run for office. I said, "What do you mean I shouldn't run for office?" (She had somebody else all picked out to be financial secretary.) "Why shouldn't I run? I have been nominated and I have accepted and my name is going to be on the ballot and why in the hell should I take it off?" She said, "Well, do you know how to keep books?" I said, "No, I don't know how to keep books? Do you?" She said, "Yes." "Well, didn't you have to learn? So, I'll learn." She never got around to telling me why I shouldn't run.

Then I went back and told the guys Mamie Harris had told me not to run and that did it! "Discrimination! We got to get her!" From then on the campaign became black against white.

I probably would not have won except that everybody on the night shift was going to vote for me because I was known. I became shop committeewoman when I was working nights and I never lost a case. I settled almost every case on the first phase of the grievance procedure because the foreman knew that I wasn't going to let up. I was going all the way up to the top—arbitration, anything. We always took the worker in when there was a grievance they brought. They saw how we fought. They'd come out and tell it. "You better join the union. I mean because if you get in trouble, Sylvia goes in there and wrecks the place. You better join." So everybody knew me.

The night shift was smaller than the day shift. If everybody on the day shift had voted, they probably would have beaten me. But the day shift didn't come out to vote in as large numbers as the night shift. The night shift didn't have anything to do but go to the union hall. They couldn't go home washing and ironing and cooking and scrubbing at that time in the morning. They had plenty of time, so they all came to vote.

I won by two measly votes. Then they demanded a recount. I won by one vote. The director of the region took me under his wing.

1217

I didn't know what to do and they were sending guys in from downtown to help me.

We had the reputation with the international for being a good local. In fact, the region gave a party for our local because we kept 90% signed up. With the turnover being what it was in those days, we still kept 90%. We were a well-organized local.

We never had check-off. We didn't want it. We said if you have a closed shop and check-off, everybody sits on their butts and they don't have to worry about organizing and they don't care what happens. We never wanted it.

1218

One day a black guy came there looking for a job—one of the skilled jobs. Mamie was called because they were going to hire him. If they hired him, the guys said, they would walk out. But [the company] wanted to hire him because they needed him and he came well recommended. Mamie said, "Fine." So she went back in and said, "He's coming here to work. Anybody that doesn't like it if a black person comes in this shop can leave right now. Turn in your union cards and get the hell out. Go." But nobody left. The guy came and he worked. Two days later he was friendly with one, and the next day with another. Soon he was getting along very well.

So this made me take a little notice of Mamie. She wasn't so bad. She was fighting for the black people so I said, "That gal is all right."

Then another thing came up with another young woman, Selma. They were having a cutback. In our contract it said that you could be cut back to the highest skill and nothing more. The highest skill for Selma was in a department where there had never been any blacks. Selma was a fiery little thing and she was single-minded that she go in there. Here too, they said that if Selma came in, they would walk out. This was on the night shift. I went down there and I said, "If you walk out, fine. We'll fill your places before you get home." They were going to wait and see Mamie in the morning. Mamie told them the same thing. They stayed. Nobody left. About two weeks later, there was an opening for a steward and they nominated Selma to be steward. Selma was elected.

The night Selma was elected I was really tired. I was sitting in the office waiting to go and Mamie came over and said, "I have a friend who is having a party. I'd like you to go to the party with me." I wasn't going to go to a party with white folks! She had to be kidding. I said, "I don't want to go." She said, "Why not?" I said, "I just don't go to parties with white folks. I've never been to one." She said, "But there's going to be colored people there too." I said, "This I have to see."

We went to the party and I enjoyed it. They were writing a letter to someone's husband who was in the Army. Everybody had to sign it. "Well, he won't know me," I said. So Mamie said, "Put down that you're Sylvia Woods and he doesn't know you but he's going to know you when he comes home."

Mamie had done these few things and I had begun to like her. She got in my good book. From then on she was instrumental in teaching me the need for unity between black and white, who was the enemy, because I thought the white people were our enemy —every white worker in America. And she taught me that that was not so. My attitude about black and white changed when I saw what Mamie was doing.

The next year when election time came up nobody ran against me but somebody ran against Mamie and I got more votes than she did. Then I began to see that if I could win an election and get more votes than Mamie with only twenty-five per cent blacks in there, if every single black person voted for me I still could not have won the election, no matter what. So all these white people had to vote for me. Now this is something. I began to think "Now why are they voting for me? Why?" And then, "They're voting for you because you're fighting for them."

We had one guy from Tennessee who went down south and overstayed his vacation. He didn't send a telegram. He came back and the company fired him. We got his job back with back pay. Then after the union got him back in the shop, he didn't want Selma in this department. I was for going down there and throwing him out bodily and Mamie said, "Let's not do it like that." (We became a really good team. I would fly off, she would rub me down. When she would get mad, I'd say, "Just a second, Mamie . . .") Mamie said, "I'll write him a letter." She wrote him a letter and she said that the union spent half of whatever the arbitration cost was to get

1219

him back in the shop. . . . Well, that guy changed and he worked
for Selma. He became one of the best union members in the shop.
We threw a party one night and he came—this southerner who didn't
want a black to do anything—he brought his wife and children. We
used to call him Tennessee. I danced with him that night. It was
really something.

We used to have a lot of absenteeism and we took the position
that you can't fire anybody for being absent. We would tell them,
"You don't have to tell any lies. You don't have to make up any
excuses. If you're tired and you are absent, you just put down
'Tired.' " The foreman would say, "But you can't say . . .'"
"But, that's the only reason I was off. I was tired. I worked seven
days straight for three months without a day off, so I am tired."

Every night I would have departmental meetings. The women
were coming off the night shift at three o'clock in the morning. They
didn't have to go home, so this was some recreation for them. We'd
have beer and sandwiches and coffee and cake or whatever. We'd
sit there and eat and talk. People would voice their grievances about
the shop, home, family or whatever. They'd love to come. Every
night we met, department by department. This kept us organized.

We had good union meetings too. We would have speakers. Either
I would speak or Mamie would speak or we would invite a speaker
to come in. We would talk about trade unionism. How were trade
unions organized? What was the very beginning? How come they
were organized? We would talk about the structure of the international union, how it was set up and how it worked and why it worked
like it did, how the cio was born. We would have a question period
where the workers could ask questions. We would discuss current
events.

We had social things too. We had a picnic and a big Christmas
dance every year. We organized a horseback riding team.

We stayed there until the day the plant closed down. I'll never
forget the day the plant closed down. Everybody came to work and
there we didn't have any job. I wasn't so worried about my not
having a job. I wondered, "What am I going to do without these
people?" Everybody just stood around the gate.

Two years after the plant closed up, we still had union meetings.

1220

We would have full crowds. We were fighting for [unemployment] compensation. We made ninety cents an hour and some, of course, made more. You would go to get your compensation and they'd offer you a job. You weren't supposed to take a job that was less than the rate you had been getting. We would fight these cases. They would throw them out and we would go down to the arbitration board and fight the cases and win them. We could call a union meeting and bring in maybe seventy-five per cent of our plant two years after it closed down. We had representation in the international because we still had the workers together.

The main thing that I would say is that you have to have faith in people. You know, I had very little faith in white people. I think that I had faith in black people. But you have to have faith in people, period. The whites, probably a lot of them feel towards blacks like I felt. But people, as a rule, come through.

You have to tell people things that they can see. Then they'll say, "Oh, I never thought of that," or "I have never seen it like that." I have seen it done. Like Tennessee. He hated black people. A poor sharecropper who only came up here to earn enough money to go back and buy the land he had been renting. After the plant closed he went back there with a different outlook on life. He danced with a black woman. He was elected steward and you just couldn't say anything to a black person. So, I have seen people change. This is the faith you've got to have in people.

The big job is teaching them. And I was not patient. That is another thing, you must be patient. I just didn't have any patience. If a worker did something, "To hell with you. You didn't come to the last union meeting, so don't tell me when you have a griev-ance. You just handle it the best way you can by yourself." But you can't do that. "You better go talk to Mamie Harris because I don't talk to non-union people and folks who don't come to the union meeting. Don't talk to me." This I learned was wrong. You have to be patient with people. People have to learn and they can't learn unless we give them a chance.

THE JOURNAL

OF

NEGRO HISTORY

Vol. XV—July, 1930—No. 3

THE NEGRO WASHERWOMAN, A VANISHING FIGURE

1223

The Negroes of this country keenly resent any such thing as the mention of the Plantation Black Mammy, so dear to the hearts of those who believe in the traditions of the Old South. Such a reminder of that low status of the race in the social order of the slave régime is considered a gross insult. There is in the life of the Negro, however, a vanishing figure whose name every one should mention with veneration. She was the all but beast of burden of the aristocratic slave-holder, and in freedom she continued at this hard labor as a bread winner of the family. This is the Negro washer-woman.

This towering personage in the life of the Negro can-not be appreciated today for the reason that her task is al-most done. Because of the rise of the race from drudgery and the mechanization of the industrial world the washer-woman is rapidly passing out. Confusing those women em-ployed in laundries with those washing at homes, the Bureau of the Census in 1890 reported 151,540 washerwomen, 218,227 in 1900, and 373,819 in 1910. In 1920, however, there were actually 283,557, but this number has comparatively de-clined.[1] Through machinery and the division of labor the steam laundry has made the washing of clothes a well or-ganized business with which the toiler over the wash tub

[1] U. S. Bureau of the Census, *Negro Population in the United States, 1790 to 1915*, p. 526; *Fourteenth Census of the United States*, Vol. V, p. 359.

269

cannot compete. The price required for this laundry service is not always lower than the charges of the washerwoman, but the modern laundry offers so many other conveniences and advantages that the people are turning away from her to the new agency. Only the most unfortunate and the most inefficient washerwoman who is unable to do anything else and must work for the lowest wages remains to underbid or obviate the necessity for introducing the steam laundry system. The Negro washerwoman of the antebellum and the reconstruction periods, then, has passed from the stage. For her, however, an ever grateful people will have a pleasant memory, and generations unborn may honor her in brass and stone.

And why should the Negro washerwoman be thus considered? Because she gave her life as a sacrifice for others. Whether as a slave or a free woman of color of the antebellum period or as a worker in the ranks of an emancipated people, her life without exception was one of unrelenting toil for those whom she loved. In the history of no people has her example been paralleled, in no other figure in the Negro group can be found a type measuring up to the level of this philanthropic spirit in unselfish service.

The details of the story are interesting. When a slave she arose with the crowing of the fowl to sweat all but blood in the employ of a despotic mistress for whose household she had to toil often until late in the night. On return home she had to tax her body further to clean a neglected hut, to prepare the meals and wash the clothes of her abandoned children, while her husband, also worn out with the heavier burdens of the day, had time to rest. In addition to this, she often took in other work by which she saved sufficient money to purchase her freedom and sometimes that of her husband and children. Often she had compassion on a persecuted slave and used such savings to secure his liberation at a high cost only to let him go free for a nominal charge.[2]

[2] Woodson, *Free Negro Owners of Slaves in the United States in 1830*, p. VI

As a slave, too, the washerwoman was the head of the family. Her husband was sometimes an uncertain quantity in the equation. Not allowed to wed according to law, they soon experienced that marriage meant living with another with the consent of the owners concerned and often against the will of the slaves themselves. Masters ordered women to take up with men and vice versa to produce numerous slave offspring for sale. When the slave hesitated because of the absence of real love the master's will prevailed. Just as such matches were made according to the will of the master they were likewise broken by the selling of the man or the woman thus attached, and in the final analysis the care of the children fell to the mother while the father went to the bed of another wife on some remote plantation.[3] To provide for her home the comforts which the custom of slavery did not allow she had to plan wisely and work incessantly. If the mother had not developed sufficiently in domestic art to earn a little money at leisure she usually fell back on "taking in washing."[4]

1225

When free during the antebellum period the drudgery of the Negro washerwoman was not much diminished. The earning power of her husband was not great since slave labor impoverished free labor, and the wife often had to do something to supplement the income of her unprofitable husband. Laboring, too, for those who were not fortunately enough circumstanced to have slaves to serve them, the free Negro woman could earn only such wages as were paid to menial workers. In thus eking out an existence, however, the washerwoman was an important factor. Without her valuable contribution the family under such conditions could not have been maintained.[5]

In the North during these antebellum times, the Negro washerwoman had to bear still heavier burdens. In the

[3] *Journal of Negro History*, XIV, p. 236-237.

[4] This was always a possible resort because this sort of work was looked upon as too menial for the whites.

[5] To appreciate how washerwomen figured in the life of the Negroes see Williams, *History of the Negro Race in America*, II, 136

South, her efforts were largely supplementary; but, in the North, she was often the sole wage earner of the family even when she had an able-bodied husband. The trouble was not due to his laziness but to the fact that Negro men in the North were often forced to a life of idleness. Travelers of a century ago often saw these black men sitting around loafing and noted this as an evidence of the shiftlessness of the Negro race, but they did not see the Negro washer-woman toiling in the homes and did not take time to find out why these Negro men were not gainfully employed. Negro men who had followed trades in the South were barred therefrom by trade unions in the North,[6] and the more en-lightened and efficiently trained Irish and Germans immi-grating into the United States drove them out of menial positions.[7]

In many of the Northern cities, then, Negro men and children were fed and clothed with the earnings of the wife or mother who held her own in competition with others. In most of these cases the man felt that his task was done when he drew the water, cut the wood, built the fires, went after the clothes, and returned them. Fortunate was the North-ern Negro man who could find acceptance in such a woman's home. Still more fortunate was the boy or girl who had a robust mother with that devotion which impelled her to give her life for the happiness of the less fortunate members of an indigent group. Without the washerwoman many ante-bellum Negroes would have either starved in that section or they would have been forced by indigent circumstances to return to slavery in the South, as some few had to do during the critical years of the decade just before the Civil War.[8]

The Negro washerwoman, too, was not only a bread-

[6] During the thirties and forties the trades unions barring Negroes were beginning to make themselves felt.

[7] Woodson, *A Century of Negro Migration*, pp. 41, 82.

[8] Some of the Northern States had laws barring Negroes who were not self-supporting. See Hickok, *The Negro in Ohio*, pp. 41, 42; and Harris, *Negro Servitude in Illinois*, pp. 10, 24, 121, 138, 148, 157, 162, 233-236

1226

winner but the important factor in the home. If the family owned the home her earnings figured in the purchase of it. When the taxes were paid she had to make her contribution, and the expenses for repairs often could not be met without recourse to her earnings. When the husband could not supply or showed indifference to the comforts of the home it was she who replaced worn out furniture and unattractive decorations and kept the home as nearly as possible according to the standards of modern times. She could be depended upon to clean the yard, to decorate the front with flowers, and to give things the aspect of a civilized life. In fact, this working woman was often the central figure of the family and the actual representative of the home. Friends and strangers calling on business usually asked for the mother inasmuch as the father was not always an important factor in the family.[9]

This same washerwoman was no less significant in the life of the community. The uplift worker sought her at home to interest her in neglected humanity, the abolitionist found her a ready listener to the story of her oppressed brethren in chains, the colonizationist stopped to have her persuade the family to try life anew in Liberia, and the preacher paid his usual calls to connect her more vitally with the effort to relieve the church of pecuniary embarrassment. While burdened with the responsibility of maintaining a family she was not too busy to listen to these messages and did not consider herself too poor to contribute to the relief of those who with a tale of woe convinced her that they were less favorably circumstanced than she. Oftentimes she felt that she was being deceived, but she had rather assist the undeserving than to turn a deaf ear to one who was actually in need.[10]

The emancipation of the Negroes as a result of the Civil

1227

---

[9] Certain fathers, however, were equally as conspicuous. See *Journal of Negro History*, XIV, 239.

[10] Church workers, understanding this weakness of the Negro women, have exploited them as a class known to be generous to a fault.

War did not immediately elevate the status of the Negro washerwomen nor did it bring them immediate relief from the many burdens which they had borne. In their new freedom certain favorably circumstanced Negroes were disposed to assume a haughty attitude toward these workers. After emancipation Negro men rapidly withdrew their wives and daughters from field work and restricted their efforts largely to the home; but the washerwomen who went out occasionally to do day work or had the clothes brought home, remained for several generations. There was yet so much more for them to do in the reconstruction of a landless and illiterate class that the importance of this rôle could not be underrated. For a number of years thereafter, then, certainly until 1900 or 1910 there was little change in the part which these women played in the economic life of the Negro.[11]

Why should the Negro washerwoman have to continue her unrelenting toil even after emancipation? This makes an interesting story. In the first place, the Negro was nominally free only. The old relation of master and slave was merely modified to be that of landlord and tenant in the lower South. The wage system established itself in the upper South, but soon broke down in certain parts because there was no money with which to pay; and the tenant system which followed with most of the evils of slavery kept the Negro in poverty. With such a little earning power under this system it was a godsend to the Negro man to have a wife to supplement his earnings at some such labor as washing. She did not always receive money for her services, but food and cast-off clothing and shoes contributed equally as much to the comfort of her loved ones. White employers and black employees were all hard put to it while the South was trying to recover from its devastation and the whole country was undergoing a new development, but one class could help the other, and both managed in some way to live.[12]

[11] The United States' Census figures are confusing because at one time launderers and laundresses in and outside of laundries are reported together, but in other cases they are separate.

[12] Many poor whites of that day were not any better off than the Negroes, but they were too proud to work.

In the course of time, too, when the problem of eking out an existence had been solved there came to the ambitious program of the freedmen other demands which made the services of the Negro washerwoman indispensable. In the first place, the freedmen were urged to buy homes, and they could easily see the advantage of living under one's own vine and fig tree and of thus forming a permanent attachment to the community. Land was cheap, but money was scarce. To make such a purchase and at the same time carry the other burdens did not permit the withdrawal of the washerwoman from her arduous task. Often she was the one who took the initiative in the buying of the home, for the husband did not always willingly assume additional responsibilities.[13]

1229

Then when the home had been purchased the children had to be educated. Negroes were ambitious to see their children in possession of the culture long since observed among the whites; and they were urged by the missionary teachers from the North to seek education which, as a handmaiden of religion, would quickly solve their problems. This often meant the education of the whole family at once; for, since the indifference and the impoverished condition of the South rendered thorough education at public expense practically impossible, the washerwoman had to come to the front again to bear more than her share of the burden. The missionary schools established by teachers from the North required the payment of tuition as well as board and room rent. Many things now supplied to students free of charge, moreover, had to be purchased in those days by their parents.[14]

Sometimes, too, when there were no children to educate, the husband was ambitious to become a teacher or minister, and he had to go to school to qualify for the new sphere.

[13] Biographical treatments in the *Journal of Negro History*, passim; and data in questionnaires filled out for the Association for the Study of Negro Life and History.

[14] Because of rapidly diminishing income the missionary schools are not as well equipped as they were in those days, and public institutions better equipped are taking their places.

The wife usually took over the responsibility of the home which she often financed through the wash tub. The Negro teacher or minister who did not receive such support in obtaining his education was an exception to the rule. Without this particular sacrifice of the washerwoman the Negro professional groups would be far less undermanned than what they are today. Many of the prominent Negro teachers, ministers, business men, and professional workers refer today with pardonable pride to sisters, mothers, and wives who thus made their careers possible.[15]

1230

In not a few cases the earnings of the Negro washerwoman went to supplement that of her husband as capital in starting business enterprises. This effort today is not easily estimated because most of such enterprises never succeeded. For lack of experience and judgment these pioneers in a hitherto forbidden field soon ran upon the rocks, and the highly prized savings of their companions together with their own accumulations sank beneath the wave only to discourage a people who had to grope in the dark to find the way. As a rule, however, the woman bore her losses like a heroine in a great crisis, being the last to utter a word of censure or to despair of finding some solution of a difficult problem. Often when the man at his extremity was inclined to give up the fight it was his courageous companion who brought a word of cheer and urged the procession onward.[16]

In cooperative business, this worker was a still larger factor. The Negro washerwoman, continuing just as she had been before the Civil War in social uplift and religious effort, served also in the capacity of a stockholder in the larger corporations of Negroes. Being already the main support of the school and church, she could easily become interested in business. At the same time the Negro teachers

---

[15] Data in the files of the Association for the Study of Negro Life and History

[16] Dabney, *Maggie L. Walker*, passim; Andrews, *John Merrick*, passim; and *The Modern Jack and the Beanstalk*, passim.

and professional classes, who in being taught solely the superiority of the other races had developed an inferiority complex, could not have confidence in the initiative and enterprise of the uneducated Negroes who launched these enterprises. The Negro working women who had not been misguided by such theories had no such misgivings. The only thing they wanted to know was whether it was something to give employment, prestige, and opportunity for leadership. They believed in the possibilities of their own group and willingly cooperated with any one who had a high sounding program. They were not the ignorant and the gullible, but the true and tried coworkers in the rehabilitation of the race along economic lines.[17]

Some of the leading enterprises like the St. Lukes Bank in Richmond, the North Carolina Mutual Life Insurance Company of Durham, and the National Benefit Life Insurance Company of Washington still count among their stockholders noble women of this type. These businesses have developed to the point that the well-to-do and educated Negroes now regard them as assets and participate in their development, but the first dimes and nickels with which these enterprises were launched came largely from women of this working class.

C. G. WOODSON

[17] *The Negro as a Business Man,* p. 90 et seq.

Dorothy Bolden, Organizer of Domestic Workers: She was Born Poor, But She Would Not Bow Down

DOROTHY COWSER YANCY

The seeds for change in the status of Black domestic workers in Atlanta, Georgia, were planted in 1880 when the Black washerwomen in the city organized the Washerwomen's Association. In 1881 this group, dissatisfied with working conditions and wages, went on strike and demanded a dollar per dozen pounds of wash. Approximately 3000 washerwomen were involved in the strike. Various tactics were used by those impacted to break this organized effort. White landlords threatened to increase the rent of Black tenants and some were evicted. The City Council introduced an ordinance which required all members of the association to pay $25 annually for a license. Finally, eight of the leaders were convicted of disorderly conduct. Five were fined five dollars each and three were fined $25 each. As a result

Originally published in *Sage*, Vol. III, No. 1 (Spring 1986), pp. 53-55.

1

of this systematic effort the strike was broken.[1] Yet, the seeds for change had been planted in Atlanta by the washerwomen and they were watered, fertilized and cultivated 81 years later by Dorothy Bolden when she founded the National Domestic Workers Union.

Dorothy Bolden's parents migrated to Atlanta from Madison, Georgia. Her father found employment as a chauffeur and cook; her mother was hired as a cook. Dorothy was born October 13, 1920, in Atlanta, Georgia, in the Vine City community. At an early age she fell off the porch of the family home and damaged a nerve in an eye which resulted in blindness for several years. Between the ages of seven and nine the eyesight returned and at age nine she entered the work force as a maid. After school recessed at 12:00 noon (the Atlanta school system had a split session), Dorothy worked for a Jewish family on Kelly Street near the Georgia State Capital. Duties included washing diapers (they had to be boiled to make them white), baby-sitting and washing dishes. Small of stature, Dorothy had to stand on an orange crate box in order to reach the dish pan. This job paid $1.50 weekly.[2] According to Dorothy, "we were just coming out of the depression . . . we needed some money. I had to help my parents survive."[3]

During her teenage years, Dorothy dropped out of high school and started working full-time cleaning the home of another Jewish family. Her wage increased to $3.00 per week and the task included scrubbing the floor by hand. Work commenced at eight o'clock and ended at sunset when the family had finished dinner and the dishes were washed. According to Bolden, "I was lucky, some went to work at 6:00 a.m. These were the days when families gave domestic workers grease from the bacon drippings, left-over food, old clothes and shoes to take home, thinking they had paid you off."[4] Bolden refers to this period in her life as the "second slavery."[5] Yet, this full-time job as a domestic was the beginning of many jobs that Dorothy would hold over the next 45 years.

As a young woman she worked occasionally as an elevator operator, waitress and laborer. She also suffered from an "itchy feet" syndrome. Distant, far away places constantly beckoned. In an effort to determine if the grass were greener outside Georgia, she headed to Illinois, North Carolina, New York, Virginia, and Alabama. Yet, she was always drawn back to Atlanta and to domestic work. When asked why, Bolden responded, "I kept going back to domestic work because I loved children and I still do."[6]

At one time in her career as a domestic worker, she was put in jail because she talked back to her employer. Bolden had a habit of talking back to

1234

people and had been told on several occasions by her mother that her tongue would be her ruin. This particular employer had indicated to Bolden when she was hired that she did not allow servants to use her telephone. According to Bolden, on the day of the incident the lady of the house was constantly giving orders in a nasty voice. She ordered Bolden to call her husband and tell him she would be late coming home.[7] According to Bolden, "I begged her pardon . . . if I couldn't call him to tell him my business . . . I couldn't call him and tell him hers."[8] At this point, other words were exchanged and the employer allegedly lunged at her. Bolden was rushed out of the house by the yardman and later arrested on Peachtree Road. According to Bolden, "They said I was 'mental' because I talked back. No one had ever talked as nasty to me as she did. I was in jail five days."[9]

1235

In 1964 the idea of an organization to fight for improved wages and working conditions for maids began to percolate in Bolden's mind. Black maids in Atlanta were earning from $3.50 to $5.00 a day for 12-13 hours work. Also in 1964 Bolden organized a boycott and protest against the Atlanta School Board when it attempted to move the eighth grade out of her community to a condemned building downtown. Bolden's fight was for a safe, decent school facility and quality education. As a result of her efforts, the school board later built a modern school in her neighborhood.[10] The organizing techniques learned in the skirmish with the school board were to serve her well in her later attempt to organize Atlanta's maids. As a result of her community involvement, Bolden became well known to the maids and other Atlanta citizens. Moreover, she had been riding the bus with other maids for years and had heard their constant complaints about "no money, no respect, and long hours."[11] According to Bolden, "I decided I had to do it,"[12] and in 1965 she started organizing Atlanta's domestic workers.

Why was she willing to take the big step? She admits to being influenced by Ben Perry, a local radio personality, the Civil Rights Movement, and Dr. Martin Luther King, Jr., her neighbor. According to Bolden, she talked to Dr. King about her idea of organizing domestic workers and he encouraged her. When he would see her at the neighborhood bus stop on the corner of Vine and Magnolia Streets, he always said, "Keep on doing what you're doing."[13] Some Black ministers in the city attempted to discourage her by arguing, "You can't organize those gossipy women."[14] Nevertheless, Bolden was determined and undaunted in her efforts.

In 1968 Bolden embarked upon a mission that would be all-consuming and set fire to her spirit. She began to organize Atlanta's maids when she held the first formal meeting of eight women at Perry Homes, an Atlanta public housing project. Meetings continued at the Butler Street YMCA and finally, in mid-1969, the growing band moved to the Wheat Street Baptist Church. The church was pastored by Rev. William Holmes Borders, a pillar of the Black community and an encouraging force behind Bolden. He made his church available as a long-term meeting place for the group at no expense. John McCowan, Executive Director of the Georgia Human Relations Council, also provided the group with office space and access to a telephone and a secretary. Prior to 1968, Bolden had approached representatives of organized labor for support and direction. They indicated that she needed to get at least ten women for a meeting. By mid-1968 several hundred women were meeting and organized labor expressed an interest. However, at this juncture Bolden and her group were not really interested in affiliating with the AFL-CIO. They had decided to stand on their own.[15]

1236

Although the idea for the organization was Bolden's, she had no interest in being president. Dorothy had six children, a husband, a father and a job to care for. Because she was unwilling to step forward and lead, the group elected Martha Parker as their first president in August, 1968. Several members pressured Bolden to assume the leadership role and at the September 19, 1968 meeting Parker resigned, and Bolden was elected president.[16] She continues today in that capacity. It was felt by the membership that the organization needed a charismatic leader and of course Bolden was a perfect fit.

Bolden's first order of business was to seek a charter for the group, determine the membership dues, and select a National Board of Directors. The group agreed that the objectives of the organization would be to:

Promote . . . organized and unionized Domestics, including all people, no limitations on the amount of members, no one can be a member unless you are a registered voter.[17]

The aforementioned aims and goals were incorporated into the charter which was acquired from the State of Georgia in 1968. According to the charter:

This corporation is organized and chartered for the purpose of enhancing, protecting, and promoting the economic, social and educational welfare of its members in Atlanta, Georgia, its environs and in the American nation as a

4

whole. The primary purpose of this organization shall be to benefit the community as measured by increased wages, better working conditions, and more benefits to its members as reflected by improving living standards rather than monetary profits to its members.[18]

Utilizing skills acquired from community organizing efforts and from participation in the Civil Rights Movement, Bolden moved to increase the organization's membership. After combining her ideas with those of the group, the following strategies were put into place. Individually, they agreed to talk up their organization on the city buses, call fellow maid-friends on the telephone, organize meetings in various communities, and distribute leaflets advertising meetings at the bus stops and other places frequented by maids. Each member was considered to be the membership chairperson on the bus that she rode to her job in the white community. Bolden advertised the group meetings on WAOK (a local radio station which is popular in the Black community). She also invited important city and state dignitaries to the local meetings.[19]

1237

Under Bolden's direction, the organization began to demand better wages. They demanded $13.50 per day and car fare if a maid worked four days a week or more for the same person. However, $15.00 per day plus car fare was requested if the employer worked one day a week for a family. Typically, women with families who request a maid for one day per week expect two days worth of work to be completed. No strikes were threatened because of the fear of losing jobs.[20] Bolden's dream was not a "union" in the true sense of the term. She used the word "union" to give the organization strength of its own . . . the word union gave it clout, and working class members understood the word. The group did not have access to any models or formulas for organizing maids. Bolden believed that they could not be organized like many other workers because they were individuals whose work isolated them from each other. They did not work in groups. Bolden argued that each maid had to be taught to negotiate and communicate her desires to her employers. Thus, members were trained to do this. This technique proved to be successful and most members got the wage increases that they requested.[21]

The organization, under Bolden's charismatic leadership, has engaged in activities on the local, state and national levels. From the organization's inception, voting and community activities were considered to be important. Thus, the group has participated in voter registration drives, protested against the Atlanta Mass Transit Authority, sent resolutions regarding their position on issues to numerous United States Congresspersons and Presidents, and worked in local and national political campaigns. Bolden has had the ear of Presidents Richard Nixon, Gerald Ford and Jimmy Carter on issues regarding workers. From 1972-1976 she served as a member of the Advisory Committee in the Department of Health, Education and Welfare to Secretary Elliot T. Richardson. In 1975 she was appointed to the Georgia Commission on the Status of Women by Governor George Busbee. Bolden also spent considerable energies in the 1970s helping to organize domestic workers in other cities.[22]

1238

Bolden's secondary purpose for organizing Atlanta's maids was to professionalize the field. She states that being a maid requires more than a knowledge of how to clean. It also requires a flexible personality, attitude and ability which allows one to cope with a variety of circumstances. However, at the same time the workers must demand and receive dignity and respect.[23] In an effort to professionalize the field, Bolden has implemented projects such as Maids Honor Day which honored the outstanding maid each year in Atlanta and sponsored the Career Learning Training Center where women interested in domestic work were trained for six months in reading, writing, mathematics, early childhood education, monetary budgeting, food preparation, first-aid training and how to carry out general household duties.[24]

After the founding of the organization, Bolden set up the National Domestic Workers Union non-profit employment service. Since 1980 this placement and counseling service has been the major function of the organization. Potential employers call Bolden and make requests and she in turn matches the requests with members on file. Since 1972 more than 13,000 maids have been served. Counseling and placement is the group's most successful venture. The initial wage for those placed is set by Bolden. Presently wages range from $35 to $60 per day with car fare. Atlanta maids are now eligible to receive the minimum wage, social security benefits, unemployment benefits and overtime. Bolden has lobbied on the local, state and national scene to make this possible.[25]

Now in retirement, Bolden still volunteers her time to run the National Domestic Workers Union Office and serves as President. When asked why she is still in business, Bolden responds, "I love people and the love of people will make you work for them. I love to fulfill other people's needs. Love is something you can't explain."[26] However, Bolden's commitment to making life better for maids can be described by a statement she made in

1976: "I was born poor, grew up poor and I am still poor, but I am not going to bow down. I am still a woman."[27] Dorothy Bolden is a tireless, "sturdy Black bridge."[28]

NOTES

1. David M. Katzman, *Seven Days a Week: Women and Domestic Service in Industrializing America* (New York: Oxford University Press, 1978), p. 196; William H. Harris, *The Harder We Run: Black Workers Since the Civil War* (New York: Oxford University Press, 1982), p. 37; Howard N. Rabinovitz, *Race Relations in the Urban South, 1865-1890* (New York: Oxford University Press, 1978), pp. 73-76.
2. Interview with Dorothy Bolden, National Domestic Workers Union, Atlanta, Georgia, July 16, 1986.
3. *The Atlanta Constitution*, January 6, 1983.
4. Bolden, Interview, July 16, 1986.
5. *Ibid.*
6. *Ibid.*
7. *The Atlanta Daily World*, March 23, 1975.
8. Bolden, Interview, July 16, 1986.
9. Interview with Dorothy Bolden, National Domestic Workers Union, Atlanta, Georgia, February 1, 1983.
10. *The Atlanta Journal and Constitution*, November 21, 1976. Interview with Dorothy Bolden, National Domestic Workers Union, Atlanta, Georgia, September 15, 1982.
11. Bolden, Interview, February 1, 1983, and Bolden, Interview, September 15, 1982.
12. *Ibid.*
13. *Ibid.*
14. *Ibid.*
15. *Ibid.* The August 1968-December 1968 minutes of the organization's meetings indicate that representatives of several labor unions attended. The minutes for the organization are located in the *National Domestic Workers Union Papers*, Southern Labor Archives, Georgia State University, Atlanta, Georgia.
16. Minutes of the meeting of the National Domestic Workers Union, meeting of September 19, 1968, National Domestic Workers Union Papers.
17. Minutes of the meeting of the National Domestic Workers Union, meeting of September 5, 1968, National Domestic Workers Union Papers.
18. National Domestic Workers Union Charter, 1968.
19. Minutes of the meeting of the National Domestic Workers Union, meetings of September 19, 1968-January 1, 1969, National Domestic Union Papers.

1239

20. Gerda Lerner, ed., *Black Women in White America: A Documentary History* (New York: Vintage Books, 1973), p. 237; Bolden, Interview, February 1, 1983.
21. Interview with Dorothy Bolden, National Domestic Workers Union, Atlanta, Georgia, June 25, 1985.
22. National Domestic Workers Union Papers. This information is disbursed throughout the papers.
23. *National Domestic Workers Handbook*, National Domestic Workers Union Papers.
24. National Domestic Workers Union Papers. This information is disbursed throughout the papers.
25. Interview with Dorothy Bolden, National Domestic Workers Union, Atlanta, Georgia, June 25, 1985.
26. Bolden, Interview, July 16, 1986.
27. *The Atlanta Journal and Constitution*, November 12, 1976.
28. See Carolyn Rodgers' poem "It Is Deep" in *Sturdy Black Bridges: Visions of Black Women in Literature*, eds. Roseann P. Bell, Bettye J. Parker, and Beverly Guy-Sheftall (Garden City, N.Y.: Anchor Press/Doubleday, 1979), pp. 377-78.

1240

Dorothy Cowser Yancy is Associate Professor and Associate Director, school of Social Sciences at the Georgia Institute of Technology in Atlanta, Georgia.

Acknowledgments

1. *Votes for Women: A Symposium by Leading Thinkers of Colored America.*
2. Anderson, Karen T. *Last Hired, First Fired: Black Women Workers During World War II.* Published by permission of the *Journal of American History* and the author.
3. Anderson, Kathie R. *Era Bell Thompson: A North Dakota Daughter.* Published by permission of the Historical Society of South Dakota. Copyright (c) 1982.
4. Blackwelder, Julia Kirk. *Quiet Suffering: Atlanta Women in the 1930s.* Published by permission of the author.
5. Blackwelder, Julia Kirk. *Women in the Work Force: Atlanta, New Orleans, and San Antonio, 1930 to 1940.* Published by permission of Sage Publications, Inc. and the author. Copyright (c) 1978.
6. Brady, Marilyn Dell. *Kansas Federation of Colored Women's Clubs, 1900-1930.* Published by permission of The Kansas State Historical Society.
7. Brady, Marilyn Dell. *Organizing Afro-American Girls' Clubs in Kansas in the 1920's.* Published by permission of *FRONTIERS: a journal of women studies* and the author.
8. Breen, William J. *Black Women and the Great War: Mobilization and Reform in the South.* Published by permission of the Managing Editor of the *Journal of Southern History.* Copyright (c) 1978 by the Southern Historical Association.
9. Brooks, Evelyn. *Religion, Politics, and Gender: The Leadership of Nannie Helen Burroughs.* Published by permission of *The Journal of Religious Thought.*
10. Brown, Elsa Barkley. *Womanist Consciousness: Maggie Lena Walker and the Independent Order of Saint Luke.* Published by permission of The University of Chicago Press. Copyright (c) 1989 The University of Chicago.
11. Bryan, Violet H. *Frances Joseph-Gaudet: Black Philanthropist.* Published by permission of *Sage* and the author.
12. Cantarow, Ellen and Susan Gushee O'Malley. *Ella Baker: Organizing for Civil Rights.* Published by permission of The Feminist Press. Copyright (c) 1980 by the Press.
13. Carby, Hazel V. *It Jus Be's Dat Way Sometime: The Sexual Politics of Women's Blues.* Published by permission of *Radical America* and the author.
14. Chateauvert, Melinda. *The Third Step: Anna Julia Cooper and Black Education in the District of Columbia, 1910-1960.* Published by permission of *Sage* and the author.
15. Clark-Lewis, Elizabeth. *'This Work Had a End:' African-American Domestic Workers in Washington, D.C., 1910-1940.* Published by permission of Cornell University Press. Copyright (c) 1987 by Cornell University.
16. Coleman, Willi. *Black Women and Segregated Public Transportation: Ninety Years of Resistance.* Published by permission of The Association of Black Women Historians and the author.
17. Ergood, Bruce. *The Female Protection and the Sun Light: Two Contemporary Negro Mutual Aid Societies.* Published by permission of the *Florida Historical Quarterly.*
18. Farley, Ena L. *Caring and Sharing Since World War I: The League of Women for Community Service—A Black Volunteer Organization in Boston.* Published by permission of *Ujoma: A Scholarly Journal of Black Studies.*

19. Feinman, Clarice. *An Afro-American Experience: The Women in New York City's Jail.* Published by permission of the Afro-American Historical Association of the Niagara Frontier.
20. Ferguson, Earline Rae. *The Women's Improvement Club of Indianapolis: Black Women Pioneers in Tuberculosis Work, 1903-1938.* Published by permission of the *Indiana Magazine of History.*
21. Ford, Beverly O. *Case Studies of Black Female Heads of Households in the Welfare System: Socialization and Survival.* Published by permission of *The Western Journal of Black Studies.*
22. Gilkes, Cheryl Townsend. *'Together and in Harness': Women's Traditions in the Sanctified Church.* Published by permission of The University of Chicago Press. Copyright (c) 1985 by The University of Chicago.
23. Gilkes, Cheryl Townsend. *Going Up for the Oppressed: The Career Mobility of Black Women Community Workers.* Published by permission of The Society for the Psychological Study of Social Issues.
24. Gilkes, Cheryl Townsend. *Successful Rebellious Professionals: The Black Woman's Professional Identity and Community Commitment.* Published by permission of Cambridge University Press and the author.
25. Gunn, Arthur C. *The Struggle of Virginia Proctor Powell Florence.* Published by permission of the author.
26. Guzman, Jessie P. *The Social Contributions of the Negro Woman Since 1940.* Published by permission of the Association for the Study of Afro-American Life and History.
27. Harley, Sharon. *Beyond the Classroom: Organizational Lives of Black Female Educators in the District of Columbia, 1890-1930.* Published by permission of the *Journal of Negro Education* and the author.
28. Harley, Sharon. *Black Women in a Southern City: Washington, D.C., 1890-1920.* Published by permission of the University Press of Mississippi.
29. Haynes, Elizabeth Ross. *Negroes in Domestic Service in the United States.*
30. Helmbold, Lois Rita. *Beyond the Family Economy: Black and White Working-Class Women during the Great Depression.* Published by permission of *Feminist Studies*, Inc.; c/o Women's Studies Program; University of Maryland; College Park, Maryland; 20742.
31. Hine, Darlene Clark. *The Ethel Johns Report: Black Women in the Nursing Profession, 1925.* Published by permission of the Association for the Study of Afro-American Life and History and the author.
32. Hine, Darlene Clark. *From Hospital to College: Black Nurse Leaders and the Rise of Collegiate Nursing Schools.* Published by permission of the *Journal of Negro Education* and the author.
33. Hine, Darlene Clark. *Mabel K. Staupers and the Integration of Black Nurses into the Armed Forces.* Published by permission of the University of Illinois Press and the author.
34. Hine, Darlene Clark. *The Call That Never Came: Black Women Nurses and World War I, An Historical Note.* Published by permission of the author.
35. Hine, Darlene Clark. *'They Shall Mount Up with Wings as Eagles': Historical Images of Black Nurses, 1890-1950.* Published by permission of the author.
36. Hull, Gloria T. *Alice Dunbar-Nelson: Delaware Writer and Woman of Affairs.* Published by permission of The Historical Society of Delaware.
37. Hunter, Tera. *The Correct Thing: Charlotte Hawkins Brown and the Palmer Institute.* Published by permission of *Southern Exposure*; P.O. Box 531; Durham, N.C.; 27702.
38. Jacobs, Sylvia M. *'Say Africa When You Pray': The Activities of Early Black Baptist Women Missionaries Among Liberian Women and Children.* Published by permission of *Sage* and the author.

39. Jacobs, Sylvia M. *Afro-American Women Missionaries Confront the African Way of Life.* Published by permission of Howard University Press. Copyright (c) 1987 by Rosalyn Terborg-Penn, Sharon Harley, and Andrea Benton Rushing.

40. Jacobs, Sylvia M. *Their 'Special Mission': Afro-American Women as Missionaries to the Congo, 1894-1937.* Published by permission of Greenwood Press, Inc.

41. Janiewski, Dolores. *Seeking 'a New Day and a New Way': Black Women and Unions in the Southern Tobacco Industry.* Published by permission of Cornell University Press. Copyright (c) 1987 by Cornell University.

42. Janiewski, Dolores. *Sisters Under Their Skins: Southern Working Women, 1880-1950.* Published by permission of the University Press of Mississippi.

43. Jones, Beverly W. *Race, Sex and Class:Black Female Tobacco Workers in Durham, North Carolina, 1920-1940, and the Development of Female Consciousness.* Published by permission of *Feminist Studies*, Inc.; c/o Women's Studies Program; University of Maryland; College Park, Maryland; 20742.

44. Kendrick, Ruby M. *'They Also Serve': The National Association of Colored Women, Inc., 1895-1954.* Published by permission of the Association for the Study of Afro-American Life and History.

45. Lee, Don L. *The Achievement of Gwendolyn Brooks.* Published by permission of *The Black Scholar.*

46. Leffall, Dolores C. and Janet L. Sims. *Mary McLeod Bethune—The Educator; Also Including a Selected Annotated Bibliography.* Published by permission of the *Journal of Negro Education* and the author.

47. Lerner, Gerda. *Early Community Work of Black Club Women.* Published by permission of the Association for the Study of Afro-American Life and History.

48. Matthews, Mark D. *'Our Women and What They Think,' Amy Jacques Garvey and the Negro World.* Published by permission of *The Black Scholar.*

49. McDowell, Deborah E. *The Neglected Dimension of Jessie Redmon Fauset.* Published by permission of the Afro-American Historical Association of the Niagara Frontier.

50. McDowell, Margaret B. *The Black Woman As Artist and Critic: Four Versions.* Published by permission of *The Kentucky Review* and the author.

51. Nerverdon-Morton, Cynthia. *Self-Help Programs as Educative Activities of Black Women in the South, 1895-1925: Focus on Four Key Areas.* Published by permission of the *Journal of Negro Education* and the author.

52. Newman, Debra L. *Black Women Workers in the Twentieth Century.* Published by permission of *Sage* and the author.

53. O'Dell, J. H. *Life in Mississippi: An Interview With Fannie Lou Hamer.* Published by permission of *Freedomways.*

54. Parks, Rosa. *Interview.* Published by permission of The Rosa and Raymond Parks Foundation and Steven M. Millner.

55. Peebles-Wilkins, Wilma. *Black Women and American Social Welfare: The Life of Fredericka Douglass Sprague Perry.* Published by permission of Sage Publications, Inc. and the author. Copyright (c) 1989 by Women and Social Work, Inc.

56. Pleck, Elizabeth H. *A Mother's Wages: Income Earning Among Married Italian and Black Women, 1896-1911.* Published by permission of the author.

57. Porter, Dorothy B. *Maria Louise Baldwin, 1856-1922.* Published by permission of the *Journal of Negro Education* and the author.

58. Ross, B. Joyce. *Mary McLeod Bethune and the National Youth Administration: A Case Study of Power Relationships in the Black Cabinet of Franklin D. Roosevelt.* Published by permission of the Association for the Study of Afro-American Life and History.

59. Saunders, Deloris M. *Changes in the Status of Women During The Quarter Century (1955-1980)*. Published by permission of *The Negro Educational Review*.
60. Seraile, William. *Henrietta Vinton Davis and the Garvey Movement*. Published by permission of the Afro-American Historical Association of the Niagara Frontier.
61. Smith, Elaine M. *Mary McLeod Bethune and the National Youth Administration*. Published by permission of Howard University Press. Copyright (c) 1980 by the Press.
62. Smith, Sandra N. and Earle H. West. *Charlotte Hawkins Brown*. Published by permission of the *Journal of Negro Education* and the authors.
63. Stetson, Erlene. *Black Feminism in Indiana, 1893-1933*. Published by permission of *Phylon*.
64. Still, Judith Anne. *Carrie Still Shepperson: The Hollows of Her Footsteps*. Published by permission of the *Arkansas Historical Quarterly* and the author.
65. Terborg-Penn, Rosalyn. *Discontented Black Feminists: Prelude and Postscript to the Passage of the Nineteenth Amendment*. Published by permission of Greenwood Press, Inc.
66. Trigg, Eula S. *Washington, D.C. Chapter—Links, Incorporated: Friendship and Service*. Published by permission of the Association for the Study of Afro-American Life and History.
67. Tucker, Susan. *A Complex Bond: Southern Black Domestic Workers and Their White Employers*. Published by permission of *FRONTIERS: a journal of women studies* and the author.
68. Woods, Sylvia. *You Have to Fight for Freedom*. Published by permission of Alice and Staughton Lynd.
69. Woodson, Carter G. *The Negro Washerwoman: A Vanishing Figure*. Published by permission of the Association for the Study of Afro-American Life and History.
70. Yancy, Dorothy C. *Dorothy Bolden, Organizer of Domestic Workers: She Was Born Poor But She Would Not Bow Down*. Published by permission of *Sage* and the author.

Index

their 1920 conference on race relations, 1169

Committee on Fair Employment Practice
establishment of, 945-946

Committee on Women's Defense Work (World War I)
and black women in the South, 133-152

community workers
study of black women and their mobility by Cheryl Townsend Gilkes, 399-423
successful rebellious professionals—Cheryl Townsend Gilkes's study of, 425-447

Congo
Afro-American Missionaries there (1894-1937), 740-755

Congregationalist American Board of Commissioners for Foreign Missions, 730

Congress of Colored Women (Atlanta, 1895), 1141

Congress of Industrial Organizations, 776, 798
and 1938 crabpickers strike, 944
military nurse corps—supports integration of, 644
and Southern tobacco workers, 772, 774

Congress of Racial Equality
and Council of Federated Organizations, 238
and freedom rides, 235

Consciencism (Nkrumah)
quoted, 873

Consolidated American Baptist Missionary Convention, 712

Cook, Coralie Franklin
and the Colored Young Women's Christian Association (Washington, D.C.), 483
National Association for the Relief of Destitute Colored Women and Children—active in, 481
on woman suffrage, 7-8

Cook, Helen Appo
Colored Women's League (Washington, D.C.)—founder of, 482
National Association for the Relief of Destitute Colored Women and Children—active in, 482
and National Colored Women's League, 817

Cook, John H.

National Association for the Relief of Destitute Colored Women and Children—active in, 482

Cook, Mercer, 1180

Cook, Vashti, 1180
and Links, Incorporated (Washington, D.C. branch)—formation of, 1178

Cooke, Michael G.
his book *Afro-American Literature in the Twentieth Century: The Achievement of Intimacy*—on Alice Walker, 903

Coolidge, President Calvin
pardons Marcus Garvey, 1085

Cooper, Anna Julia
quoted, 706
background of, 262
her book *A Voice from the South, By a Black Woman of the South*, 261, 262, 273; quoted, 502
Brown v. *Board of Education*—Cooper quoted on, 272
and the Colored Social Settlement of the District of Columbia, 483
her educational philosophy, 270
and Frelinghuysen University, 266-271, 484-485; quoted on 266, 267
industrial education—quoted on, 270
women's movement—Cooper quoted on, 248
World's Congress of Representative Women (1893)—her speech there quoted, 173

Cooper, Lane
Alice Dunbar Nelson's thesis advisor, 692

Cooper, Lula E. (African missionary), 721

Cooperative Women's League of Baltimore, 1169

Coppin, Fanny Jackson
Africa—missionary to (1902-1904), 736
her home for training black domestics, 521

Coppin, Levi Jenkins (first African Methodist Episcopal Bishop in South Africa), 736

Cornelius, Lucille
quoted on Women's Department of the Church of God in Christ, 393

The Correct Thing To Do, To Say, To Wear (Brown), 696, 702, 708, 1136-1137

Corregidora (Jones), 258

Coterie Club (Topeka, Kansas)

and the Colored Social Settlement of the District of Columbia, 483

and the Colored Young Women's Christian Association (Washington, D.C.), 483

National Association for the Relief of Destitute Colored Women and Children—active in, 481

Francis, Doris
biography of, 1183

Francis, Dr. Lionel A.
and the Universal Negro Improvement Association, 1086

Franklin, Alice M., 1074

Fraternal Hospital (Montgomery, Alabama)
their nurse training described, 599-600

Frazier, E. Franklin, 428
on black middle class, 422

Frazier, Lynn J. (North Dakota governor)
and Era Bell Thompson's father, 38

Frederick Douglass Home
and NACW, 822

freedom rides, 235

Freedom Summer, 238

Freeman, Minnie
biography of, 1186

Frelinghuysen University
and Anna Julia Cooper, 266-271, 484-485
early years of, 264-266

Friends American Inter-racial Peace Committee
and Alice Dunbar Nelson, 682

From Mammies to Militants: Domestics in Black American Literature (Harris), 907-908

Gainer, Ruby Jackson
her salary discrimination suit, 469

Gaines, G.L.
and the Universal Negro Improvement Association, 1081

Gaines, Irene McCoy
quoted, 823
NACW president, 823

Gale, Zona, 13

Gantt, Eliza
mother of Lucy Gantt Sheppard, 746

Garnet, Henry H.
and George A. Hackett, 1075

Garrison, James A. (uncle of Era Bell Thompson), 34, 36

Garrison, Mary Lou (cousin of Era Bell Thompson), 37

Garrison, Mrs. Memphis T.
president of the West Virginia State Teachers Association, 461

Garrison, Mina (grandmother of Era Bell Thompson), 36

Garvey, Amy Ashwood (first wife of Marcus Garvey), 1077

Garvey, Amy Jacques
and Davis, Henrietta Vinton, 1077
her feminist philosophy, 1167-1168
Negro World—her department in, 866-877, 1167
photograph of, 867
and Russia, 871
and the Universal Negro Improvement Association, 1167

Garvey, Marcus, 318, 868
and Davis, Henrietta Vinton, 1075-1086
Parks, Rosa on, 964
photograph of bust of, 867
and Russia, 871
and the Universal Negro Improvement Association, 1075-1086

Gaudet, Adolphe P. (husband of Frances Joseph-Gaudet), 195
and Gaudet Normal and Industrial School for Black Youth, 195

Gaudet Normal and Industrial School for Black Youth
and Episcopal Church, 197-198
history of, 193, 195-198

Gayle, Addison
quoted on Jessie Redmon Fauset, 879

General Cable Corporation
and black women workers, 31

General Federation of Women's Clubs, 149
their exclusion of Josephine St. Pierre Ruffin from 1900 convention, 100, 102

Genovese, Eugene
quoted on Christianity, 159

Georgia State Federation of Colored Women
activities during World War I, 146, 150

Geschwender, J.A.
quoted, 400

Gibson, Donald B.

Webster, S.W., 1062
Weeden, Allie
biography of, 1186
welfare system
black female heads of households in, 365-376
Wells-Barnett, Ida B., 318, 387, 858, 1163
and anti-lynching movement, 99, 857
and black women's club movement, 858
Harding, President Warren—meets with to demand anti-lynching legislation, 1170
her railroad suit, 296-297
the Woman's Improvement Club (Indianapolis)—she addresses, 347
Welty, Eudora, 911
quoted, 897
West, Hollie I.
on Mary McLeod Bethune, 853
West, Major Harriet M.
and Women's Army Auxiliary Corps, 462
Western and Southern Missionary Baptist Convention, 712
Western Electric
white female job action, 21
Weston, George A.
and the Universal Negro Improvement Association, 1084
White, Deborah Gray
quoted, 176
White, Eartha M., 471, 979, 981
and the Committee on Women's Defense Work (World War I), 142, 147, 148-149, 151
White, Viola, 970-971
White, Walter, 631, 639, 890
quoted, 632
quoted on the National Youth Administration, 1112
and Nelson, Alice Dunbar, 683
Parks, Rosa on, 970
on white suffrage leaders, 1162
Whiteman, Paul
and William Grant Still, 1157
White on Black: The views of twenty-two white Americans on the Negro (Thompson), 47
White Rose Mission
and Victoria Earle Matthews, 859
Whitman, Charles S.
and the Circle for Negro War Relief, 651

Whitten, Jamie (Congressman), 956, 957
Wiggins, Ella Mae, 791
Williams, Aubrey
and the National Youth Administration, 1037, 1039, 1095, 1096, 1097, 1104, 1107, 1108, 1110
Williams, Camilla
wins Marian Anderson Award, 465
Williams, Carrie Clifford
engraving of, 97
Williams, Dr. Daniel Hale
founds hospital nursing school, 661-662
quoted on black nurses, 662
Williams, Edward Christopher (first black library school graduate), 449
Williams, Fannie Barrier, 173, 318, 500
quoted, 480
her book *A New Negro for a New Century*—quoted, 872
Williams, Mary
and the Female Protective Society (Alachua County, Florida), 306
Williams, Mary Lou (jazz pianist), 464
Williams, Sherley Anne
on blues singers, 250-251
her poem on Bessie Smith, 250
Williamson, Sarah C. (African missionary), 721
Wilson, Emma
and Mary McLeod Bethune, 1094
Wilson, Emma J., 856
Wilson, President Woodrow
anti-black feelings attributed to, 494
his commitment to segregation, 649
Winston, Dr. Michael
and Links, Incorporated essay contest, 1180
Wintz, Gary De Cordova
quoted on Jessie Redmon Fauset, 879-880
womanist consciousness
Alice Walker and Chikwenye Okonjo Ogunyemi on, 172
Woman's Committee (Committee on Women's Defense Work—World War I)
and black women in the south, 133-152
Woman's Committee of the Council of National Defense
Alice Dunbar Nelson's trip for, 682
Woman's Convention of the National Baptist Convention

1283

Black Women in United States History: A Guide to the Series

PUBLISHER'S NOTE

The sixteen volumes in this set contain 248 articles, in addition to five monographs. This *Guide to the Series* is designed to help the reader find *every* substantive discussion of a topic of interest in the articles. Included in the subject index are general topics such as education and family life, as well as individuals to whom articles are devoted. Geographical locations are included when they are an important part of the article. Professions are also included. Thus, one can look up Fannie Lou Hamer (three articles), Kansas (two articles), or nursing (four articles). The more than 200 authors represented in the index to authors are a who's who of contemporary scholarship.

For topics in the five monographs and for specific discussions in the articles, please see the comprehensive indexes for every title. The more than 10,000 entries in these indexes make this series a virtual encyclopedia of black women's history.

Contents of the Series

Vols. 1-4. **BLACK WOMEN IN AMERICAN HISTORY: FROM COLONIAL TIMES THROUGH THE NINETEENTH CENTURY,** Edited with a Preface by Darlene Clark Hine

3

Volumes 1-4, continued

24. Foster, Frances Smith. *Adding Color and Contour to Early American Self-Portraitures: Autobiographical Writings of Afro-American Women.*
25. Fox-Genovese, Elizabeth. *Strategies and Forms of Resistance: Focus on Slave Women in the United States.*
26. Fry, Gladys-Marie. *Harriet Powers: Portrait of a Black Quilter.*
27. Goldin, Claudia. *Female Labor Force Participation: The Origins of Black and White Differences, 1870 and 1880.*
28. Goodson, Martia G. *Medical-Botanical Contributions of African Slave Women to American Medicine.*
29. Goodson, Martia G. *The Slave Narrative Collection: A Tool for Reconstructing Afro-American Women's History.*
30. Gregory, Chester W. *Black Women in Pre-Federal America.*
31. Griggs, A. C. *Lucy Craft Laney.*
32. Gundersen, Joan R. *The Double Bonds of Race and Sex: Black and White Women in a Colonial Virginia Parish.*
33. Gutman, Herbert G. *Marital and Sexual Norms among Slave Women.*
34. Gwin, Minrose C. *Green-eyed Monsters of the Slavocracy: Jealous Mistresses in Two Slave Narratives.*
35. Hanchett, Catherine M. *'What Sort of People and Families . . .' The Edmondson Sisters.*
36. Harris, William. *Work and the Family in Black Atlanta, 1880.*
37. Hartgrove, W. B. *The Story of Maria Louise Moore and Fannie M. Richards.*
38. Hartigan, Lynda R. *Edmonia Lewis.*
39. Hine, Darlene Clark. *Co-Laborers in the Work of the Lord: Nineteenth-Century Black Women Physicians.*
40. Hine, Darlene Clark. *Female Slave Resistance: The Economics of Sex.*
41. Horton, James Oliver. *Freedom's Yoke: Gender Conventions Among Antebellum Free Blacks.*
42. Jacobs, Sylvia M. *Three Afro-American Women Missionaries in Africa, 1882-1904.*
43. Johnson, Michael P. *Smothered Slave Infants: Were Slave Mothers at Fault?*
44. Jones, Jacqueline. *'My Mother Was Much of a Woman': Black Women, Work, and the Family Under Slavery.*
45. Kennan, Clara B. *The First Negro Teacher in Little Rock.*
46. Kulikoff, Alan. *Beginnings of the Afro-American Family.*
47. Lawson, Ellen N. *Sarah Woodson Early: 19th Century Black Nationalist 'Sister'.*
48. Lawson, Ellen N. and Merrell, Marlene. *Antebellum Black Coeds at Oberlin College.*
49. Leashore, Bogart R. *Black Female Workers: Live-in Domestics in Detroit, Michigan, 1860-1880.*
50. Lebsock, Suzanne. *Free Black Women and the Question of Matriarchy: Petersburg, Virginia, 1784-1820.*
51. Mabee, Carleton. *Sojourner Truth, Bold Prophet: Why Did She Never Learn to Read?*
52. Massa, Ann. *Black Women in the 'White City'.*
53. Matson, R. Lynn. *Phillis Wheatley—Soul Sister?*
54. Matthews, Jean. *Race, Sex and the Dimensions of Liberty in Antebellum America.*
55. Mills, Gary B. *Coincoin: An Eighteenth Century 'Liberated' Woman.*
56. Moses, Wilson Jeremiah. *Domestic Feminism Conservatism, Sex Roles, and Black Women's Clubs, 1893-1896.*
57. Newman, Debra L. *Black Women in the Era of the American Revolution in Pennsylvania.*
58. Obitko, Mary Ellen. *'Custodians of a House of Resistance': Black Women Respond to Slavery.*

Volumes 1-4, continued

59. Oden, Gloria C. *The Journal of Charlotte L. Forten: The Salem-Philadelphia Years (1854-1862) Reexamined.*
60. Parkhurst, Jessie W. *The Role of the Black Mammy in the Plantation Household.*
61. Perkins, Linda M. *Heed Life's Demands: The Educational Philosophy of Fanny Jackson Coppin.*
62. Perkins, Linda M. *The Black Female American Missionary Association Teacher in the South, 1861-1870.*
63. Perkins, Linda M. *The Impact of the 'Cult of True Womanhood' on the Education of Black Women.*
64. Perkins, Linda M. *Black Women and Racial 'Uplift' Prior to Emancipation.*
65. Pleck, Elizabeth H. *The Two-Parent Household: Black Family Structure in Late Nineteenth Century Boston.*
66. Porter, Dorothy B. *Sarah Parker Remond, Abolitionist and Physician.*
67. Quarles, Benjamin. *Harriet Tubman's Unlikely Leadership.*
68. Riley, Glenda. *American Daughters: Black Women in the West.*
69. Reiff, Janice L., Michael R. Dahlin, and Daniel Scott Smith. *Rural Push and Urban Pull: Work and Family Experiences of Older Black Women in Southern Cities, 1880-1900.*
70. Schafer, Judith K. *'Open and Notorious Concubinage': The Emancipation of Slave Mistresses by Will and the Supreme Court in Antebellum Louisiana.*
71. Scalander, Judith. *Antebellum Black Press Images of Women.*
72. Seraile, William. *Susan McKinney Steward: New York State's First African-American Woman Physician.*
73. Shammas, Carole. *Black Women's Work and the Evolution of Plantation Society in Virginia.*
74. Silverman, Jason H. *Mary Ann Shadd and the Search for Equality.*
75. Sloan, Patricia E. *Early Black Nursing Schools and Responses of Black Nurses to their Educational Programs.*
76. Soderlund, Jean R. *Black Women in Colonial Pennsylvania.*
77. Sterling, Dorothy. *To Build A Free Society: Nineteenth-Century Black Women.*
78. Sumler-Lewis, Janice. *The Forten-Purvis Women of Philadelphia and the American Anti-Slavery Crusade.*
79. Tate, Claudia. *Pauline Hopkins: Our Literary Foremother.*
80. Terborg-Penn, Rosalyn. *Black Women Freedom Fighters in Early 19th Century Maryland.*
81. Thompson, Priscilla. *Harriet Tubman, Thomas Garrett, and the Underground Railroad.*
82. Tucker, David M. *Miss Ida B. Wells and Memphis Lynching.*
83. Vacha, John E. *The Case of Sara Lucy Bagby: A Late Gesture.*
84. Wade-Gayles, Gloria. *Black Women Journalists in the South, 1880-1905: An Approach to the Study of Black Women's History.*
85. White, Deborah G. *The Lives of Slave Women.*

Vols. 5-8. BLACK WOMEN IN AMERICAN HISTORY: THE TWENTIETH CENTURY, Edited with a Preface by Darlene Clark Hine

1. *Votes for Women: A Symposium by Leading Thinkers of Colored America.*
2. Anderson, Karen T. *Last Hired, First Fired: Black Women Workers During World War II.*
3. Anderson, Kathie R. *Era Bell Thompson: A North Dakota Daughter.*
4. Blackwelder, Julia Kirk. *Quiet Suffering: Atlanta Women in the 1930s.*

Volumes 5-8, continued

5. Blackwelder, Julia Kirk. *Women in the Work Force: Atlanta, New Orleans, and San Antonio, 1930 to 1940.*
6. Brady, Marilyn Dell. *Kansas Federation of Colored Women's Clubs, 1900-1930.*
7. Brady, Marilyn Dell. *Organizing Afro-American Girls' Clubs in Kansas in the 1920's.*
8. Breen, William J. *Black Women and the Great War: Mobilization and Reform in the South.*
9. Brooks, Evelyn. *Religion, Politics, and Gender: The Leadership of Nannie Helen Burroughs.*
10. Brown, Elsa Barkley. *Womanist Consciousness: Maggie Lena Walker and the Independent Order of Saint Luke.*
11. Bryan, Violet H. *Frances Joseph-Gaudet: Black Philanthropist.*
12. Cantarow, Ellen and Susan Gushee O'Malley. *Ella Baker: Organizing for Civil Rights.*
13. Carby, Hazel V. *It Jus Be's Dat Way Sometime: The Sexual Politics of Women's Blues.*
14. Chateauvert, Melinda. *The Third Step: Anna Julia Cooper and Black Education in the District of Columbia, 1910-1960.*
15. Clark-Lewis, Elizabeth. *'This Work Had a End:' African-American Domestic Workers in Washington, D.C., 1910-1940.*
16. Coleman, Willi. *Black Women and Segregated Public Transportation: Ninety Years of Resistance.*
17. Ergood, Bruce. *The Female Protection and the Sun Light: Two Contemporary Negro Mutual Aid Societies.*
18. Farley, Ena L. *Caring and Sharing Since World War I: The League of Women for Community Service—A Black Volunteer Organization in Boston.*
19. Feinman, Clarice. *An Afro-American Experience: The Women in New York City's Jail.*
20. Ferguson, Earline Rae. *The Women's Improvement Club of Indianapolis: Black Women Pioneers in Tuberculosis Work, 1903-1938.*
21. Ford, Beverly O. *Case Studies of Black Female Heads of Households in the Welfare System: Socialization and Survival.*
22. Gilkes, Cheryl Townsend. *'Together and in Harness': Women's Traditions in the Sanctified Church.*
23. Gilkes, Cheryl Townsend. *Going Up for the Oppressed: The Career Mobility of Black Women Community Workers.*
24. Gilkes, Cheryl Townsend. *Successful Rebellious Professionals: The Black Woman's Professional Identity and Community Commitment.*
25. Gunn, Arthur C. *The Struggle of Virginia Proctor Powell Florence.*
26. Guzman, Jessie P. *The Social Contributions of the Negro Woman Since 1940.*
27. Harley, Sharon. *Beyond the Classroom: Organizational Lives of Black Female Educators in the District of Columbia, 1890-1930.*
28. Harley, Sharon. *Black Women in a Southern City: Washington, D.C., 1890-1920.*
29. Haynes, Elizabeth Ross. *Negroes in Domestic Service in the United States.*
30. Helmbold, Lois Rita. *Beyond the Family Economy: Black and White Working-Class Women during the Great Depression.*
31. Hine, Darlene Clark. *The Ethel Johns Report: Black Women in the Nursing Profession, 1925.*
32. Hine, Darlene Clark. *From Hospital to College: Black Nurse Leaders and the Rise of Collegiate Nursing Schools.*
33. Hine, Darlene Clark. *Mabel K. Staupers and the Integration of Black Nurses into the Armed Forces.*
34. Hine, Darlene Clark. *The Call That Never Came: Black Women Nurses and World War I, An Historical Note.*

Volumes 5-8, continued

Volumes 5-8, continued

68. Woods, Sylvia. *You Have to Fight for Freedom.*
69. Woodson, Carter G. *The Negro Washerwoman: A Vanishing Figure.*
70. Yancy, Dorothy C. *Dorothy Bolden, Organizer of Domestic Workers: She Was Born Poor But She Would Not Bow Down.*

Vols. 9-10. BLACK WOMEN'S HISTORY: THEORY AND PRACTICE, Edited with a Preface by Darlene Clark Hine

1. Aldridge, Delores. *Black Women in the Economic Marketplace: A Battle Unfinished.*
2. Allen, Walter R. *Family Roles, Occupational Statuses, and Achievement Orientations Among Black Women in the United States.*
3. Allen, Walter R. *The Social and Economic Statuses of Black Women in the United States.*
4. Armitage, Susan, Theresa Banfield, and Sarah Jacobus. *Black Women and Their Communities in Colorado.*
5. Biola, Heather. *The Black Washerwoman in Southern Tradition.*
6. Bracey, John H., Jr. *Afro-American Women: A Brief Guide to Writings from Historical and Feminist Perspectives.*
7. Brown, Minnie Miller. *Black Women in American Agriculture.*
8. Collier-Thomas, Bettye. *The Impact of Black Women in Education: An Historical Overview.*
9. Dickson, Lynda F. *Toward a Broader Angle of Vision in Uncovering Women's History: Black Women's Clubs Revisited.*
10. Dill, Bonnie Thornton. *Race, Class, and Gender: Prospects for an All-Inclusive Sisterhood.*
11. Dill, Bonnie Thornton. *The Dialectics of Black Womanhood.*
12. Fox-Genovese, Elizabeth. *To Write My Self: The Autobiographies of Afro-American Women.*
13. Higginbotham, Evelyn Brooks. *Beyond the Sound of Silence: Afro-American Women in History.*
14. Hine, Darlene Clark. *An Angle of Vision: Black Women and the United States Constitution, 1787-1987.*
15. Hine, Darlene Clark. *To Be Gifted, Female, and Black.*
16. Hine, Darlene Clark. *Opportunity and Fulfillment: Sex, Race, and Class in Health Care Education.*
17. Hine, Darlene Clark. *Lifting the Veil, Shattering the Silence: Black Women's History in Slavery and Freedom.*
18. Jackson, Jacquelyne Johnson. *A Partial Bibliography on or Related to Black Women.*
19. Katz, Maude White. *The Negro Woman and the Law.*
20. Katz, Maude White. *She Who Would Be Free—Resistance.*
21. King, Deborah K. *Multiple Jeopardy, Multiple Consciousness: The Context of a Black Feminist Ideology.*
22. Ladner, Joyce A. *Racism and Tradition: Black Womanhood in Historical Perspective.*
23. Lewis, Diane K. *A Response to Inequality: Black Women, Racism, and Sexism.*
24. Marable, Manning. *Groundings with my Sisters: Patriarchy and the Exploitation of Black Women.*
25. Palmer, Phyllis Marynick. *White Women/Black Women: The Dualism of Female Identity and Experience in the United States.*
26. Patterson, Tiffany R. *Toward a Black Feminist Analysis: Recent Works by Black Women Scholars.*

Volumes 9-10, continued

27. Reagon, Bernice Johnson. *My Black Mothers and Sisters, or On Beginning A Cultural Autobiography.*
28. Reagon, Bernice Johnson. *African Diaspora Women: The Making of Cultural Workers.*
29. Rector, Theresa A. *Black Nuns as Educators.*
30. Render, Sylvia Lyons. *Afro-American Women: The Outstanding and the Obscure.*
31. Scales-Trent, Judy. *Black Women and the Constitution: Finding Our Place, Asserting Our Rights.*
32. Shockley, Ann Allen. *The Negro Woman in Retrospect: Blueprint for the Future.*
33. Smith, Eleanor. *Historical Relationships between Black and White Women.*
34. Snorgrass, J. William. *Pioneer Black Women Journalists from 1850s to the 1950s.*
35. Strong, Augusta. *Negro Women in Freedom's Battles.*
36. Terborg-Penn, Rosalyn. *Historical Treatment of Afro-Americans in the Woman's Movement, 1900-1920: A Bibliographical Essay.*
37. Terborg-Penn, Rosalyn. *Teaching the History of Black Women: A Bibliographical Essay.*
38. Thornbrough, Emma Lou. *The History of Black Women in Indiana.*
39. Walker, Juliet E. K. *The Afro-American Woman: Who Was She?*
40. Yellin, Jean Fagan. *Afro-American Women 1800-1910: A Selected Bibliography.*

Vol. 11. **Daughters of Sorrow: Attitudes Toward Black Women, 1880-1920,** by Beverly Guy-Sheftall

Vol. 12. **Jane Edna Hunter: A Case Study of Black Leadership, 1910-1950,** by Adrienne Lash Jones; Preface by Darlene Clark Hine

Vol. 13. **Quest for Equality: The Life and Writings of Mary Eliza Church Terrell, 1863-1954,** by Beverly Washington Jones
including Mary Church Terrell's selected essays:

1. *Announcement* [of NACW].
2. *First Presidential Address to the National Association of Colored Women.*
3. *The Duty of the National Association of Colored Women to the Race.*
4. *What Role is the Educated Negro Woman to Play in the Uplifting of Her Race?*
5. *Graduates and Former Students of Washington Colored High School.*
6. *Lynching from a Negro's Point of View.*
7. *The Progress of Colored Women.*
8. *The International Congress of Women.*
9. *Samuel Coleridge-Taylor.*
10. *Service Which Should be Rendered the South.*
11. *The Mission of Meddlers.*
12. *Paul Laurence Dunbar.*
13. *Susan B. Anthony, the Abolitionist.*
14. *A Plea for the White South by A Coloured Woman.*
15. *Peonage in the United States: The Convict Lease System and Chain Gangs.*
16. *The Disbanding of the Colored Soldiers.*
17. *What It Means to Be Colored in the Capital of the United States.*
18. *A Sketch of Mingo Saunders.*
19. *An Interview with W.T. Stead on the Race Problem.*
20. *The Justice of Woman Suffrage.*
21. *Phyllis Wheatley—An African Genius.*
22. *The History of the Club Women's Movement.*
23. *Needed: Women Lawyers.*
24. *Dr. Sara W. Brown.*
25. *I Remember Frederick Douglass.*

Vol. 14. **To Better Our World: Black Women in Organized Reform, 1890-1920,** by Dorothy Salem

Vol. 15. **Ida B. Wells-Barnett: An Exploratory Study of an American Black Woman, 1893-1930,** by Mildred Thompson

including Ida B. Wells-Barnett's Selected Essays

1. *Afro-Americans and Africa.*
2. *Lynch Law in All Its Phases.*
3. *The Reason Why the Colored American is not in the World's Columbian Exposition.*
   Chapter IV. *Lynch Law,* by Ida B. Wells
   Chapter VI. *The Reason Why,* by F.L. Barnett

4. *Two Christmas Days: A Holiday Story.*
5. *Lynch Law in America.*
6. *The Negro's Case in Equity.*
7. *Lynching and the Excuse for It.*
8. *Booker T. Washington and His Critics.*
9. *Lynching, Our National Crime.*
10. *How Enfranchisement Stops Lynchings.*
11. *Our Country's Lynching Record.*

Vol. 16. **Women in the Civil Rights Movement: Trailblazers and Torchbearers, 1941-1965**

Edited by Vicki Crawford, Jacqueline A. Rouse, Barbara Woods; Associate Editors: Broadus Butler, Marymal Dryden, and Melissa Walker

1. Black, Allida. *A Reluctant but Persistent Warrior: Eleanor Roosevelt and the Early Civil Rights Movement*
2. Brock, Annette K. *Gloria Richardson and the Cambridge Movement*
3. Burks, Mary Fair. *Trailblazers: Women in the Montgomery Bus Boycott.*
4. Cochrane, Sharlene Voogd. *'And the Pressure Never Let Up': Black Women, White Women, and the Boston YWCA, 1918-1948.*
5. Crawford, Vicki. *Beyond the Human Self: Grassroots Activists in the Mississippi Civil Rights Movement.*
6. Grant, Jacquelyn. *Civil Rights Women: A Source for Doing Womanist Theology.*
7. Knotts, Alice G. *Methodist Women Integrate Schools and Housing, 1952-1959.*
8. Langston, Donna. *The Women of Highlander.*
9. Locke, Mamie E. *Is This America: Fannie Lou Hamer and the Mississippi Freedom Democratic Party.*
10. McFadden, Grace Jordan. *Septima Clark.*
11. Mueller, Carol. *Ella Baker and the Origins of 'Participatory Democracy.'*
12. Myrick-Harris, Clarissa. *Behind the Scenes: Doris Derby, Denise Nicholas, and the Free Southern Theater.*
13. Oldendorf, Sandra. *The South Carolina Sea Island Citizenship Schools.*
14. Payne, Charles. *Men Led, But Women Organized: Movement Participation of Women in the Mississippi Delta.*
15. Reagon, Bernice Johnson. *Women as Culture Carriers in the Civil Rights Movement: Fannie Lou Hamer.*
16. Standley, Anne. *The Role of Black Women in the Civil Rights Movement.*
17. Woods, Barbara. *Modjeska Simkins and the South Carolina Conference of the NAACP.*

Author Index

Boldface indicates volume numbers and roman
indicates article numbers within volumes.

Subject Index

Boldface indicates volume numbers and roman indicates article numbers within volumes.